Law, Power and Culture
Supporting Change from Within

Palgrave Macmillan Socio-Legal Studies

Series Editor

David Cowan, Professor of Law and Policy, University of Bristol, UK

Editorial Board

Dame Hazel Genn, Professor of Socio-Legal Studies, University College London, UK

Fiona Haines, Associate Professor, School of Social and Political Science, University of Melbourne, Australia

Herbert Kritzer, Professor of Law and Public Policy, University of Minnesota, USA

Linda Mulcahy, Professor of Law, London School of Economics and Political Science, UK

Carl Stychin, Dean and Professor, The City Law School, City University London, UK

Mariana Valverde, Professor of Criminology, University of Toronto, Canada

Sally Wheeler, Professor of Law, Queen's University Belfast, UK

Law, Power and Culture
Supporting Change from Within

Fauzia Knight
Independent Scholar, UK

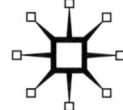

© Fauzia Knight 2014

All rights reserved. No reproduction, copy or transmission of this publication may be made without written permission.

Crown Copyright material is licensed under the Open Government Licence v2.0.

No portion of this publication may be reproduced, copied or transmitted save with written permission or in accordance with the provisions of the Copyright, Designs and Patents Act 1988, or under the terms of any licence permitting limited copying issued by the Copyright Licensing Agency, Saffron House, 6–10 Kirby Street, London EC1N 8TS.

Any person who does any unauthorized act in relation to this publication may be liable to criminal prosecution and civil claims for damages.

The author has asserted her right to be identified as the author of this work in accordance with the Copyright, Designs and Patents Act 1988.

First published 2014 by
PALGRAVE MACMILLAN

Palgrave Macmillan in the UK is an imprint of Macmillan Publishers Limited, registered in England, company number 785998, of Houndmills, Basingstoke, Hampshire RG21 6XS.

Palgrave Macmillan in the US is a division of St Martin's Press LLC, 175 Fifth Avenue, New York, NY 10010.

Palgrave Macmillan is the global academic imprint of the above companies and has companies and representatives throughout the world.

Palgrave® and Macmillan® are registered trademarks in the United States, the United Kingdom, Europe and other countries.

ISBN: 978–0–230–30453–6

This book is printed on paper suitable for recycling and made from fully managed and sustained forest sources. Logging, pulping and manufacturing processes are expected to conform to the environmental regulations of the country of origin.

A catalogue record for this book is available from the British Library.

A catalog record for this book is available from the Library of Congress.

Typeset by Cambrian Typesetters, Camberley, Surrey

Printed and bound in Great Britain by TJ international Ltd, Padstow

To my late mother, Nora Shariff, and to my father,
Sultan Shariff

Contents

Map		ix
Acknowledgments		x
1	**Introduction**	1
	Background	2
	Theoretical contributions	4
	Theoretical departures	6
	Physical sites of the research	10
	Chapter outlines	12
2	**Power, Resistance and Legal Pluralism: Processes of Freedom and Constraint**	17
	Power	18
	Resistance	22
	Legal pluralism	29
3	**The Santal: Processes of Subordination in the State**	34
	The Santal: migrating to alterity	35
	Subordination and the state	41
	Vulnerability of otherness	52
	Conclusion	55
4	**The Primary Construction of Inequality: Kinship, Law and Ritual in the Santal Family and Village**	57
	The Santal family	58
	The village	66
	Conclusion	78
5	**Resisting from Without: The Illusive Promise of the Alternative Legal Order**	79
	The individual: disputing across legal orders	80
	Critical tensions in cultural meanings: witchcraft related crimes	92
	Disputing in the context of group survival	97
	Conclusion	100

6	**The Realization of Needs from Within: The Power Product and Non-compliance**	**101**
	The power product	103
	Non-compliance	115
	Optimization and the rational subject	121
	Conclusion	125
7	**A Tripartite Theory: Power Practices and Embedded Change**	**127**
	Three forms of power practice	129
	Culture as a dynamic context for change within	137
	Conclusion	144
8	**Forced Marriage: Engaging with Renegotiations Within**	**146**
	Dilemmas of state intervention in forced marriage cases	147
	Power practices and the South-Asian marriage process	154
	Renegotiating relations of dependence and nature	160
	Conclusion	164
9	**Conclusion**	**167**
Glossary of Terms and Key Authors		171
Bibliography		174
Index		187

Acknowledgments

Writing this book has been a decade-long journey, and there are many people I would like to thank who have guided its trajectory, directly and indirectly.

The primary data on which the book is drawn originated in a doctoral study based at the university of Warwick and its genesis owes much to two scholars who nurtured my early ideas and supported me through my fieldwork. I was very fortunate to work with Professor Abdul Paliwala and Professor Upendra Baxi. Professor Abdul Paliwala supervised me with careful thought and great care and has remained a mentor and friend. Much of the inspiration for the theoretical themes in this book was introduced to me by Professor Upendra Baxi, a scholar like no other I have met, always one step ahead of my thoughts, able to see through them and beyond them.

An ethnography is never truly sole-authored in that it relies on the people who host the researcher to share their worldview. The Santal people in the four villages where I stayed, and those I met during my pilot trip and elsewhere, shared their experiences with me openly and I am very grateful to them. I would like to thank in particular: Samuel Baske and his wife Shanti (and their son, who was born while I was living with them), Babu Lal Tudu, Sitoram Hembrom, Chonchol Hembrom and his wife, Katherine Baske, Rupai Baske and *gogo*. I also owe much to friends and family who supported my fieldwork: Professor Doctor Moazzem Hossain Khan and *bhabi*, Akash and Ovik, Mahboob Uddin Ahmed Bir Bikram, Professor Buddhadeb Chaudhuri, Doctor Aparna Dasgupta and all the inspirational people I met at the People Institute for Development and Training. I would also like to thank my friend Sonkar Sengupta, who loved the Santal people and devoted his life to working with them, and some of the charismatic people I interviewed along the way, including: Basu Dev Besra, Meghna Guhakurta, Ashish Nandy, who generously gave their time and thoughts.

My fieldwork was only possible thanks to generous funding from the Economic and Social Research Council (Research Fellowship grant number R42200134457 and Post-doctoral Fellowship grant PTA-026-27-1531), Ford Foundation (Delhi, grant number 980-0350-3) and the University of Warwick. A special thanks to Professor Gowher Rizvi, then at Ford Foundation, who enthusiastically supported my research.

I was invited at various stages of the research to give seminars and lectures (Adivasi Land Rights in North West Bangladesh, Oxfam/RDC Seminar, Dinajpur, in January 2002; International Post Graduate

Programme in Human Rights at University of Kolkata, in January 2003; Conference on Disadvantaged Peoples at North Bengal University, in March 2003; Asian Seminar Series at London School of Economics, in November 2003; Asin Dasgupta Memorial Lecture at the Anthropological Survey of India, in December 2003; Anthropology of Law, Birkbeck College, London, in May 2004). Thanks to the participants for their feedback and contributions.

Although much of the data presented here is drawn from my early research, its development into a book has been a process in itself. I would like to thank Professor Werner Menski who mentored me during my post-doctoral studies at the School of Oriental and African Studies. Teaching on his course 'Ethnic minorities and the law' introduced a new dynamic from which many ideas in this book have developed. I would also like to thank my colleagues at the London School of Economics, and in particular Doctor Mathijs Pelkmans, Professor Deborah James and the students of AN226, whose discussions of resistance and power helped challenge and mature my ideas in the final stages of writing. In my work on forced marriage, I give thanks to Matthew Gould and James Watt at the Foreign and Commonwealth Office, Fawzia Samad, Baroness Uddin, Lord Ahmed and Roger Ballard, who recognized the importance of community involvement in state interventions on forced marriage.

On a personal level my family have made many sacrifices in supporting me during the writing of this book and I want to thank them. I owe a great deal to my husband, Matthew, who supported me unquestioningly through years of study and fieldwork and many years of writing and rewriting and my in-laws Gilly and Roger. My late mother, Nora Shariff, who died months before I finished this book, is my constant inspiration: an Irish woman fluent in Bengali whose *dhal,* and generosity, is the talk of East London! She taught me the art of practical perseverance and patience without which I could not have written this book. My father, who has made it his life's work to help others, taught me through his own example, the importance of humanity, and nurtured a life-long interest in the country of my birth, Bangladesh. He accompanied me on my first trip to India and made everything easy, never ceasing to amaze with his ability to connect in a profound way with people we met, through their shared experience of Partition. Thanks to my sister, Razia, who read draft chapters in the final stages of writing, for thought-provoking discussions about agency and a shared love of all things Foucault! And to Nabi Newaz, my thoughtful brother-in-law, who grew up in close proximity to the Santal. Had he not suggested the Santal to me for this study, this book would not have been. Last but not least, my daughter who sat patiently on my lap as I finished off just one more paragraph!

Although I only came to know my Commissioning Editor, Rob Gibson, and Series Editor, David Cowan, very late on in this process I am very grateful for the patience, generosity and care they took in supporting its production. The anonymous reviewer gave some tantalizing and eye-opening final comments that helped with an important transformation of the book into its current state.

I would like to thank everyone I interviewed and spoke with during my fieldwork. All names have been changed and all specific settlement names anonymized.

Parts of earlier versions of chapters in this book were published in the journals *Field Methods* (Shariff, 2014), *Social and Legal Studies* (Shariff, 2012), *Journal of Legal Pluralism* (Shariff, 2013 and 2008) and *Law, Social Justice and Global Development* (Shariff, 2007).

1
Introduction

In 2000 the UK government set up a dedicated unit to assist women and men facing forced marriages in the UK and abroad. A world first, the Forced Marriage Unit (hereafter the Unit), as it later became known, sought to provide a way out for young South-Asian women and men who were facing a marriage arranged by their parents to which they did not consent. Due to early intervention by women's groups, who warned against negotiating with families, assisting in these cases often took the form of extracting these men and women from their families and communities. But the wishes of the young person in each case were paramount and it soon became clear that the complex of emotional ties, feelings of filial piety and duty and interdependencies made such assistance a painful and sometimes unattractive prospect for the person concerned. The conceptual tools of 'injustice', 'inequalities', 'rights' and 'victims' used to defend government interventions often seemed too simplistic and failed to engage with the experiences of the young men and women themselves.

While race relations and feminist theorists have grappled with these dilemmas through a study of the ideological conflicts they represent, a deeper understanding of the social relationships at the base of the conflicts, put in their social and cultural contexts, can be a more fruitful way to identify prospective trajectories for policy. Studying social relations through the intersections of culture, power and law provides an illuminating framework to do this. The potential of this approach is demonstrated here through a case study of the Santal people in South Asia where the dynamics of power and freedom provide a fertile base for analysing the shortcomings of state assistance. The renegotiation of power relations within the Santal family and village, as well the use of state law in disputes with other Santal and non-Santalis, provides a rich resource on which to examine social relations as a means of constraint and a context for change. An investigation of the forms of power relations and the possibilities for renegotiating these in the South-Asian context are used here to suggest alternative ways in which the problem of 'forced marriage' can be understood in the UK.

Background

The research on which this book is based began over a decade ago. I was seconded to the British Foreign and Commonwealth Office to help set up a unit dedicated to developing government policy and to handling, forced marriage cases. The government's interest in forced marriage had emerged from an increase in requests for assistance from young British South Asians who were being forced into a marriage abroad. These requests posed an awkward challenge for the state. There was a clear human rights imperative to assist the young women, and occasionally men, but also a recognition that any intervention would draw the state into scrutiny as it intervened in family relations within a cultural community with distinct social norms, about which it had very little institutional knowledge. In recognition of this, the first working paper produced by the government was drafted by a working group whose members were all of Asian and South-Asian heritage. The two members of the House of Lords who co-chaired the group recognized that, while there was a place for the state in assisting in forced marriage cases, the bigger challenge was to transform the social relations within the migrant communities that allowed them to occur. The working paper was addressed to British migrant communities in the first person plural and made it clear that ending forced marriage was not solely a government task but one for those communities primarily.

Their foresight was well founded and the limits of state assistance were immediately apparent in the Unit's work. During the first year, our efforts to repatriate young men and women who contacted the Unit for help were repeatedly thwarted because many did not commit entirely to the process of rescue we offered. The assistance we gave was grafted onto a complex of pressures and commitments in the South-Asian family which these individuals were seeking to navigate. While these men and women valued state involvement, they were concerned about the impact this would have on family relations, and how their needs would be met if they separated from their families.

At the end of the first year we commissioned research into community perceptions of forced marriage (Samad and Eade, 2001), which examined the complex emotions surrounding the South-Asian marriage process. That research revealed a rich and varied experience of pressure tied in with sentiments of filial love. Participants in the research, citing poor race relations and a rise in Islamaphobia in Britain post-9/11, also raised serious suspicions about the state's interest in intervening in forced marriage cases. This suggested a need for greater dialogue with, and within, communities to shift practices in social relations internally and improve trust in state processes. Instead, the state began to exclude migrant communities from its work in this area and replaced dialogue with regulation and punishment. (I have written about this elsewhere, see Shariff, 2012.)

I left the Foreign Office in 2002 to begin my doctoral fieldwork on the Santal in South Asia but these dilemmas preoccupied me and fed into my doctoral work. My doctorate began as an examination of how individuals within a minority community use law to help themselves. My work with the Foreign Office had taught me to challenge any presumption that state law held the solution, or would be trusted to deliver a desired outcome. I began to investigate the ways in which those disadvantaged within Santal society sought to help themselves both through Santal institutions and through institutions of the state. The research again revealed a complex picture of negotiations. The state was part of the picture but recourse to the state was patchy and usually non-committal.

Researchers in the field of legal anthropology, and particularly legal pluralism, had been considering these same challenges since the 1970s. In a critical paper in 1973, Sally Falk Moore warned that to make real lasting social change state policy needed to engage with the multiple overlapping normative orders in societies' many social fields, and the social relationships through which they are negotiated. She noted that the insistence that the state had the solution and that individuals within these social fields, with some prompting, would voluntarily avail themselves of state assistance, failed to acknowledge that the normative order of the social field, and the power relations they encompassed, attracted a great deal of authority over the individual. In the decades since then legal anthropologists have shown that a preliminary investigation into the normative aspects of a social field reveals a world of complex, sometimes contradictory, but, importantly, negotiated relationships into which state law seeks to intervene.

The Santal provided an interesting case study for examining this phenomenon. Having a rich history of cultural distinctiveness and turbulent migration, they are now settled largely in the eastern states of India and north-west of Bangladesh. Despite being diasporic they manage to maintain a highly prized uniqueness, and each Santal village functions as a microcosm of the Santal people, independent but connected to its others. A system of village officers facilitates the maintenance of Santal customs and rituals, but the people are bound together through mutuality of support, shared language, a shared history and origin myth and a sense of belonging. This does not detract from their identity as Bangladeshis and

Indians, and they can and do reach out to the state. But it is at the level of social relations in the village that each individual seeks primarily to have their needs met.

Theoretical contributions

Perhaps the principle concept on which this book draws is the concept of power. It seeks to answer the question: 'How do power relations condition but also facilitate social change within cultural minorities?' In doing so, it re-evaluates agency in the cultural context, but it also seeks to help us understand better how power directs the individual to fulfil their needs within existing power relations. This is particularly revealing for policy because it demonstrates why the conventional approach to assisting minorities within minorities, from the outside, is deeply flawed. Through a tripartite theory of power it challenges the assumption that changes in social relations within cultural communities must involve recourse to a legal system outside the minority community, or other norms originating outwith the community. It also challenges the assumption, associated with this, that resistance and agency are only valuable when they promote standards set by those outside cultural minorities.

Through a study of the process through which individuals seek to have their needs met within power relations in two diverse settings (a tribal minority in South Asia and immigrant communities in Britain), it demonstrates that, although recourse to external normative orders such as the state does occur, internal adjustments and renegotiations are prevalent. The complexity of this process and the problems of resisting through external forums such as the state demand a more detailed understanding of how the individual experiences power. While theory on micro-power assists with this, it treats social settings as isolated and micro-power as singular in its effect. This book demonstrates, however, that power practices are heterogeneous and shifting, and their exposure to alternative normative social fields leaves them open to contestation. The book identifies three types of power practice – relations of force, dependence and nature – and examines how individuals respond to these and the potential for social change in plural socio-legal contexts. Social change in this context may not mean immediate shifts in social relations that meet the demands of equality and human rights standards, but reflects a gradual change in how practices are understood.

While much of the book draws on the concept of power and its corollary, resistance, my findings make a critical departure from the literature in this area. At the heart of this paradigm is the idea that power circulates through relationships, creating positive as well as negative effects and is always subject to change. This dynamic nature of power and the seed of change within it is central to my argument. However, the term resistance has created a false ideal of the process through which change occurs and has been heavily critiqued. While resistance suggests a 'fighting back', anti-power, in fact much of the negotiating I have examined takes place within a context of acceptance.

Rather than anti-power, I see negotiations in the context of power relations as part of an acceptance of the power relation. The individual's drive for survival, biological but also social, means that power relations evolve through pressures that reflect individual needs but are themselves fundamentally accepted and invested in. This is not to say that there is never resistance, anti-power. But this takes place in the context of certain moments in the relationship only, what I call relations of force. In fact, people invest in relationships and for the most part attempt to realize their needs within them rather than outside them.

This book therefore distinguishes 'resistance', as a form of anti-power that challenges the relationship from the outside, from 'renegotiation', which is performed within power relations. External resistance relates to circumstances in which the individual takes recourse to a forum outside the power relation, an action that is against and potentially may end the power relationship or allow the individual to exit from it. I distinguish this from internal renegotiations, which form part of the dynamic process of change within power relations. This allows us to think differently about social change. In doing so, I challenge empirical researchers to overcome the tendency to treat internal renegotiations as coincidental to power and not worthy of analysis. This tendency has occurred as a result of the critical response to literature on 'everyday resistance' (see Abu-Lughod, 1990). In her paper, 'The Romance of Resistance', Lila Abu Lughod urges ethnographers to use resistance as a diagnostic of power. Indeed, although her work intends to thwart overzealous attempts to celebrate resistance, this book is evidence that the study of internal renegotiation and external resistance provides both a richer picture of power and greater appreciation of the importance of individual negotiations for understanding the direction of change.

Uniquely, this book draws on empirical research amongst an understudied chthonic people, the Santal, in India and Bangladesh. It examines power relations within the normative social fields of the Santal family and village as well as in the state, where they occupy a minority status, and identifies different ways in which renegotiations are attempted, trajectories of negotiation, across these socio-legal fields. These trajectories of negotiation are used to examine power. Correlations between these and different types of power practice are explored. These findings are then applied to the practice of forced marriage, by Pakistani and Sylheti Bangladeshis primarily, within Britain. Despite the very different context, trajectories of negotiation and power practices prevalent in Santal society are also identifiable within these communities. The practice of forced marriage, or force in the context of arranged marriages, provides a topical case study in which to test out the correlation between these power practices and trajectories of negotiation. Internal renegotiations and external resistance through recourse to the British state are both present, but again the empirical data reveals that power directs renegotiation inwards.

Theoretical departures

As an empirical study this book is necessarily light on theory. Nevertheless, analysis of data takes place within the context of theoretical discourse. I look at the main theoretical concepts that underpin this book in Chapter 2. However, my subject touches on some important themes that I have not been able to elaborate on. Below I attempt to explain how and why I have avoided some of the more obvious themes as a basis for this study.

Minority rights: the group and its individuals

Minority rights were an early preoccupation for me and when I first conceptualized this research my interest was in understanding why certain minorities were able to exert their interests more effectively than others. With a background in international human rights law, my attention was drawn to the then ongoing debates on the Draft UN Declaration on the Rights of Indigenous Peoples (hereafter the Draft Declaration). I attended the annual session of the UN Human Rights Commission in 1997 when the Draft Declaration was in its third year of consideration before the commission. The governments that had accepted to negotiate on it were seeking to soften its language to avoid costly obligations towards well-organized indigenous and tribal groups. The Draft Declaration's aim of 'self-determination of indigenous people' was particularly contentious. It was seen by states as providing an opportunity for indigenous peoples to claim autonomy from the state. The declaration had been drafted by representatives of indigenous people and was unquestioned as an authentic expression of their wishes and concerns. In fact, it reflected the agenda of organizations predominantly from Latin America, Canada and Australia, where indigenous rights had a particular history. Their demands for rights over the lands and resources of their ancestors reflected their own history of loss, characterized by colonization, brutal (in some cases genocidal) assimilation and domination by European migrants.

Tribal and chthonic peoples from the two largest tribal belts in the world in Africa and Asia had little representation[1] and it seemed to me that the Draft Declaration did little to address the different priorities of indigenous people in these continents. Furthermore, the inclusion of self-determination in Article 1 of the Draft Declaration provided an opportunity for some states in those continents to exclude themselves from its provisions as they claimed that the Draft Declaration applied to colonized peoples who had never achieved independence. Bangladesh was amongst the countries that stated that the victory of self-determination from the British in 1947 meant that Bengalis, as indigenous peoples of that territory, had already achieved their independence.[2]

The exclusion of chthonic ethnic peoples from the debate was not only a problem of representation but was symptomatic of their underprivileged position in the international tribal rights movement and in their own states. I felt that there was a need to examine the question of their rights in its socio-political as well as legal context, to understand the forces behind their exclusion. My enquiries, which began as an investigation of the socio-political dynamics of group exclusion, soon turned to an examination of exclusion within those minority communities themselves. Minority rights literature has historically challenged the centrality of the individual and the state in human rights discourse by forefronting group rights (Shachar, 2001). Indigenous peoples' rights provisions in international law seek the protection of individuals from state interference, but only as members of groups: their ability, collectively, to enjoy the territories, natural resources and way of life of their ancestors. My investigation therefore took me away from a minority rights/indigenous rights focus. In writing about the individual within the group I found the work of political theorists provided greater scope for investigating the individual within the group and my focus changed from rights to the renegotiation of power.

Writing culture: intersections and subjectivity

My research on the Santal focuses on three normative social fields: the family, the village and the state. My initial concern when starting the research was that I uncover the forces that sustain inequality, from the experiences of the Santal people, in each of these normative social fields. I was interested in inequality as it occurs at the level of the state, but my preoccupation with uncovering the forces at work on the individual led me

---

1 The Chakma of the Chittagong Hill Tracts in Bangladesh were one of the few exceptions.
2 See Report of the Working Group established in Accordance with Commission on Human Rights Resolution 1995/32, E/CN4/1997/102 para. 52 – Bangladesh.

to look at how the village and family work also as sites of inequality. Examining the social field of the Santal family and village inevitably involved investigating material on Santal culture. In 1871 Reverend Lars Olsen Skrefsrud, a Norwegian missionary of the Lutheran Church who lived and worked amongst the Santal from 1867 until his death in 1907, took down a record of Santal customs from a Santal man called Kolean whom he described as having the most comprehensive appreciation of Santal culture of anyone he had come across. These traditions of the Santal, recorded verbatim in Santali and based on oral traditions, were later translated by Skrefsrud's successor, Reverend Paul O Bodding. This text now accounts for one of the most insightful records of Santal customs and I drew heavily on this work for my analysis. While this text is an indigenous account of Santal customs, applying it to my own theme of discovering power relations within the family and village required a certain amount of interpretation and updating in light of what I experienced in the villages where I stayed.

Writing about culture inevitably involves an external process through which meaning is constructed (Wagner, 1981). My reconstruction of Santal culture in this book has resulted in a particular reading of interactions I found in Santal society that are reflective of practice theory. Andreas Reckwitz (2002) describes cultural theories as falling into four categories: those which locate the social in the minds of human subjects (culturalist mentalism); those which locate the social in signs, symbols, discourses and communication (cultural textualism); those which locate the social in interactions and particularly speech acts (cultural intersubjectivity); and those which locate the social in social practices, routinized behaviour, ways of knowing, doing, thinking (practice theory). Practice theory relates to the works of Michel Foucault and Pierre Bourdieu amongst others. Whereas other forms of cultural theory intellectualize culture from a standpoint of Western traditions (Western ideas of mind or consciousness, post-Cartesian philosophy, texts and communicative action), Reckwitz tells us that practice theory does not invite analysis of these elements of practice, but rather explores their embeddedness (Reckwitz, 2002, p. 258). The individual is a carrier of practices, a participant. While practice theory acknowledges the individual as actor, acting out social practices, the individual is also an agent (rule-following or deviant) in the social process and a point at which different social practices cross over.[3] My research examines the individual in this context as a point at which social practices associated with different normative or legal orders intersect. I treat social practices as power practices

---

3 Reckwitz (2002, p. 256) cites Simmel's 'networks' of social circles rather than social practices.

and examine how different power practices affect agency in the context of intersecting normative orders.

I limit my analysis of normative orders to the family, village and state and have not been able to elaborate on the wider effect of non-governmental organizations (NGOs) and missionaries in the way power struggles are won and lost – although I do consider specific NGO interventions in the villages where I stayed. Undoubtedly, local, national and international development and human rights organizations and donors affect the balance of power between the subordinated and the elite at all three levels I discuss. In Bangladesh, pro-poor NGO initiatives in rural areas (although not specifically in tribal areas) have had a significant influence on power struggles and, in India, NGOs have added considerably to intellectual and political debates over tribal rights. Their intervention means that global and transnational power struggles and debates link into micro-struggles. This reinforces my conclusion that intersecting normative orders play a crucial role in renegotiating power relations, but I do not address its effect here.

Women: a gendered debate?

Women have, in the final analysis, played a fairly central role in my discussion of trajectories of negotiation and power relations. Their position of disadvantage within the family, village and state has made them important subjects. When I carried out my research my focus was on the problems people faced and the role of law in addressing them. It was only as I began to write up that women's situation, which I made an effort to elaborate on in the text, took the prominence it now has. When I carried out my fieldtrips from 2002–2004 I had not yet formulated my legal orders as a structure for analysing the Santal's situation. At that time, my main focus was on responses to inequality in the village and in relations with the state.

The navigation of power relations by women of culture, designated 'third world', has been the subject of much dispute in feminist literature. While third-world scholars have rebutted the presumption of the third-world woman as passive victim (Ong, 1988; Liddle and Rai, 1998), the re-invention of women as active agents has also been contested. While social and anthropological studies have evidenced women's capacity to negotiate in the context of power relations, feminist theorists and empiricists keen to emphasize the potency of power have favoured viewing agency as a subtext of power relations (Abu-Lughod, 1990). Agentic action and discourse is seen as problematic and even counter-productive.

These questions are central to this book. However, this book is not a book about women but about disadvantage, in its multiple dimensions. It is a book about the subaltern, and includes women in so far as they are subordinated. Feminist standpoint theory, which suggests that women have an alternative viewpoint on the world that is missing from scientific evaluation, is closer to what I hope to achieve here. In a sense what I am doing is arguing for a subaltern standpoint, which includes women's experiences of power, but I do not insist on a gendered perspective, only on a subaltern one.

Physical sites of the research

My study is based on multi-sited rapid ethnographic research in four villages. Multi-sited ethnography is well suited to research that seeks to contextualize the study of practices by one group of people in a wider socio-political context (Ortner, 1995). This form of ethnography has its own challenges and gifts and I explore these elsewhere (Shariff, 2014). As well as collecting data through participant observation, semi-structured interviews and focus groups in the villages, I interviewed judges, academics and activists in the towns nearest to the villages. I also triangulated my research wherever possible, including with the use of historical and archival texts. The villages where I collected most of the data I present in this book were rural villages in the regions of Rajshahi, Bangladesh, and the Santal Parganas, India.

Gaining access to the villages was often complicated. I wanted to avoid any perception that I was directly connected with NGOs, politicians or others whose agendas may have impacted on my work in the village – any of these identities would have affected the way I was perceived and how villagers answered my questions. I often used snowballing techniques to get access to a village through someone unconnected with any significant political agenda. For example, a relative in Rajshahi university introduced me to a Santali student who gave me access to my first village where he and his family lived. In another village I got an introduction through the brother of an employee of an NGO working in another district. I generally kept several options open for accessing the village so that I would not have to rely on any single gatekeeper.

Inevitably, the nature of my introduction affected how I was viewed in the villages, and even where I seemed to have no connections to authority some villagers nevertheless had suspicions about why I had come and whom I was working for. I tried to minimize these by talking openly about my research and by participating in village life in a way that distinguished me from NGO workers, missionaries, government agents, local politicians and other researchers. I participated in household chores, collected water, prepared meals and so on and slept on the floor, eating with the family and avoiding any changes to their daily routines. I maintained little contact with those outside the village and, apart from a compulsory visit to the *thana* (police station area) police or union chairman to give notice of my stay in the village, I kept away from government officials during my stay. Nevertheless, the fieldwork had its challenges and I talk elsewhere about the precariousness of establishing fieldwork relations (Shariff, 2014).

The first village where I stayed, which I will call Thakurban, is 50 kilometres from the nearest large town in north-west Bangladesh. The village was established shortly after the turn of the twentieth century when many Santal migrated from the Santal Parganas. Thakurban was a majority Santal village, with a number of Paharia[4] families in the village who seemed to cohabit without any tension. The surrounding villages were all chthonic and mostly Santal villages. The land on which the village was built was made up of government land, missionary land and land owned by villagers. The area was immensely fertile and, although only a few villagers still owned their own land, they all found work in the area as cultivators (day-labourers, or, if they had access to a bull and plough, sharecroppers). The majority of people in the village were Christians and the village had a small church with a priest from the village. It also had a primary school run by an NGO with two women teachers from the village.

The second village where I stayed is over 60 kilometres from the nearest large town. Unlike Thakurban, this second village, which I call Dhanban, was, according to the villagers, established in the mid-twentieth century in an area densely populated with Hindus, Muslims and other *adivasis*.[5] The Santal in the village had little or no land and mostly worked as day-labourers. The village was built on government land and had occasional two-storey houses owned by Muslims dividing the smaller Santal ones. Exceptionally, the village had a *Parganait* – one of the highest officials in the Santal village hierarchy – who oversaw all the Santal villages of the area. There was a government-run primary school and a secondary school very near the village, though these were unaffordable for most and only a few of the Santal children attended. Because of the ethnic mix of the area, there were always Muslims and other non-Santal in the village. The village had a Santal priest and a few Christian families. Dhanban – unlike Thakurban, which was only ten minutes walk from a bus into town – was not well connected to the town. An hour's walk through villages and across paddy fields led to a dirt road. From there, only hand-pulled carts (called *'vans'*)

---

4 The Paharia are one of the poorest and numerically smallest of the chthonic people in north-west Bangladesh.
5 The term literally means 'indigenous people' or 'aborigines' but it has been used as a political term to associate chthonic peoples with the wider politics of indigenous rights.

and rickshaws took villagers to small nearby towns. The nearest motor transport was more than 5 kilometres away.

In India, the first village I stayed in is in the Santal Parganas almost 30 kilometres from the nearest town. Situated in an inhospitable area of dry plains land far from the nearest road or transport link, punctuated with cobra and scorpion-ridden hills, the village offered little local work for the villagers. Many migrated seasonally to West Bengal, Orissa and elsewhere to work as cultivators or unskilled labourers. The area was frequently troubled by malaria and many families had lost children and parents. There were three men in the village who had studied to degree level but none had found jobs. The village, which I call Lahara, had a government school that some children from the village attended, but it was closed during my stay. The village and area were, almost completely populated by Santali families. The villagers were very politically aware and it was the only village where my presence was challenged in a threatening way. Unlike Bangladesh, where NGO and missionaries were pervasive, there was no NGO or missionary presence in or near the village. The village land was owned by its occupants.

The fourth village where I stayed is 30 kilometres by train and over 60 by car from the nearest town. There were more skilled workers there, many of whom migrated frequently for work. The area was mixed and the village itself, which I call Madhura, had Muslim and Hindu households. The village was built on land owned by its inhabitants. The *pradhan* (government land revenue collector) of the area was a Santal. The village was situated near to a large fee-paying NGO school. The NGO provided jobs for a few villagers and had built a small irrigation system in one part of the village to irrigate one area, which stood out lush green in the sandy desert landscape of the area. There was also a government school in the area, but I was told the teacher rarely worked.

Chapter outlines

I begin in Chapter 2 by introducing three theoretical concepts that run through the book. Foucault's theory of micro-power is explored to demonstrate how power relates to concepts of law and norms, how it functions as a fluid, changeable force within social interrelationships and, crucially, the integral dimension of freedom within Foucauldian power relations. Links are made between this idea of 'freedom' within power relations and the somewhat contentious concept of individual/everyday resistance, which differs in important ways from theories of collective resistance. Feminist critiques of everyday resistance and agency that see these acts as unable to change power structures and relations are explored and critiqued. Finally, the concept of legal pluralism is put into historical and global context and its relevance to ideas of micro-power and resistance within culturally and normatively plural societies is examined. The introduction of these concepts and exploration of how they interrelate will allow the non-expert reader to be introduced to some of the theoretical themes underlying the book. Coverage is aimed at giving enough background understanding of the concepts to engage the non-expert while also demonstrating to those already familiar with these themes how the book intends to utilize these concepts and how they relate to each other.

In Chapter 3 I set the scene of the Santal's current subordinate socio-economic and political position and relations with the state. This chapter explores the historical backdrop to the Santal's subordination and key legislation and events (from British rule through to Partition and Bangladesh's independence) affecting their social and economic status. The chapter discusses the socio-legal, political and cultural dimensions to the processes by which Santal subordination is formed and perpetuated within the local and national state in the current day. This includes an examination of the relationship between lack of political recognition and resource allocation, historic linkages between wealth, power and kinship in the region, 'othering' of the Santal as a cultural, linguistic and religious minority politically and socially, and state failure to respond to targeted land-grabbing and violence.

While Chapter 3 focuses on the state as a site of inequalities, Chapter 4 illustrates how inequalities are formed and perpetuated in the Santal family and village. In the family, inequality between men and women is given (cultural) meaning through forms of marriage, division of labour, benefits, prohibitions and dependencies, and self-enforced through the visibility of key events and daily rituals. In the village, mechanisms of inequality have more complex sources. Advantages in power relations may be structural (village office-holders such as the headman, deputy and guardian of morals have certain privileges) or can be acquired through marriage strategies designed to extend a kinship group's size or influence within a given village, non-filial village friendships, and knowledge and experience of Santal norms and customs or those of state institutions. These may also be denied, especially to women, through taboos and customs relating to control over land and suspicions relating to witchcraft practices. These are illustrated with examples.

In Chapter 5 the Foucauldian notion of freedom within power relations is explored by examining the potential for resisting in the context of power relations in one normative order, such as the family, through recourse to another, such as the state. Examples from fieldwork amongst the Santal are used to demonstrate the possibilities and challenges of using an alternative legal order to resist from without. Other examples where recourse to an alternative legal order brings about critical tensions in cultural meanings and beliefs are also explored. These are examined in light of Laura Nader's (1990) theory of 'harmony ideology' on the cultural pressures against dispute resolution outside the community and Marc Galanter's (1984) 'litigotiation', negotiation alongside litigation, as a context for dispute settlement. Conclusions are drawn on the potential but also the shortcomings of this form of resistance for social change and the risk for the individual of excommunication from the community.

Chapter 6 examines the alternative possibilities of renegotiating from within the normative order (and power relation) where it occurs. The chapter explores the ideas of counter-power (benefits available to the less privileged individual in the context of power relations), and non-compliance. Examples taken from the fieldwork amongst the Santal are used to identify the scope of counter-power and demonstrate scenarios of non-compliance within the normative orders of the family and state. The chapter then goes on to consider the inherent limitations to renegotiating from within the power relation and feminist critiques of everyday resistance as unable to produce real change. Conclusions are made about how internal renegotiations can nevertheless provide a vital contribution to social change through transformations in perspective.

The material in Chapters 5 and 6 is used in Chapter 7 to identify three types of power practice and link these to the three trajectories of negotiation identified. *Relations of force* describe power relations where the individual feels they are being compelled to conform by force or fear, or that the dominant party's will is imposed on them. This type of power relation leaves very little room for negotiation and is more likely to be resisted through recourse to an *alternative normative order* outside of the power relation. This has repercussions for its utility as a means of social reform from within which are explored in some detail. *Relations of dependence* occur when the individual recognizes their disadvantage but accepts it (in part) in order to gain some perceived advantage in a relationship of mutual dependence. Here individuals are more likely to use *counter-power* to renegotiate their position as this depends on a strong interdependency between the parties. They may in some circumstances take recourse to an alternative normative order but may not take this to its conclusion as it risks fracturing the power relationship on which they depend in some way. Finally, *relations of nature* involve the individual misrecognizing their subordination as a natural state flowing from their gender, class, or caste, for example. This is most likely to be challenged, if at all, through recourse to moments of *non-compliance*. This trajectory of negotiation does not challenge the inequality of the power relation per se but acts to stop misuse of privilege by the more dominant party or temporarily prevent them from enforcing their will.

The chapter uses this theory to draw conclusions as to what these correlations mean for strategies in social change. It demonstrates that identifying these different forms of power relation in any given situation of injustice or inequality and understanding how each relates to trajectories of negotiation is crucial as a starting point for understanding actor-led change. Where inequality within a cultural group is misrecognized as a relation of nature, for example, providing law and policy in the state legal order, which relies on individuals to take the more drastic avenue of recourse to an alternative legal order, is likely to be problematic.

Chapter 8 examines how this theory may illuminate the topical debate on forced marriage in Europe. In order to demonstrate that the theoretical findings from Asia may be transferable to the Global North, this chapter demonstrates that the same three modes of power/domination (relations of force, dependence and nature) and trajectories of negotiation (use of alternative legal orders, counter-power and non-compliance) are identifiable in the context of the marriage process within South-Asian families in Britain. The chapter illustrates how pressure to marry is experienced and responded to in different ways. It explores evidence, for example, of young South Asians who perceive their power relations within the family as a relation of dependence, and seek to renegotiate pressures to marry in accordance with their parent's choice by drawing on a perceived religious (textual rather than cultural) entitlement to 'consent' to the marriage (using counter-power). In other examples, those who do not wish to marry but misrecognize their subordinate position in the marriage process as part of a relation of 'nature' (as a cultural norm or consequence of their younger age, naivety) are more likely to resort to tactics of non-compliance: agreeing to the marriage but setting their own limits to how they conform to role expectations within it. Meanwhile those who experience their subordinate position in marriage choice as imposed or forced upon them (relations of force) are more likely to take recourse to the alternative legal order of the state (police, Home Office or Foreign Office) or to remove themselves from the family to prevent the marriage from happening – with the implications of 'exit' from the (power relation) family and community that this entails. These findings have important implications for government strategies to assist in cases of forced marriage.

I hope in presenting the trajectories of negotiation present in the South-Asian and British contexts to begin to address what Sherry Ortner (1995, p. 190) refers to as 'ethnographic refusal', the failure to investigate the internal politics, subjectivities (fears and projects) and culture of dominated groups in resistance theory. The result is not a thorough ethnography of

Santal struggles or forced marriage, or a comprehensive theory of microresistance. What I hope to achieve here is to raise the possibility of analysing trajectories of negotiation, and power, through the three forms of power practice I have presented. My aim is also political. To persuade policy-workers, and those who research with policy in mind, to take more pains to look and listen to the internal battles within minority cultures and find ways to invest in existing negotiations.

2
Power, Resistance and Legal Pluralism: Processes of Freedom and Constraint

In this chapter I introduce three theoretical concepts that run throughout this book: the concepts of power, resistance and legal pluralism. My aim is to introduce these concepts to those coming to this book from other areas of specialism and, for those already familiar with these concepts, to demonstrate how they enrich our understanding of change within cultural minorities. Together the three concepts provide a fertile basis on which to examine a fundamental question that haunts every study of micro-resistance: how do we conceptualize the resisting subject as both culturally constituted and yet free to challenge cultural precepts?

This question poses some epistemological challenges that the concepts of power, resistance and legal pluralism help us to overcome. Firstly, we need to reimagine the subject not as a 'culturally constituted' construct, but rather as an entity that has constituted itself within culture. This means accepting that culture conditions a person's socialization but does not always determine their behaviour. Secondly, it is very rare now that a cultural minority exists in isolation without exposure to other social groups. Most people born today experience a variety of cultural influences over their lifetimes. We now think of the world as a global village and, whether through personal travel, living in multicultural cities or education through global media, most people have some exposure to other cultures. Even those living in more remote locations are likely to interact with people outside their immediate social group, either voluntarily or not, through trade, the necessity to find work, to give children an education, and to get medical assistance. While these may only be transitory or incidental, they may also draw people into alternative fields of socialization, where they engage in new relationships capable of altering their experience of social relations.

People are also often born into complex intersecting identities, associated with ethnic, religious or linguistic heritage, filtered through gendered and nationalized identities. These form the backdrop for sets of social relationships in which the individual is given a place, for instance, as citizen of the nation, and follower of a faith, with benefits and duties. These identities often also engage social positioning, which situate the individual in a dominant or less dominant position, for example, member of a linguistic minority or a non-dominant ethnic group. What is hidden within these experiences are subtle, and not so subtle, pressures to belong, and in that belonging to embrace certain postulates (value systems) that seek to define or distinguish particular fields of social relations. These pressures, a fertile pre-occupation of feminists and race relations theorists, act on the individual, both positively, to define them, but also to restrict, and to redirect. Here, I introduce the theoretical concepts that help us understand this, the concepts of power, and its corollary freedom, manifested through resistance, and of the plurality of normative social fields, legal pluralism.

Power

Studies of power tend to ask not what power is, but how it functions in society and on the individual. Power is presented as a force that constitutes us into relations of inequality which permeate all human relations and which direct and govern our actions. It shapes the way we constitute ourselves as individuals with collective identities. It directs the way we perceive, think, act and react. While most of us tend to think of our actions as restricted only in the sense that they are regulated by laws emanating from a central authority, much of what we do is directed by rules we consider 'legally neutral' and belonging to the domain of civil society (Gramsci, 1971, p. 242). Without the need for explicit sanctions, civil society exerts pressure over us through customs and ways of thinking and acting. That pressure co-exists with and often re-enforces the sovereignty of state.

This link between social pressure and the state is fundamental to the work of the Marxist theorist Antonio Gramsci. In his *Prison Notebooks*, written in the context of violent anti-socialist repression by the fascist government of Italy in the 1920s, he uncovers an intimate relationship between social forces and state governance. He presents the state as a critical interlocutor in using social regulation to meet the economic needs of production and in developing its subjects into a productive group with minimum external coercion. In analysing the process through which this is achieved, he posits social regulation as capable of addressing a key dilemma for the state:

> how will each *single individual* succeed in *incorporating himself into the collective man*, and how will *educative pressure* be applied to single individuals so as to obtain their consent and their collaboration, turning *necessity and coercion into 'freedom'*? (emphasis added) (Gramsci, 1971, p. 242)

His question is primarily concerned with governance but it includes a number of key insights into power that go to the heart of its nature and application, and I use it here as a springboard to explore the concept of micro-power.

Firstly, the focus of power on the single individual within the collectivity evokes the individualizing nature of power, making the individual into a person who is to account for his/her actions. Secondly, the application of educative pressure as a means of obtaining collaboration refers to the fact that those in positions of seniority control their subordinates through intellectual and moral leadership, which *teaches* them how to think. Thirdly, the urge for the individual's incorporation into the collective man refers to the way in which the individual – unimportant on his or her own – becomes part of a productive unit, which is greater than him/herself. Finally, the aim of turning necessity and coercion into freedom refers to the need for coercion to appear to be absent, and hints at the centrality of freedom in the process of domination.

Underlying Gramsci's insight is the acknowledgment that power functions through structures but also through individuals (Stone, 1966, p. 592). Power is an amorphous energy that exerts pressure over all people collectively and individually, not only directing their actions but also conditioning their ability to react (Mitchell, 1990). This idea is most clearly elucidated in Michel Foucault's early work on the emergence of disciplinary power, *Discipline and Punish*. In this book, Foucault examines the historical process of informalization of punishment in Western society: developing from violent public floggings and executions by the monarch in the Middle Ages to the more invisible disciplinary mechanisms of social control used in the eighteenth and nineteenth centuries. By the nineteenth century individual actions were being organized by institutions of disciplinary power. Disciplinary power allowed domination to result not from the imposition of direct control from above but at the most basic level of society, between individuals. Schools, hospitals, workplaces, all acted as autonomous institutions where the effect of power was to normalize behaviour through surveillance, subtle forms of punishment and examination.

Foucault uses many different examples to explain this, but most pertinent for my study is Jeremy Bentham's model of the panopticon. He uses this to explain how the mechanics of power function permanently and automatically in society without needing a specific operator or surveyor. Bentham's panopticon is based on a fixed architecture: peripheral buildings/cells and a central tower with windows that an observer can see out of but people cannot see into. The two key elements of this mechanism are that *power is visible* (the tower always in sight) and at the same time *unverifiable* (the individual in the cell never knows at any moment if he or she is being spied on or not). The combination of the individual being always potentially visible and the viewer(s) potentially invisible (unverifiable surveillance) makes the individual control him/herself as well as surveying others.

Visibility as a tool of self-regulation was combined with subtle forms of punishment for those who did not conform, micro-penalties focusing on regulating timing (lateness, absences), activity (inattention, negligence, lack of zeal), behaviour (impoliteness, disobedience), speech (idle chatter, insolence), body (cleanliness, attitudes, irregular gestures), sexuality. Punishment took the form of subtle forms of humiliation, corporal punishment and deprivations. Disciplinary power is described by Foucault (1977, p. 183) as a force that: 'compares, differentiates, hierarchizes, homogenizes, excludes. In short, it normalizes.' It controls people's behaviour in comparison to others and in relation to what are shown as 'natural' rules to be followed. Foucault calls this educative process 'normalizing judgement'.

These regulatory processes are at once contrived by those in positions of status and have a semi-autonomous life of their own through processes of social exchange. In Robert D Putnam's book *Making Democracy Work* (1993, pp. 172–3), he identifies that people cooperate with others because they want to achieve the benefits of collective action – pooling resources and experiences. People form relationships and create networks of interpersonal communication and exchanges with others in society that are part of what he calls the 'norms of generalised reciprocity'. These relationships may be horizontal, between people of equivalent status, or vertical, linking people in a relationship of hierarchy and dependence (Putnam, 1993, p. 173). In societies where people's position in society is determined at birth (for example, through caste, gender or ranking amongst siblings), relationships of hierarchy and dependence are pervasive. Yet incentives for reciprocity remain even where the relationship perpetuates one groups' subordination. In Pierre Bourdieu's (1977) study of social exchanges in Kabylia, Algeria, he identifies that the vertical exchanges between the dominating and subjugated groups, which he calls 'symbolic violence', are euphemized, taking the form of gifts, invitations and courtesies.

Bourdieu's conception of the relationship between the individual and structures is explored elsewhere through his concept of *habitus* (Bourdieu, 1984; 1992). This concept sees social norms as a product of common experiences shaped by history. Social construction is temporal because the principles that organize practices can be, and are, adapted. For Bourdieu (1992, p. 53), social practices evolve and change. While there may be attempts to transform the habitus, according to Bourdieu, these are limited by past and present realities and inscribed within current practices, which confine and condition what is conceived of as possible or probable in the future. Attempts at transformation are therefore themselves conditioned by the structures of the habitus in the present. Thus, in Bourdieu's work, as in the early work of Foucault, structure is emphasized to the exclusion of the individual (see McNay, 2000, p. 8; but on Foucault see also Allen, 2000).

A critical problem that arises is that this deterministic conception of power treats power as a function of the state–society–individual nexus rather than as a phenomenon that attaches to relationships, in their different forms, at all levels. It treats power as polymorphic, an objectively knowable entity that changes its form (Castelfranchi, 2003), rather than as something that grafts onto, engages with, and is transformed by complex existing bodies (Butler, 1993). As such it prevents deeper understanding of the multiple and simultaneous ways power manifests in, plays on, and is renegotiated by the individual. Eric R Wolf (1999, p. 5) differentiates different types of power that function through structures and through individuals. In his book *Envisioning Power*, Wolf says that when we think of power as an aspect of relationships we can begin to differentiate how power works in different types of relationships. The modality through which power is woven into social relations changes. He distinguishes four modalities of power in social relations. Tactical or organizational power refers to the power that controls the context through which some direct the actions of others. Structural power meanwhile operates within the settings and domains of relationships and orchestrates them, specifying the direction of their flow. Wolf likens structural power to the power over people as a resource, labour (in Marxist terms), and over ideas. But he recognizes two other modalities of power, which relate to the individual as subject of power. Firstly, there is the personal power of potency or capability in the Nietzschean sense, which he sees as determining how a person enters into the play of power. Secondly, there is Weberian interpersonal power, how people interact within the context of the powerplay and the ability of one individual to impose his or her will against another.

Power as a force that seeks to organize and structure society en masse is distinct from power as it functions at the intimate level of the self. While in *Discipline and Punish* Foucault focuses on the individual's 'normalization' within institutions, in his later work he makes a shift towards an active self-constituting subject (McNay, 1991). A more 'specific, diffuse idea emerges of individuals actively constructing their day-to-day existences in a relatively autonomous fashion' (McNay, 1991, p. 82). This emphasis on the active, independent subject is particularly visible in *The History of Sexuality*. Here, Foucault (1981) shifts emphasis away from the idea of individuals as 'docile bodies', which he formulates in *Discipline and Punish* (1977), and towards a more active individual, the 'self'. In fact, both conceptions of power, presented in his earlier and later work as structural and as individual, are important. The direction power takes in these two *loci* need not be contradictory, as we have seen. One may reinforce the other. However, differentiating them allows us to see that they may not, either, always be complementary. That is to say that it is not power but the relationship to which it attaches that needs to be examined. Personal and interpersonal power exist in a way that is functionally distinct from structural power and need not have convergence with structural power as its aim.

With this is the understanding that power itself is not predictable and power within any relationship is constituted within that relationship and may shift between the parties. In his later work on technologies of the self, Foucault shows that in order to understand how power works we need to make a shift from the study of power itself to the study of power relations. He describes power relations as relationships between 'partners' whereby each person is prompted to follow the path of others, but this takes place in a game where the rules are not fixed (1994b, p. 337). Power 'incites', 'seduces', 'makes [some responses] more probable or less', it acts on a 'field of possibilities' in which 'a whole field of responses, reactions, results, and possible inventions may open up' (1994b, pp. 340–1). This differs from Weber's concept of interpersonal power, which involves the imposition of will by one against, and against the will of, another. Power in the Foucauldian sense is not linear in this way but rather circular, 'never in anyone's hands', and individuals are conduits of its articulation rather than targets in its trajectory (Foucault, 1980, p. 98). To understand this further we turn now to the concept of resistance.

Resistance

Whether in studies of history, sociology or political science, resistance was for a long time equated with popular movements for liberation from a particular form of time-and-space specific oppression. In this context it was framed with reference to moments of 'crisis' when the subjugated rose up in revolt against their oppressors. Resistance occurred during episodes in history when a chain of events, beginning perhaps with rumours or minor incidents, escalated into a collective demonstration of might/action (see, for example, Horowitz, 2001). There was also a tendency to treat revolt and resistance as a study of elite practices.

Subaltern historians writing in post-colonial South Asia challenged this, reformulating the way in which historical agents were identified. They uncovered the locus of struggle in the villages and houses of ordinary people who were dismissed in historical texts as 'rebels', 'insurgents' and 'bandits' acting spontaneously without real consciousness (Guha, 1983, p. 4). Through these studies less visibly organized forms of resistance were attributed with hegemony (leadership) in the Gramscian sense, and actions that were previously considered indiscriminate, unprovoked and unorganized attacks were re-imagined as conscious acts of resistance.

This work relied heavily on Gramsci's theory of consciousness. Consciousness for Gramsci functions on two levels: an embryonic conception of the world which is only rarely manifested when groups come together and take some form of action; and a conception of the world which is borrowed from the hegemonic ideology, putting the group in a position of intellectual subordination that group members manifest verbally and think themselves to be following. Action is a rare event of collective revolt, and thought is the everyday submission to external hegemonic ideology. In other words, Gramsci sees groups as conforming to the ideology of a hegemonic group but as having their own embryonic consciousness which manifests itself through 'occasional' 'flashes' of action taken by a group acting as an organic totality (Gramsci, 1971, p. 327).

Both the Gramscian and subaltern approaches focus on resistance as a rupturing event, a rare moment when the harshness of domination breaches the limits of what is otherwise accepted by the dominated. But this contrast of acceptance and revolt under-represents what happens in between these periods of violent resistance. Alternative theories began to emerge based on ethnographic research that found resistance in everyday practices, questioning the presumption that power relations were uncomplicated and unchallenged between these moments of upheaval (Haynes and Prakash, 1991). James Scott's work in the area of social movement theory – and most notably his study of peasant resistance in Malaysia, *Weapons of the Weak* (1985) – showed that the emphasis on peasant rebellion was misplaced. Peasant resistance was an 'everyday' occurrence, manifested through daily tensions between the dominator and subjugated.

This shift in focus to individual or everyday resistance allowed for an understanding of resistance other than at the level of collective revolt. It acknowledged resistance within relationships, as a counter-force to domination, anti-power: domination and resistance occurring at the level of individual relations, and not merely during moments of collective action. This also signified a shift towards recognition of resistance as an act that occurs within as well as outside power relations: based on the premise that collective resistance brings the individual outside (exterior to) the power relation and individual resistance occurs within the power relation (Fitzpatrick, 1988, p. 184).

It is in this respect that studies of everyday resistance seem to depart most dramatically from traditional literature on resistance. This distinction has created a popular retort that individual resistance is unlikely to represent an escape from or dramatic change to the relationship in the way that collective revolt intends to (Haynes and Prakash, 1991, p. 3). Individual resistance is merely part of an ongoing renegotiation within power relations that fails to disrupt the status quo and may even reduce people's ability to perceive their disadvantage.[1] What this shift in the status quo might look like is unclear. In reality, as we will see in Chapter 3, even collective resistance, while it may have a more disruptive immediate effect on the techniques of domination used by the hegemonic power, is unlikely to end inequality. Foucault (1994a, p. 123) acknowledged that even revolutions could leave essentially untouched the power relations that provide the foundations for the functioning of the state. Even where collective resistance does achieve the destruction/replacement of the hegemonic elite of the time, this may do little more than instigate a paradigm shift from one set of elite, and power relations, to another. Because power relations are part of the fabric of social relations, new forms of domination appear in the place of old.

Gramsci saw such paradigm shifts as nevertheless serving a purpose if they replaced an elite ideology with the embryonic ideology of the people. Resistance for him was 'a struggle of political "hegemonies" … first in the ethical field and then in that of politics proper, in order to arrive at the working out at a higher level of one's own conception of reality' (Gramsci, 1971, p. 333). Intellectual revolution is performed not by confronting one philosophy with another but by confronting the social forces behind them and the ideology, 'common sense', which these forces generate (Hoare and Smith, 1971 pp. 321–2). The individual or social group is assisted in realizing his/her/its embryonic ideology through an elite of intellectuals who are able to organize and lead the masses. But there is a problem with this since, by Gramsci's own admission, intellectuals are also functioning as a social group in themselves. The force of power relations works across the various social groups in society to subjugate the intellectual elite of subordinate social groups.

This position is put forward by Gramsci (1971, p. 55) in *The Problem of Political Leadership in the Formation and Development of the Nation and the Modern State of Italy*. Here he explains:

---

1 Christine White says that small acts of resistance are counter-productive because they make individuals *feel* they are resisting but in fact blinds them to the reality of the extent of their powerlessness (cited in Mitchell, 1990, p. 555).

> there does not exist any independent class of intellectuals, but every social group has its own stratum of intellectuals, or tends to form one; however, the intellectuals of the historically ... progressive class ... exercise such a power of attraction that, in the last analysis, they end up by subjugating the intellectuals of the other social groups; they thereby create a system of solidarity between all the intellectuals, with bonds of psychological nature (vanity, etc.) and often of a caste character (technico-juridical, corporate, etc.). (Gramsci, 1971, p. 60)

For Gramsci, this situation occurs spontaneously during the historical period when the social group is progressive, attempting to increase its domains of conquest to new areas of economic and productive activity. Collective resistance led by an intellectual elite is not then a straightforward escape from domination. The individual is still depending on an elite for intellectual leadership, and that elite will share some if not many of the techniques of domination of the previous elite.

However, the cultures and the political structures and legal orders they encompass are not static, they develop and change, and individual resistance can play an important role in directing change. I should point out here that I am not negating the role of collective *identity* – which is often at the root of subordination – as a basis for resistance. Individual renegotiations occur in the context of a person's identity based on ethnicity, social class, age, gender, sexuality, mental and physical health and so on. Individual acts of resistance take place in the context of group oppression and may impact on the actions and thoughts of the collectivity. I am contrasting individual resistance, which takes place as a *renegotiation* of power relations, with collective strategies that seek a radical change in power relations through mobilization of a group or part of a group.[2]

I do depart from the literature on individual resistance in two important ways, however. Firstly, whereas I have said above that a theoretical distinction has been made between 'individual resistance' as a phenomenon that is internal to power relations and 'collective resistance' that is exterior to power relations, my theory relies on the fact that individual resistance can be an external or an internal process. That is to say that I do not agree that collective resistance is exterior to power relations and individual resistance internal. I explore individual external resistance to power relations through the use of external forums in Chapter 5. Secondly, and following from this, I reserve the term individual 'resistance' for the phenomenon of resisting

---

2 Nevertheless, as we will see, some trajectories of renegotiation, in particular the use of alternative legal orders (ALOs) discussed in Chapter 6, are more likely to rupture the relationship.

the power relation from the outside. I make this distinction in order to demonstrate that trajectories of renegotiation that take place within the power relation are very different in nature. Whereas external 'resistance' denotes a form of anti-power that rejects and works against the power relation, individual renegotiations within power relations rely on and work through the power relation, a form of acceptance.

Nevertheless, I do focus on resistance and renegotiations at the level of the *individual* alone and there is another reason for this. Power is, in its very nature, an individualizing force. As discussed earlier, power works on the individual so that he or she becomes both the object and the instrument of its exercise (Foucault, 1977, p. 170). This 'individualization' is a way for the hegemonic power to control the inefficiency of the collectivity and neutralize its organizing forces. Resistance and renegotiations that occur at the level of the individual take advantage of the individualizing force of power and use its momentum against itself.

However, the individual still faces pressure to contribute to the collectivity by conforming to the dominant ideology. The effect of power is to make the individual feel that he or she is only useful as part of a collectivity, but that he or she is accountable as an individual for his/her part in the functioning of the collectivity. Gramsci (1971, p. 201) shows that the individual is devalued in the production process: the collective work is what is important, the individual can be replaced at any time. But while his/her identity as a 'collective worker' is nurtured, his/her responsibility as an individual is also emphasized. The individual is made to feel responsible for the collectivity reaching its aim, fulfilling its function. This puts pressure on the individual and I discuss this in Chapter 5.

Because of this, analysing how power relations engender domination over the individual is critical to understanding how the individual responds. By domination I mean the forces inherent in the nature of power relations that put one person or group in a position of advantage over another at any given moment.[3] The position of advantage or degree of advantage is not fixed: it may be changeable or even reversible. Where the initial inequality is vertical and its field of application is vast and well established – such as between master and slave from the seventeenth to nineteenth century in America – reversal may be near impossible, but the

---

[3] Foucault, in fact, rarely mentions domination and seems to define it as an extreme: domination exists when 'an individual or social group manages to block a field of relations of power, to render them impassive and invariable and to prevent all reversibility of movement ... in such a state that practice of liberty does not exist or exists only unilaterally or is extremely confined and limited' (1988, p. 3). Nevertheless, he does acknowledge domination in male–female and adult–child relationships – see Delsing (1991, n. 173) – and uses the term occasionally in the context of power relations.

more horizontal the inequality – such as between a well-established scholar and an early career academic – the more chance there is of reversal. Foucault (1988, p. 12) illustrates this in the context of an interview with a young scholar. He tells the interviewer that, while his own seniority in age gives him an initial advantage and may have made the younger academic intimidated, in the course of the interview it is Foucault who may become intimidated by the questioning of the young academic.

This leads us onto a more contested question: how does this domination, which gives space for resistance, act on the individual? Writers looking at the effects of power and resistance often make a distinction between domination acting over the physical body of the individual and domination over their mind, ideology, culture that is between *coercion* and *persuasion* (Mitchell, 1990). Scott (1985, pp. 317–18) adopts a similar distinction in *Weapons of the Weak* in which he examines everyday resistance of peasants in a village which he calls Sedaka, in the rice-producing Muda region of Malaysia. He shows the subordinate of Sedaka as having an internal consciousness or rationality that the local elite are not able to dominate. Their behaviour suggests that they are conforming to the dominant ideology but they are able to think critically about their relationship with their exploiters. They engage in 'calculated conformity' to relations of inequality in the village. Timothy Mitchell (1990, p. 545) rejects the starting point that domination functions within a dualism of mind and body. He says the notion of the individual as a *physical body*, which can be coerced, with an autonomous *consciousness*, forces us to see power as an external process working on the body.

Mitchell (1990) argues for a different dualism at the heart of modern domination. He argues that domination occurs through the development of an unphysical frame that seeks to control practice and is external to the actual practices of the people in society. Thus, he sees the tension as being between this objective unphysical frame (in the form of rules and regulation of aspects of production which were previously flexible and sensitive to changes in nature) and the actual practices of people in society. For Mitchell, these new forms of domination, coming from a more distant state, appear fixed and enduring, whereas older forms of domination, which grew organically through social relations, were negotiated and flexible. He does not talk about how this dualism contributes to resistance but suggests that, being fixed from the outside and not subject to local influence, new forms of domination are not negotiable. He sees them as 'enframed' by external regulatory entities, 'self-reproducing' and controlled by official policing. The distancing of the process of enframing rules and controlling compliance from the locale of social practices means that governing has become regularized, achieves uniform repetition (Mitchell, 1990, p. 571).

The distancing of the regulation from social practices is said to ensure its stability and reduce and replace locally constructed social practices. Mitchell acknowledges these new practices as constructing a binary world, but sees the externally framed, fixed realm of new modes of domination as coinciding with existing meanings and ideologies. This is true to some extent but the imposition of a new set of ideologies from a source exterior to the locale of social practices is a process that involves struggle and contestation. External rules and ideologies are unlikely, at least not in the first instance, to be adopted and accepted. I have written elsewhere that the imposition of external ideologies is resisted on both an individual and group level. The source of exterior domination, whether in the immediate locale of social relations or in a more distant locale of regulation by a dominator such as the state, does not affect the fact of resistance, only its mode of operation (Shariff, 2013).

All regulation must at one point or another be implemented and its application takes place if not through then in the presence of existing social practices. But the exposure to external rules and ideologies is important. The coinciding of rules that Mitchell refers to creates a fertile ground for transformation. How that transformation occurs and the new social practices that emerge from it, however, are not pre-determinable. New practices emerge from existing ones and different types of relationship are affected by transformations in different ways.

Carla Risseeuw (1988, p. 266) goes some way to illustrating this. In her discussion of resistance amongst the female coir workers in Sri Lanka, she distinguishes different types of power relation. Domination over women as workers, exercised by traders, is experienced separately from the domination over women in the household, exercised by husbands and in-laws. She shows that women are trained by their mothers to realize the exploitative nature of the relationship between them and the traders, but fail to realize their exploitation as wife and family member in their husband's household. Risseeuw uses Bourdieu's theory of the *orthodoxy* (dominant opinion), *heterodoxy* (opposing opinion) and *doxa* (outside the discourse) to explain this. She sees the women's exploitation in the household as falling under the doxa, that which is not discussed, so that the woman does not see herself as making a decision or choice.

Globalization and the spread of information technology means that the realm of the doxa, which for Bourdieu dominated social structures, is shrinking and individuals are constituted in a context of plural orthodoxies and heterodoxies, which provide multiple alternative ways of conceiving society. While some cultural influences will dominate their lives, this exposure to different domains of discourse, or an alternative view on one's position, I will argue, is a vital component of renegotiating power relations, particularly where inequalities are internalized, and does have the potential to facilitate change. This is because that which is treated as doxa in one domain may be treated as orthodoxy in another. It is in the nature of discourse that it simultaneously produces power and has the ability to undermine it, or expose its fragility (Foucault, 1981).

Legal pluralism

In 1986 John Griffiths wrote a compelling paper outlining and critiquing the emerging theory of legal pluralism.[4] Reflecting on the broad and diverse social situations that had been researched under this term he wrote:

> Society is neither the homogeneous whole supposed by legal centralism nor the neat federative structure of segmentary associations supposed by institutionalist theory and by writers such as Pospisil and Smith. It is rather a chaotic mess of competing, overlapping, constantly fluid groups more or less inclusive, with entirely heterogeneous principles of membership, social functions, etc. and with a baffling variety of structural relationships to each other and to the state. (Griffiths, 1986, p. 27)

By the time he wrote this, legal pluralism was a well-established term and subject to a wide range of interpretations and uses. The term was first coined by the late legal anthropologist Franz Von Benda Beckmann[5] to describe the juxtaposing of customary, religious and colonial laws in nineteenth- and twentieth-century Malawi. The term proved versatile and, while well suited to the study of ex-colonial societies, was rapidly adapted to the study of law in society in the West. Sally Falk Moore (2001, p. 95) describes the discovery of legal pluralism as a turning point in legal anthropology when studies of class and domination in Western legal institutions challenged the presumption that the state was the only source of obligatory rules. Legal pluralists argued that society consisted of many smaller social sites where norms were generated. These sites existed between the state and the individual and constituted social fields to which the individual was attached, 'belonged'. They possessed not only their own customs and rules but also the means of coercing or inducing compliance (Moore, 1978, p. 57). Legal monists, who see state law as the only source of 'law', and jurisprudential scholars, who seek to understand the nature and meaning

---

4 He has since written a paper in which he states that it is not law, but social control that is the proper subject of the sociology of law (Griffiths, 2006).
5 *Rechtspluralismus in Malawi: Geschichtliche Entwicklung und heutige Problematik*, PhD dissertation, completed 1970 at the University of Kiel.

of law, question whether the term 'legal' is appropriate for describing norms constituted within society.[6] A prominent legal anthropologist, Simon Roberts, also argued that non-state norms are by their nature so different to state norms that insisting on calling them 'law' takes away from their unique characteristics (Roberts, 2005).

However, the intersections between state law and social norms and the difficulty in identifying an empirically observable line between the two (Woodman, 1998) has meant that attempts to conceptually separate 'laws' and 'norms' within legal pluralist investigations have remained in the margins, and mostly the pursuit of theoretical scholars (see, for example, Teubner, 1992; also Tamanaha, 1993; 2001; Melissaris, 2004; 2009). Legal pluralism, emerged as an antidote to monism and centralism, concepts that privileged state law as a tool of social control (Griffiths, 1986; Merry, 1988). Legal pluralists continue to use the term 'legal' order to describe sites of norms outside the state and have produced a rich resource of literature covering a truly global terrain (see *Journal of Legal Pluralism* and the work of the Commission on Legal Pluralism). Over the past 30 years the concept has developed to cover a wide range of subjects. While the earliest discussions of legal pluralism focused on colonial and customary law, or state and tribal law, today it covers the study of sports associations, trade unions, families, multiculturalist societies, development organizations and alternative dispute resolution in the West.

There have been some attempts to create a globally relevant map of legal pluralism. Boaventura de Sousa Santos suggests six basic forms of legal orders (which he calls 'structural places'), which are structurally autonomous but interrelated, for capitalist societies: domestic law of the 'householdplace' which governs relations between husband and wife, their children and among kin; production law of the 'workplace'; exchange law of the 'marketplace'; community law of the 'communityplace', where social relations revolve around (re)production of territories and identities; territorial (state) law of the 'citizenplace' which constitutes the public sphere and obligation between the state and citizens; and systemic law of the 'worldplace'.[7]

Although interlinked, the power relations that constitute an individual in each of these legal orders belong to that legal order. As such, we can talk about the legal order of the householdplace with its rules of relationship separately from the legal order of the communityplace. For example,

---

6 Tamanaha (2000) and Melissaris (2004), for example, advocate 'rule-system pluralism' and 'legal discourses' respectively as alternative terms to legal pluralism.
7 Santos (1995, p. 417; and 2002, p. 374). Some inconsistencies and inadequacies have been found in Santos' elaboration of these structures and the distinction he makes between the laws existing in each 'place' (see, for example, Tamanaha, 2000).

relationships in the rural village of a community such as the one I studied, the Santal, that subordinate women through a system of patriarchal leadership, are not the same as those that subordinate the woman belonging to the same village as a 'wife' in the context of her family. The two may be linked and may reinforce each other, they may even be structured by the same principle of patriarchy, but they are nevertheless constituted through relationships within quite distinct legal orders. The technologies of domination that subordinate the woman overlap, but differ.

Santos integrates into his definition of these distinct places the characteristic of porosity. That is to say that as individuals we experience these overlapping legal orders in a way that forces us to transition and trespass between them constantly and they become 'mixed in our minds' (2002, p. 437). He calls this phenomenon 'interlegality'. Interlegality has far-reaching consequences as 'mixing' spills out into the development of these legal orders, for example, the global legal space as it emerges appropriates local legal vernaculars. The legal spaces that he describes borrow from each other, albeit that this process is uneven and the combinations of codes it produces are unstable. Francis Snyder points out that socio-legal orders are 'usually intertwined in the same social micro-processes ... the apparent autonomy of a small social field is itself always shaped and determined by a wider system' (cited in Griffiths, 1985, p. 18). This intimate relationship between legal orders is a core characteristic of legal plurality. Speaking of the relationship between state and non-state law, Moore (1978) coined the phrase 'the semi-autonomous social field' to describe non-state law, pointing to the interconnectedness between state law and social norms. The connections between legal orders provide some points of cross-fertilization. Nevertheless, each legal order also seeks to develop in contradistinction to its alternatives. Santos (2002, p. 374) says 'the specificity of each structural place lies in the form of unequal exchange that is the specific form of power in action that marks the social relations it constitutes'. While it may co-opt the rules of compliance from state law, for example, non-state law may choose rules that directly contradict those of its neighbouring legal orders. This distinction is the source of its power.

How can this distinction between legal orders assist the individual? There is a whole body of literature on forum-shopping, or legal pluralism in subjectivity, that illustrates and demonstrates the importance of legal pluralism for the resisting subject. Legal pluralism produces a condition whereby the individual is confronted with multiple, possibly conflicting, regulatory orders. Masaji Chiba (1998) notes that a person living in a number of legal orders is an active agent of the law who makes a choice between the alternative legal rules available to him/her. These alternatives provide options, as well as dilemmas,[8] for the pursuit of their individual goals. This is well illustrated through empirical studies such as those included in Olivia Harris's (1996) edited volume *Inside and Outside the Law*. In that volume, Thérèse Bouysse-Cassagne (1996) examines how indigenous Inca women in Latin America voluntarily registered their children under official law as 'illegitimate' offspring of Spanish officers, *mestizajes*, ostracizing them from the Inca community, in order to gain benefits offered by the Spanish conquerors. Elsewhere Diane Austin-Broos' (1996) study of tribal women in Australia found that they lived by both their own Aranda law and God's law, giving one or the other priority according to which gave them the most benefit in a given situation. In some instances transition between legal orders may be more permanent.

Chiba (1998) notes that the choice between legal orders can be made to *support* one particular set of standards or to *reject* another one. A 'rejective choice' may take the form of evasive behaviour or actual destructive behaviour through recourse to norms outside the social field. Evasive action may put the individual in direct conflict with the legal order being rejected. Sophie Day (1996) found that street prostitutes voluntarily suffer regular fines given by police, choosing to break the state law as part of their inclusion within the social field of prostitution where they make their living. Destructive behaviour may provide a strong signal to the legal order of its failings. In Ray Abrahams' (1996, p. 44) study of criminality, people who chose vigilante justice over state due process to deal with criminality in their neighbourhood were signalling the state's inability to meet their needs. Chiba (1998, p. 239) goes on to say that, where rejective choices are accumulated, they can result in collective resistance, even to the point of revolution.

Alternative legal orders as well as being manipulated or chosen can also be shaped to meet an individual's needs. Jo-Anne Fiske and Patty J Ginn (2000) analyse a court case in the Canadian province of British Columbia in which a Catholic bishop who had had a relationship with a young aboriginal member of staff in his boarding school redefines his conviction for indecent assault and rape through a Catholic discourse. He describes himself as someone who gave many years to work for the aboriginal people and sees the conviction as a result of his misfortune, paying a heavy price for failing to respect the vow of chastity he took. Fiske and Ginn note his crime was reconceived as being against the church and the woman was

---

8 See Hellum, 1995, p. 18; Vanderlinden, 1989, pp. 153–4; Chiba, 1998. Cf. Ashley et al., 2003, on legal pluralism as an obstacle to access to justice in the southern African context in rural areas where complex socio-political negotiations take place on an uneven playing field.

transformed from victim to temptress. Although he was initially sentenced, he was acquitted of indecent assault on appeal and before he could be retried for the rape charge the complainant agreed to drop charges in return for an alternative justice procedure (healing circle with the First Nations community) and an apology. His trial demonstrated an ability to manipulate the state law process to create a different socio-legal meaning to his conviction, his failure to meet the requirements of Catholic prescripts, which suited his definition of his crime. His alternative discourse took shape in 'active resistance' to the formulation of his crime through state law. The alternative meanings drawn from Catholic narratives denied the woman in the case an acceptance of the harm he had done to her. He took himself into another discourse, avoiding the label of criminal abuser and denying the woman recognition of the injustice.

The point I wish to make here is that legal pluralism, and plural legalisms, provide a complex and fertile context for the process of power and resistance. Ultimately, the individual in cultural communities is an active subject of the relationships that work to include and exclude, subordinate and direct them. The plurality of norms and discourses that interweave through the social spaces he or she inhabits provide multiple opportunities for resistance. In the chapters that follow, I explore the distinction and interconnections between these legal orders and how the resisting subject navigates through them. I return in Chapter 7 to consider how different relational experiences of power, power practices, affect and shape resistance and renegotiations and why legal pluralism is critical to this process.

3
The Santal: Processes of Subordination in the State

The day I arrived to carry out my research in Rajshahi, north-west Bangladesh, the town was buzzing with the news that a large slum, where the poorest had erected temporary housing near the university, had been cleared overnight. What had been a thriving corner of the town near the university's Vinodpur Gate, where slum dwellers had set up small shopfronts and stalls, was engulfed in dust. The remains of makeshift buildings lay in bits, the slum's previous inhabitants watched from the sidelines in numb shock. Slum clearance appears regularly in Regional Development Plans for improvements to roads, water supply and sewage drainage, provision of housing, education and health facilities (see, for example, Ara et al., 2007), but is often met with public protest. Bystanders claimed 25 protesters had died during the slum clearance as a result of heavy-handed police intervention.

These were urban slums and the inhabitants were not cultural minorities, but I was to find that this turbulent scene of the violent force of the state against landless poor reflected regional tensions over land distribution. It also illustrated challenges for representation of disadvantaged communities in local and national politics that were key to the Santal's struggle for justice. For cultural minorities and adivasis[1] like the Santal living in rural areas, these tensions have played out through historical struggles with local elites. Such struggles have been characterized by exploitation, displacement and exclusion, in which the state has been complicit or negligent.

A long history of internal migration and dispersal within the subcontinent and shifting territorial boundaries of the state during post-colonial

---

[1] The Santal I lived with described themselves first as Santali then as Indian or Bangladeshi, however, the term adivasi was more likely to be used at meetings or conferences where rights and state obligations were in debate.

partition and the Bangladeshi war of independence from Pakistan have resulted in the Santal occupying an area now spanning three countries (including five states of India, the north-west region of Bangladesh and parts of Nepal). Despite numbering over 6 million, their linguistic, religious and cultural minority status in countries where status-based resource allocation and representation is the norm has left them with multiple disadvantages. Below I examine the circular nature of displacement and exclusion, from the pre-colonial period to the present, which has provided a turbulent context for the Santal's settlement experience and strengthened internal drivers for cultural exclusivity.

The Santal: migrating to alterity

Oral histories of the Santal's origin – such as the origin myth, recorded by missionaries and colonial officers – which mix fact with the mystical, suggest that the Santal undertook regular periodic resettlement up to the twentieth century. For the Santal people it is not the potential accuracy of the origin myth that gives it its potency but the fact that it resonates with experiences of adversity and exclusion still experienced today. The Santal believe that their race was created by *Thakur* (god) and underwent centuries of displacement. The origin myth, with its messages of morality, adversity and godly interventions, is revealing as a foundation of the Santal sense of cultural distinctiveness. It tells of the first Santal couple Pilcu Haram and Pilcu Budhi who lived in Hihiri Pipiri where they learnt to brew rice beer (still an important part of life-cycle ceremonies) and produced seven sons and seven daughters. The brothers and sisters bore children and the human race multiplied and migrated to Khoj-Kaman. But the people began to degenerate and Thakur sent down fiery rain killing all except one couple who had been sent a message to hide in the mountain of Harate. The surviving couple produced a new human race. Over a series of voluntary and involuntary migrations the origin myth tells of the Santal dividing into 12 clans, seven named after the first seven sons of Pilcu Haram. These clans were associated at one stage in their history with particular professions and are still used today to identify lineage.

According to the origin myth, in between the violent episodes in which the Santal are forced to move to avoid assimilation, the Santal develop their customs and traditions. Old traditions are occasionally discarded in favour of new practices learnt from their Hindu neighbours. But many customs are said to emerge as a result of conflict with Hindus and Muslims. At one stage of their migration story, the Santal face extinction trying to cross a high range of mountains. They ask the spirit of the mountain (Marang Buru, literally meaning big mountain) to show them a way through. The next day a path through the mountain appears and they now worship the spirit of Marang Buru, represented by a sacred grove called the *jaher than,* in every village. Spiritual interventions such as this, which are thought to have ensured their survival, provide a foundation for their present-day spiritual beliefs. In the later stages of their migration story, a long stay in Campa, thought to be in the present Punjab, where they built forts to protect themselves from their enemies, ends abruptly after a fierce battle with Muslims and Hindus. The origin myth and migration story functions as a reminder to all Santal of a shared struggle for survival and women in the villages can be heard today singing mournful laments over the lost battles of their ancestors and giving thanks to the spirit of Marang Buru.

Attempts have been made to trace the Santal's migratory history through historical texts (O'Malley, 1910; Bodding, 1942; Kochuchira, 2000). A colonial administrator, Herbert Risley (1891, p. 225), claimed to have found evidence dating back to 1340 of a large Santal colony in Hazaribagh district, near to the current-day homeland of Santal Parganas, Jharkhand. Colonial reports by Sir William Wilson Hunter and L S S O'Malley provide detailed information on their settlement in the Santal Parganas from the eighteenth century. Many Santal moved into the plains area of the Damin-i-koh in response to a call by the British. Although no accurate census data for the Santal in the Santal Parganas was available until 1891, colonial estimates of their numbers suggest an increase from 3000 in 1838 to 663,000 by 1901 (Hunter, 1868, p. 154; O'Malley, 1910, p. 99).

Hunter's *Annals of Rural Bengal* states:

> The Permanent Settlement for the land tax in 1790 resulted in a general extension of tillage, and the Santals were hired to rid the lowlands of the wild beasts which, since the great famine of 1769, had everywhere encroached upon the margin of cultivation. (1868, p. 152)

The initial Santal settlers to the area profited from the arrangement, having an abundance of cattle and rich yields. But their success brought traders and money-lenders (*mahajans*) to the area from Bengal and elsewhere who took advantage of their inexperience of trade (O'Malley, 1910, pp. 45–6). According to Hunter (1868), the traders used measuring tools with false bottoms or used uncalibrated weights to cheat the unsuspecting Santal. In leaner periods the mahajans gave loans and later forced families into bonded labour to repay their debts at exorbitant interest rates (Kochuchira, 2000, p. 73). They kept ledgers as proof of the rising debt and sometimes forged deeds of sale or mortgage to take the Santal's land in repayment. The British courts were often too far away to offer redress and the police and court messengers anyway sided with the mahajans to enforce the debt (Hunter, 1868, p. 159; O'Malley, 1910, p. 46).

In the plains surrounding the Damin-i-koh, Bengalis and others who migrated to the area used their wealth to become landlords and the Santal were forced to leave or remain as bonded labourers. Exploitation through extortion and abuse by mahajans, traders and revenue collectors (*zamindars*)[2] ignited mass support for calls for a Santal homeland, which was instrumental in what was to be a critical turning point in Santal history. Initially, the Santal in the Damin-i-koh began to attack and steal back wealth from their immediate oppressors, the mahajans and traders. These thefts were treated as simple criminal acts and the Santal involved were arrested and punished. In 1854 the Santal requested unsuccessfully that the government recognize and respond to their complaints.

When this failed the Santal turned rebels. In June 1855 two Santal brothers, Sidhu and Kanu, claiming to have been visited by their god (Thakur), called for attacks on Bengalis and mahajans to take back Santal land. A short rebellion ensued and the British responded with heavy-handed attacks by the army. By mid-August a combination of the army's attacks and assistance and funds from zamindars and European indigo-planters brought the insurrection almost to a close. The government announced that, while all *criminals* would be punished, a pardon would be given to Santal who had not committed criminal offences if they reported to the authorities. Seeing the offer as a trap, the Santal rejected the pardon and the insurrection began anew. On 10 November the government announced martial law, but it took two months before the Santal were finally overcome. Many Santal were convicted and jailed (Sinha, 1990).

Despite their military triumph the British recognized the need for tighter laws in the area to stop further exploitation. They established the Santal Parganas under Act 37 of 1855 as a separate district overseen by a deputy commissioner outside the jurisdiction of most general government regulations and legislation. While initially rules to introduce uniform weights and measures for use by traders and limit interest rates to 25 per cent addressed the Santal's grievances, by 1861 these had been abandoned. Further unrest after 1871 led to legislation in the form of the Santal Parganas Settlement Regulation 111 of 1872, setting fixed rents and fixing land titles. Between 1872 and 1879 many Santal tenants and headmen were reinstated and

---

2 Another factor was the construction of railways in the Damin-i-koh. The railway construction has been written about as a site of oppression, abductions, rape and murder against the Santal (Kochuchira, 2000, p. 78) but also as a source of wealth for the Santal railway workers, provoking unrest amongst Santal who remained on their original land as bonded labourers (Sinha, 1990, p. 26).

given security of tenure and *raiyati* land (land historically cultivated by tenant farmers) was made non-transferable under the Santal Parganas Rent Regulation II of 1886, and III of 1908. In 1949 the tenancy laws were replaced with the Santal Parganas Tenancy (Supplementary Provisions) Act (SPTA 1949) which gave a degree of security to the Santal but did not prevent land alienation altogether.

While this settlement in the Santal Parganas was the most significant in the Santal's recent history, the migration of several thousand Santal to the Barind tract, in what is now Bangladesh, had important implications for those who settled there. According to Abdus Sattar (1983, p. 71), the violence of the Santal insurrection (*hul*) of 1855 led some Santal, fearing for their safety, to leave the Santal Parganas for Rajshahi, now in north-west Bangladesh. Around this time there was also a call by the British administration to bring Santal to the area to clear and cultivate forest and wasteland. Mr Gait, census superintendent of 1901, wrote that in the mid-nineteenth century:

> it occurred to the manager of a Government state that the waste land might be reclaimed if Santals were imported and settled there. The experiment was made and proved such a success that the influx has continued ever since ... (cited in Siddiqui, 1972, p. 52).

In 1901 there were 7000 migrants from the Santal Parganas in Rajshahi and this doubled by 1911. The official Census of India 1931 states financial problems forced Santal in the Santal Parganas to migrate to the Barind tract, including parts of Dinajpur, Rajshahi, Bogra and Malda, after 1901 (Ray, 1975, p. 3 citing W G Laccy, Census of India ,1931, 1(3) 'Ethnographical: The Santal'). The Santal migrants remained in the area, being permitted by the zamindars to cultivate the newly cleared land for three to four years rent free. Mr Gait, expressing a condescension often found in records of the time, wrote 'this exactly suits the taste of these unsophisticated aborigines, who do not mind the physical labour involved in breaking down the jungle, but have a great aversion to the payment of rent' (O'Malley, 1916, p. 52). Once the rent-free term expired, the Santal moved on to new areas.

Critically for them, the Santal and other adivasis were not the only migrants to the area – in 1911 migrants from the Santal Parganas constituted only 15 per cent of those living in Rajshahi: Muslims predominated, constituting 78 per cent of the population, one of the highest ratios of Muslims to non-Muslims in North Bengal. In 1916, O'Malley noted that migrants came from Bihar and United Provinces searching for employment on roads. Many of them become *chaukidars* – village police. While the Hindus outnumbered Muslims in the towns, the Muslims dominated rural areas, comprising 98 per cent of the rural population. This had an enormous impact on the lives of the Santal, in particular in relation to their land holdings.

Islam was brought to Bengal by invading armies from north India in the thirteenth century and had become the dominant religion in Greater Bengal by 1872 (Madan, 1998, p. 972). By 1900 over half of all Bengalis (inhabiting Greater Bengal) were Muslim and by 1947 Islam had become an important political identity for Bengalis seeking to take power from the middle-class Hindus of Bengal. The suggestion by the British to partition Bengal in 1905 was welcomed by the Muslim elite as an opportunity to take some control away from the middle-class Hindus. These ambitions were nurtured under the Muslim League in the years before the end of British rule when religious identity became a crucial factor in the distribution of power and territory. Independence from British rule in 1947 marked the division of Bengal into two parts: Muslim East Bengal (known as East Pakistan until 1971) and Hindu West Bengal (India).

When Pakistan was created in 1947, Jinnah, founder of the two-nation theory, gave a speech declaring that Hindus and Muslims would be considered equal citizens. Despite this, in 1950, after his death, large-scale communal riots and disturbances throughout East Pakistan resulted in politically sanctioned, unprecedented emigration of Hindus from the country (see further Barkat et al., 1997, p. 19). The number of Hindus in East Pakistan decreased by 2.5 million between 1941 and 1951. The vacuum left by the Hindus and other religious minorities was filled by Muslim businessmen from Bihar. One million Muslims came to East Pakistan during partition and more came after the communal riots in 1950 and after the 1965 war (Whitaker, 1982, p. 7). The Muslim Biharis were appointed by the Pakistani authorities to replace the educated Hindus in key jobs in the administration, railway workshops and jute mills. They also found work as small traders, clerks, civil-service officers, skilled railway and mill workers and doctors. They were unpopular amongst the Bengalis and adivasis, seen as symbols of West Pakistani domination (Timm, 1991, p. 10). Sapha, an elderly man I met in a village near Thakurban, referred to 'a different kind of Muslim' coming to the area after partition. The Biharis were seen as more ruthless and money-grabbing and more powerful than the other local Bengali Muslims. They were also loyal to the Pakistan government and many joined the *razakars*, the auxiliary force assisting the Pakistani army, and later supporting the suppression of the Bangladesh independence movement (Whitaker, 1982, p. 8).

The out-migration of Hindus and incoming of Bihari Muslims changed the social landscape of the areas where the Santal lived in what is now north-west Bangladesh. The battle for resources where the Santal were living – and particularly in the rural areas – was characterized by confrontation between the remaining Hindus and other non-Muslims including the Santal and the growing Muslim majority. Many Santal left the region during this period: census data showed those belonging to other religions – including the Santal who were recorded as animist or Christians – fell most sharply between 1941 and 1951 from 4.4 per cent to just 0.26 per cent. Some Santal in the villages where I stayed remember neighbours leaving for India to avoid attacks by incoming Muslims and returning later to find their land had been taken. Sapha, who remembered the years after partition told me:

> When the trouble started ... Santals and Hindus left for India ... the adivasi people have become weak as a result. They became afraid to live. Their land is now occupied by the *diku* [non-adivasi] enemies. They could not sell their lands when they left for India empty handed.

The problems were exacerbated by state-authorized land reclamation policies. After the British left in 1947 legislation was drafted to facilitate the acquisition of properties left behind by fleeing Hindus and other religious minorities. Santal land acquisition was sanctioned under Article 1(b) East Bengal Evacuees (Administration of Immovable Property) Act 1951, which defined evacuees as any person 'ordinarily resident in East Bengal, who, owing to communal disturbances or fear thereof, leaves ... East Bengal for any part of India, [including] the legal heirs of such persons'. The Evacuee Property Management Committee took charge of property unilaterally or through application by any third party, and could let out the property at its will (Barkat et al., 1997). Uprisings such as the Nachol insurrection of 1948–1949[3], the communal riots of 1964,[4] the indo-Pakistan war in 1965, and the Bangladeshi independence war of 1971 provided further opportunities for expropriation of adivasi land. Proceedings of the Bengal assembly of 1951 noted that the legislation was misused by the Muslim elite (see also High Court cases listed in Barkat et al., 1997, p. 24) who took advantage of

---

3 The Nachol Insurrection was a peasant movement against landlords in Nachol, Rajshahi. The peasants proposed a new system, the *Tabhaga*system, whereby the produce of the harvest would be split not in two as was habitual, but in three parts: one for the land owner, one for the sharecropper and another one for the sharecropper to cover the costs of labour, seeds etc. (see brief description in Timm, 1991, p. 21). The landowners resisted the change with support from the police. The sharecroppers attacked the small police force. Landlords retaliated and many Santal villages were burnt down. Many, including Ila Mitra, a Hindu woman who led the movement, were arrested and jailed. Others fled to India.

4 A holy hair of the prophet Hazarat Mohammad (SM) was stolen from Hazarat Bal in Shreenagar, Kashmir, and fighting between Muslims and non-Muslims spread over the border into East Pakistan affecting the Santal in the north-west.

religious minorities' insecurity and temporary migration during these periods of instability to take over land.

During the Bangladesh war of independence in 1971, Ahsan Ali (1998, p. 67) writes 'almost all houses of Santal villages of Barind were gutted and the Santals ... fled away for fear of life to India' returning only after things had settled. When East Bengal became part of Bangladesh in 1971 the new government adopted the Pakistani Acts in the form of the Vesting of Property and Assets Ordinance 1972 (VP Act) and other Acts. Adivasis of the north and north-west, including those who were forced to flee temporarily to India as refugees to save their lives, and those who remained behind, had their lands placed on the vested property lists (Timm, 1991, p. 21). A senior land settlement officer found that 75 per cent of the 'enemy property' listings in one thana had been fraudulently created. The problem was so acute that the government promised to restore some properties illegally seized under the VP Act (Timm, 1991, p.21). But surveys carried out during the rule of General Ershad in the 1980s listing the properties to be restored were discontinued at the end of his dictatorship. A repeal of the Act was passed in 2001 by Sheikh Hasina but opposition parties boycotted the session in which the new Act was implemented and government has since failed to progress plans to return property or compensate those who lost their property. The failure to address abuse under the VP Act and other aspects of the Santal's inability to access justice have meant that adivasis and Hindus in northern Bangladesh have suffered continued land loss (Ain O Salish Kendra et al., 1997, p. 40) and this has had a lasting impact on the Santal's status in the region.

Subordination and the state

Despite some attempts to introduce positive discrimination and other rights for minorities, the Santal experience comparatively high levels of poverty and illiteracy in both countries. In Bangladesh this has been exacerbated by lack of recognition and persecution of religious minorities.

Minority rights in India and Bangladesh

After the British left, in the newly formed state of India, policies of positive discrimination at central government level provided the Santal with some recognition as a Scheduled Tribe (ST) in the states of Orissa, Bihar and West Bengal. Some areas, including the Santal Parganas, were also designated Scheduled Areas (s. 6(1) fifth schedule, Constitution of India), making them exempt from some Acts of Parliament and allowing the legislature and the governor to modify the law applicable in those areas to better protect the rights of STs over land, forests and water sources. Under the Constitution,

Scheduled Tribes and Castes (STCs) across India benefited from reservations in public offices (ss 15 and 16), the House of People, Legislative Assemblies and village *panchayats* (councils) (ss 330(1), 332 and 243D). Promotion of educational and economic interests and protection from social injustice and exploitation were also provided for under the Directive Principles of the Indian Constitution (s. 46), which are used to interpret other constitutional provisions. Under the Seventh Five-Year Plan provision was made for stipends and scholarships (including national overseas scholarships), books, stationery, uniforms and a book bank to benefit STCs. Although the politics of positive discrimination in India have been controversial (see Shah, 2010, p. 18), these provisions have contributed to a reduction in the percentage of ST population living below the poverty line: from 72.4 per cent to 52.6 per cent between 1977–1978 and 1987–1988 (though this remains high compared with the 33.4 per cent figure for the population as a whole) (Singh and Singh, 2011, p. 347).

Critically, however, the impact of these policies on STs has varied from one state to another. In Jharkhand state, formed out of the southern districts of Bihar in 2000, 60 per cent of STs still live below the poverty line (Singh et al., 2012, p. 2). Despite improvements in literacy and employment after the Fifth Five-Year Plan and Tribal Sub-Plan for the Jharkhand region of Bihar in the 1970s to 1980s, the southern districts remained proportionately poor compared with the rest of Bihar (Prakash, 2001, pp. 221–44). At their peak in 1981 illiteracy rates for STs in the southern districts were 79 per cent and 92 per cent for ST women. Given that over 91 per cent of ST in Bihar lived in the southern districts, the regional disparities in wealth were not only a reflection of geographic disadvantage but of ethnic disadvantage also.

The creation of Jharkhand in November 2000 was the result of a long struggle for greater rights for STs in Bihar, dating back to the Simon Commission in 1928. However, at its inception the developmental goals for the new state were set to meet the economic aspirations of the Hindu nationalist BJP (Bharatiya Janata Party), which took over administration of the new state, and not the manifesto of the adivasi-led Jharkhand Mukti Morcha (JMM, meaning Jharkhand Liberation Front), which had fought hard for independence to improve the lives of the region's STs. Jharkhand, meaning forest track, is one of the least-developed but most resource-rich regions in East India, providing over 40 per cent of national coal production (Newman, 2010) and the creation of a new state has opened avenues for exploitation of resources by international mining companies (see further Ekka, 2000; Prakash, 2001). In government offices in the state glossy pamphlets flaunt these riches to foreign investors and the official state website describes the region as 'famous for its rich mineral resources like

Uranium, Mica, Bauxite, Granite, Gold, Silver, Graphite, Magnetite, Dolomite, Fireclay, Quartz, Fieldspar, Cola, Iron, Copper etc. Forests and woodland ...' (Government of Jharkhand website). While the new state has made great efforts to attract transnational mining companies, it has not placed the same emphasis on poverty alleviation for STs, which, according to the 2001 census, represented a minority of 26.3 per cent of the population in the state.

While India's express policies for STs have had a mixed result, they have at least facilitated statistical analysis of the economic status of minorities. Adivasi rights legislation, and recognition, in Bangladesh is, by comparison, conspicuous by its absence. The independence war of 1971 promised a new nation built on principles of nationalism, socialism, democracy and secularism.[5] The fostering of an inclusive national culture had particular poignancy for the charismatic and visionary new leader of Bangladesh, Sheikh Mujibur Rahman, as it marked the end of a period of rule from West Pakistan during which Bengali language and culture had been subjected to radical assimilationist policies. As a result, much effort was made to preserve and nurture the Bengali culture in the newly constituted state. Sheikh Mujib's secularism advocated a celebration of religious diversity, for example, introducing recitations from the holy books of Islam, Hinduism, Buddhism and Christianity at the start of broadcasts by state radio and television. But the brutal assassination of Sheikh Mujib and his family in an army-led *coup d'état* in 1975 was a turning point in Bangladesh's history and the beginning of a creeping Islamization of Bangladeshi identity.

In 1975 General Zia-ur-Rahman replaced secularism as a principle of state policy with a call for 'trust and faith in the Almighty Allah'. Islam was declared the state religion in 1988 (Madan, 1998). This was supposed to defuse the power of fundamentalist political parties, but it had the effect of increasing anti-minority land-grabbing and injustices against minorities (Timm, 1991, p. 25). It was seen by some as a declaration that Bangladesh was for Muslims alone. More time was allotted in the media for recital from the Qur'an than other holy books, and Islamic studies was made compulsory from classes one to eight for Muslim students (Mohsin, 2000). Two major incidents (attacks on Hindus after the Babri Mosque incident in India in 1990 and assaults on Christians by pro-Iraqis in 1991) tested the government's stance on religious minorities. In both instances the government was slow to react. Some ministers provoked anti-Hindu assaults while President Ershad preached in mosques to 'we Muslims', increasing animosity against non-Muslims (Timm, 1991, p. 25).

---

5 State Principles, Article 8(1) and Bangladesh Constitution 1972, Preamble, para. 2.

The development of a Bangladeshi identity resonating with the country's Muslim majority has eclipsed government policies on minorities. Census data records only religion and language and the state is accused of undercounting as part of a policy of marginalization (Anwar, 1984, p. 370; Maloney, 1984, p. 8; Timm 1991, p. 11). Fearful of moves by distinctive cultural minorities such as the Chakma people living in the eastern region of the Chittagong Hill Tracts to assert their right to self-determination, Bangladesh is one of the few countries to have abstained from the UN Declaration on the Rights of Indigenous Peoples (Barman and Neo, 2012, p. 58). In July 2011 the government announced it would replace all references to adivasis (literally meaning indigenous people) in government publications and laws with *khudro nritattik Jonogosthi* (ethnic minorities). While some progress has been made to facilitate negotiations for greater rights for the Chakma people, this has been slow and arduous and has not been part of a wider policy of adivasi rights (Barman and Neo, 2012, p. 25).

There are no special provisions to address discrimination against minority communities per se. Broadly speaking, equality provisions under the Bangladesh Constitution provide that all citizens are entitled to equal treatment under the law (Article 27), including equality of opportunity in respect of public employment (Article 29) and freedom from discrimination by the state on grounds of race, caste, religion, sex or place of birth, as well as positive discrimination for 'backward' sections (Article 28). However, it is widely recognized that they are treated as culturally inferior (Anwar 1984, p. 369; Timm, 1991, p. 16) and lower-caste. They are commonly referred to as *upo-jati* (literally meaning sub-caste) and occasionally *junglies* (forest dwellers). While I was carrying out my research, Santal people in rural and urban areas were routinely refused food in Bengali eateries, or served on disposable plates made out of leaves, and made to eat sitting on the floor while others sat on stools and benches. Santal students reported being refused service in restaurants or tea stalls on university campuses (see Das, 1996, p. 39; Barman and Neo, 2012, p. 44).

Human rights organizations in Bangladesh, monitoring the rights of minority communities, report violence against minorities and insecurity as pervasive (Khan and Rahman, 2011). Newspapers regularly report incidents of violent attacks against minorities (Shakil and Hasnat, 2013, pp. 13–14).[6] The Santal villagers I met described going to the police and court as an ordeal, not only because of the cost but because of threats of retaliation resulting in what one Santal man described to me as *'amader adivasi bhoi'*

---

6 An attack on a Santal village in Niamtpur thana near the village where I stayed was reported by http://Kapaeeng.org/media-and-human-right-team-visits-to-investigate-niamotpur-incident.

(our adivasi fear) – the grammar suggesting a fear that belongs to, or is characterized by 'us tribals', denoting exclusivity.

Recognition, resource allocation and representation

Despite these differences in government policies post-independence in the two countries, subordination and discrimination continue to characterize daily experiences of citizenship for most Santal in both countries. Identity, recognition, representation and resource allocation are key factors in the exclusion of minority communities (Taylor et al., 1994; Kymlicka and Norman, 2000). The experience of citizenship is affected by the state at a local as well as a national level – the state directing micro-forces, including relations between citizens – reinforcing endemic inequalities. At the local level of the villages the clearest expression of Santal and other adivasis' exclusion in both countries is the monopoly of non-adivasis over the most important commodity, land.

A survey carried out for the Ministry of Rural Development in India showed that, despite legislative provision for the protection of land rights under the SPTA 1949, between 1950 and 1995 52,600 acres of land in the region's capital, Dumka, was taken by the government for public purposes (irrigation/dams, public utilities, government buildings, schools and colleges, industry/mining, forests etc.). Further land-loss through transfer to private individuals has taken place as a result of mortgages, leases, illegal encroachment/eviction and sale (mostly in the form of a gift) in contravention of the spirit of the SPTA 1949. S L Batra (1999, p. 115) found that from 1991–1996 most land-loss in Dumka to private individuals resulted from mortgage agreements made to cover medical costs (48 per cent) or household expenditure (30.8 per cent). While no clear data exists on the extent of land-loss by adivasis in Bangladesh, land alienation during key periods of conflict in the north-west has been a critical problem underlying Santal disadvantage there and reports of land-grabbing and brutal attacks on Santal villages by non-adivasis are still prevalent (Barman and Neo, 2012, pp. 100–08).

The impact of this land alienation is twofold: landownership and control over land (through mortgages) determine both the economic dependence of villagers and their political and status subordination. Those with land holdings in the village can employ and set the terms of employment for poorer villagers, who also act as political retainers in that they are dependent on the landholder in these quasi-feudal conditions. The rich peasant landowners as businessmen are able to diversify their economic activity, gain greater access to and influence over officials and are better equipped to deal with the unpredictability of agricultural yields. The landowner also usually acts as money-lender, increasing the poorer villager's dependency on him and often acquiring control over the latter's land through mortgages in return for unpaid interest payments on the debt. Wood writes that these mortgage transactions provide the most common basis for land transfer from poor to rich since the market price for the land would be beyond the reach even of the richest peasant landlords (Wood, 1994, pp. 79–83). The economic structure ultimately reinforces both the political and economic interests of dominant village groups (Westergaard, 1986, p. 154).

Wood notes beyond the village that the paternalistic nature of relations between rich peasants and petty bourgeoisie gets reflected in the recruitment of political leaders from the village and the structure of political power between the state and the countryside. The mutual relationship of dependence between the state and certain ethnic societal groups creates a vortex of power as the state needs to acquire resources belonging to societal groups to survive and societal actors who control the relevant resources exert influence on the state and its policy activities. The degree of influence a group is able to have depends on the importance of the resources held, concentration of and access to those resources, uncertainty of supply of resources, and abundance of those resources. Even where the concentration of resources is high and the societal actors in possession few, the state still has the choice of adopting cooperative or coercive policies. Which policy it chooses depends on the size and political importance of the societal group or actor (Prakash, 2001, pp. 9–10).

Naila Kabeer (2002, p. 19) distinguishes the countries of the Global 'West' from the 'South' in that, while individual/liberal ideals were achieved organically in the former, in the latter they were imposed and now live alongside persistent pre-colonial (and pre-state) society where kinship ties were the basis for resource allocation. The inequality in distribution of resources is exacerbated by corruption and nepotism. This means that, where a group is culturally subordinate in the status system, this is directly translated into subordination in distribution of wealth – Nancy Fraser (2000, p. 109) says mis-recognition in the status order is translated into mal-distribution in the class structure. In such a society, kinship is the overriding principle for distribution of resources and therefore cultural status dictates economic position.[7] Henri Claessen and Peter Skalnik (1978) call this 'the early state', where politics and kinship overlap.

---

7 Fraser says that neither this nor its opposite – *'economism'*, a fully marketized society where the economic structure dictates cultural status – exist in their pure states in contemporary society as modern societies are in reality hybridized, differentiated and pluralistic and individuals are not assigned to a single status group (Fraser and Honneth, 2003, pp. 55–6). However, it does provide a context in which battles for political recognition and access to resources take place.

In such states the economic advantage of rich peasants gives them access to political advantage and even absorption into the kinship of the elite society. The values of the political and economic leadership at the local level come to mirror those of the state. There is what Antonio Gramsci (1971, p. 60) calls a 'system of solidarity between ... intellectuals', such that this structure is perpetuated to the exclusion of the subordinate because elite groups' associations with other elite groups mean that, where a shift in power occurs, ruling classes hand down power to other ruling classes. At the end of British rule, power was handed to the existing ruling classes in Pakistan and this was repeated with the independence of Bangladesh. Each ruling class in turn has no interest in changing the social structure so the inequality of power in the state does not alter significantly (Westergaard, 1986, p. 156).

Both India and Bangladesh have nevertheless made efforts to improve representation for the poorest and most disadvantaged groups in local level governance, though these have been fraught with difficulty. As a cultural minority in both countries, accounting for 0.6 per cent of the population of India (1991 Population Census) and 0.19 per cent of the population of Bangladesh[8], the Santal have little political representation in central government in either country. However, their representation at local and regional levels varies and is subject to negotiation. In India, while the Santal are rarely represented in political bodies, in Jharkhand, where Santal have been prominent in the struggle for creation of the state, some now hold positions of influence and control.[9] Six Santal members hold positions in the state government including the deputy chief minister, three MPs, and two ministers. In north-west Bangladesh, data is less easy to access but I found that some Santal in the areas where I researched had achieved election at the most local unit of decentralized government, the *Union Parishad* (UP), though they had not progressed through the political ranks.

At the village level in India there is a complex system of local public bodies with various, sometimes overlapping, jurisdictions. The village panchayat is the official body of decentralized government administration at the village level in India. Under the 11th Schedule of the Indian Constitution, panchayats carry out schemes for economic development and social justice including: land improvement and reforms; minor irrigation; animal husbandry, social forestry, small-scale industries, rural housing; drinking water; roads and bridges; poverty alleviation programmes;

---

8 Bangladesh Population Census 1991, vol. 1, 'Analytical Report', September 1994, p. 196.
9 Only two Santal MPs exist outside Jharkhand: Laxman Tudu MP in Orissa and Pulin Bihari Baske MP in West Bengal, http://npibeta.nic.in/my-government/indian-parliament/lok-sabha?page=18.

education; libraries; cultural activities; markets and fairs; family welfare, health and sanitation; women and child development; and social welfare (see Constitution Article 243G and Bihar Panchayati Raj Act 1993).

The Panchayat Raj has developed from a traditional system of panchayats indigenous to village life. It has undergone two major phases of institution-building in the past century. Post-independence, panchayats administered the government's development projects and under the Indian Constitution (73rd Amendment) Act 1992 panchayats were recognized as institutions of self-government. The purpose of the 73rd Amendment was to create a three-tier system of governance at the local level: village, intermediate and district level panchayats. This pan-Indian structure created a body directly elected by villagers to function as an institution of self-government. In tribal Scheduled Areas another institution, the Gram Sabha, was created under the Provisions of the Panchayats (Extension to the Scheduled Areas) Act, Act No 40 of 1996. In Scheduled Areas the Gram Sabha is considered the nucleus of activity with distinct powers and functions and consists of all the voters of a village, hamlet or a group of hamlets 'comprising a community and managing its affairs in accordance with traditions and customs' of the local inhabitants (Singh, 2000, pp. 29–30). Although it represents all peoples in the area regardless of ethnicity, its powers and functions relate directly to issues of particular concern for adivasi communities: indebtedness; land alienation; displacement; alcoholism; access to water, forests and other natural resources; management of village markets; and control over local plans and resources, including tribal sub-plans.

In Lahara and Madhura where I carried out my research, there was a Gram Sabha representing several villages. It was active in considering the progress of works carried out by the Panchayat and putting together committees of experts and experienced persons to help monitor and recommend projects. In Madhura, the Gram Sabha was referred to by Santal villagers as having a monopoly to decide who benefited from government projects. However, adivasis formed a minority in the area and the Gram Sabha was made up entirely of non-adivasis and the decision-making rarely involved them. The next level of local governance did little better as a representative body. No panchayat elections had been officially held in Santal Parganas since 1978 (see the local newspaper *People's Democracy*, 24 August 2003) – although elections were at the time imminent and unofficial postholders seemed to be actively working in the area. In Madhura a *mukia* (head of the panchayat) and *serpanch* (administrator), claiming to have been elected, were carrying out some work in the villages. Alpha Shah (2010, p. 202, n. 31) notes Jharkhand is the only state in India not to have held panchayat elections and there is an ongoing dispute about whether seats should be reserved for adivasis in Scheduled Areas and whether the panchayat system is able to support local customary structures.

As head of the Santal village, the *manjhi* has been an important point of contact between the Santal villagers and the outside world. In the aftermath of the Santal Hul 1855, manjhis of villages in Santal Parganas were nominated by the British as pradhan – revenue collector – of their village in an attempt to reinvent the manjhi as primarily a government agent (Somers, 1977, p. 99). In reality the project was not consistently applied or persistent enough to replace the Santal post of manjhi with the government defined one. During my fieldwork the two co-existed. In Lahara the pradhan was a non-Santal and in Madhura he was a Santal from the village, but was not the manjhi. According to K K Sinha (2000, p. 84) tribal village councils (like the Santal's Village Council) in the Santal Parganas have had difficulty integrating into the institutions of the Panchayat Raj.

The lowest level of government in Bangladesh, the UP was functioning more consistently, although periodic changes in administrative policies that have accompanied transfer of power between the two leading parties have left many unsure about how it fits into overall governance structures. The UP or Union Council, is part of a three-tier system of rural governance, originally comprising a police district (thana), sub-district (*upazilla*) and district council (*zilla parishad*). From 1982 to 1990 many upazillas were renamed *zillas* (districts) and thanas promoted to upazillas. The upazilla system was then abolished in 1991 and sub-districts reverted to thanas. A change in government in 1996 led to a proposal to reinstate the three-tier system. The current UP consists of a chairman and 12 members, and reservations were introduced for three women members, elected on a three-yearly basis (s. 5 Local Government (Union Parishads) Ordinance 1983).

While adivasis, including adivasi women, have been elected as UP members, minority representatives are less likely to be given positions of influence or to use their position to instigate particular projects for adivasis. Sitakant Mahapatra (1986, p. 49) writes that in rural areas:

> Santals rarely participate or intervene effectively during [public policy] discussions. Being less articulate, it becomes difficult for them to conceptualize the aspirations of their locality, and to put it across forcefully during the deliberations of either the Samiti or the Panchayat.

Sapha, the elderly Santal man mentioned above whom I met near Thakurban, had served as a UP member for 15 years and described to me how he was excluded from projects and was unsupported by other members when he raised adivasi concerns before the UP. He knew three other Santali UP members, and all of them had received the same treatment and had had fabricated criminal cases brought against them to try to intimidate them into relinquishing their posts. The husband of a Santal woman UP member told me his wife was allocated only small projects, none specifically relating to adivasis, and she mostly assisted the chairman.

Lack of education, self-confidence and finances are important factors in poor representation of adivasis. The literacy rate amongst adivasis in Rajshahi, Bangladesh, in 1986 was approximately 7 per cent, compared with the national average of around 22 per cent (Timm, 1991, p. 16).[10] The literacy rate for STs in the Santal Parganas districts of Godda and Deoghar, India, was approximately 20 per cent and 21 per cent respectively (1991 Census) compared to an average of over 38 per cent in the state of Bihar (Census of India 1991, pp. 116 and 130). Literacy rates were important in determining the likelihood of participation in local politics. While Santal men and women can be elected, far fewer Santal whom I interviewed consider putting themselves forward for an election in Bangladesh than in India (17 per cent and 42 per cent respectively). The most common reason given for *not* considering candidature was not having an education (a common answer for women) or not feeling capable of carrying out the work, though some also mentioned not being able to pay the deposit (500 taka for UP member posts and 1000 taka for the chairman/woman's post: Union Parishads (Election) Rules 1983 s. 12(1)). For some in Bangladesh, ethnicity played a role: several respondents thought they would have little chance of being elected because they are Santals in a majority Muslim country. This hesitance to run for election is exacerbated by the fact that, where a Santal candidate does run for election she or he may not get support from her or his own people.

I met a Santal UP candidate, Samuel, near Thakurban who told me that he struggled to compete with the Muslim candidates. He was young, well-spoken and had begun a degree course – making him one of the few educated Santal in the area. He owned three *bigas* (just under 1 acre) of land and worked as an agriculturist like most Santal. He was sincere and dedicated and was slim from a hard physical life and dressed in *lungi* (a long piece of cloth covering the legs tied around the waste) and vest, typical cultivator's clothes, making him indistinguishable from others in the village. I asked if he felt confident of getting support from the Santal voters

---

10 The Chakma, indigenous people of the Chittagong Hill Tracts (CHT), the largest adivasi people in Bangladesh, are an exception in this respect with literacy rates higher than the national average. They have a distinct history in the CHT region, and much of the advocacy work done to promote their rights focuses on their particular needs in that region. I do not address their very specific issues in this book but there are many resources on the plight of the people of the CHT (Roy et al., 2000; Mohsin, 2003).

in the ward. He said he was not and my assistant Luke confirmed that, although he was a good candidate who would do the job well, many Santal had already promised their votes to others. One of the local landowners had put himself forward as a candidate and had put pressure on those working on his land to support him. Other landowners who were friends of that candidate or had particular allegiances to a certain party instructed those working on their land how to vote.

While Santal villagers I interviewed saw the link between voting for a Santal candidate and gaining greater benefits for their own people, a majority of interviewees said they were more likely to vote for someone they thought was 'good', 'nice' or 'honest' or would give them some assistance in the short term. Some mentioned receiving clothes from non-Santal candidates whom they described as 'good' people. Luke said some Santal are more impressed by non-adivasi candidates who promise them gifts and benefits – although there is no guarantee of benefits beyond the gifts or money given during election. But this seemingly short-term strategy may hide a deeper understanding of the limits and possibilities of voting strategies. Firstly, the multiple linguistic, cultural and class barriers to effective participation in local government for Santal members may mean it is more effective to invest their support in non-Santal candidates. Secondly, there was evidence that voting was not always a matter of individual preference or limitations.

This is not to say that strategic voting is absent. Despite pressures on villagers to vote for employers and landlords, when asked directly for whom they would vote, some villagers told me that the decision about whom to vote for was made at a village meeting where all the potential candidates were compared. A survey carried out by K T K Hossain and S Z Sadequ (1984, p. 164) in Rajshahi confirmed manjhis were actively participating in local level politics through their ability to mobilize voting. This was corroborated by the deference paid by prospective candidates to Santal governance structures. I saw for myself that candidates targeted village leaders in the belief that this would secure them blocks of votes. Manjhis and *parganaits* (Santal regional headmen) in both countries also depended on good relations with candidates to ensure that their interests were protected – and especially in Bangladesh to avoid antagonizing potential powerholders. This process seemed to reinforce the separation between adivasis and non-adivasis but also to bolster the authority of the manjhi as village head.

In Dhanban (Rajshahi) and Lahara (Santal Parganas) where I was staying close to election time, the manjhi and parganait met with local candidates. The manjhi of Lahara, India, had a visit from the local (ex-)mukia who spent the day in the village drinking with the manjhi and chatting. He told me that the mukia was looking for village support in the forthcoming elections, which the manjhi had agreed to give. The mukia had brought baby chicks to be cooked and I was invited to join in the luxury of feasting on this delicacy. During the meal the manjhi pointed out to me repeatedly how close he and the ex-mukia were. He told me 'he is a diku but he is my friend ... they are all my friends, the Block Development Officer, the thana police ...'. They were both eager to show an open, friendly relationship in a time and place where there was much animosity between Santal and non-adivasis. It was clear that the manjhi saw his friendship with the mukia as re-enforcing his own importance. In Dhanban, Bangladesh, the manjhi and parganait had a private meeting with the existing UP chairman shortly before the UP elections. The meeting was more formal and secretive – I was not allowed in. At the end they told me they had reached an agreement.

The importance of the manjhi's voting preference may be considerable. If, for example, his agreement with the candidate is that his village will vote at the time in favour of one candidate in return for benefits or preferences of distribution of jobs and welfare benefits in the area, then the villagers may be persuaded to vote collectively. Regardless of whether the villagers follow the manjhi's suggestion, the perception on the part of the candidates and those in office may nevertheless be that the manjhi does hold the power to direct their votes. This in itself is enough to give him some bargaining power locally to improve benefits for the Santal.

However, this process of relying on the manjhi as representative has its pitfalls. On the one hand, it binds the manjhi to an elite grouping in which the pressures of affiliation may draw him away from his primary duty to the villagers and make him less likely to challenge those who come into power even if they fall short of their promises. On the other, it reinforces the sense of separateness between the Santal and other citizens which I explore further below.

Vulnerability of otherness

Nadini Sen (c. 2002, p. 3) writes: '[t]he way people see themselves as citizens has a significant impact on the practice of citizenship'. Their perception of themselves is a result of a process of socialization, which is affected by others' perception of them and their perception of others (Jenkins, 1996). The experience of citizenship for Santal in Bangladesh was one area where the differing approaches to minority rights did seem to have a significant impact. The Santal in Jharkhand had gained some recognition of their plight through the creation of the Santal Parganas in the nineteenth century and of Jharkhand in the twentieth century and this gave them a fearlessness and militancy coupled with self-assurance that was less easily challenged than in Bangladesh. The sheer diversity of India's population and a tradition of incorporation of difference into the national identity also makes their difference less remarkable there. In Bangladesh, however, the insistence on a single unifying identity has pushed the Santal, determined as they are on maintaining their cultural distinction, to the social margins.

There has been a common perception in Bangladesh of adivasis as primitive people who do not speak Bangla properly and have an inferior culture/religion. Many consider them to be migratory people with no permanent home and not original inhabitants of Bangladesh (Timm, 1991, p. 16). The way they wear the national dress – men wearing their lungi tugged high above the knees, and women wearing a sari lifted up to the knee, sometimes with no blouse – differentiates them from the more modestly dressed majority Muslims. Their animist religious worship and lack of eating and drinking taboos, in particular regarding pork, vermin and alcohol, which clash directly with Muslim norms, are also particularly problematic symbols of distinction.

The Santal's own sense of otherness, reflected in their dedication to a very distinct language, culture, political and normative organization, and their sense of uniqueness, portrayed through their folk tales and origin myth, shield them from this but also reinforce their cultural counter-positioning. While the Santal call themselves *hor* or *horhopon*, meaning man or sons of mankind, they refer to non-adivasis as dikus. Historically, the term diku was used to refer to one who exploited and cheated the adivasis. Mahapatra (1976, p. 47) describes the diku as 'the indifferent or hostile outsider who is to be shunned'. In Santal folklore dikus are 'looters ... troublemakers ... deceivers ... exploiters, cheats, unreliable and those who have a sense of superiority and inspire fear' (Sen et al., 1969, pp. 123 and 127).

Different approaches to crime and its punishment make law a critical site of contestation in which tensions between the Santal and non-adivasis are played out. I found that state law was regularly misused by non-adivasis to intimidate Santal villagers. In Thakurban village two years before my visit a group of men had entered the village in the night and attempted to steal from one of the houses. A crying baby woke up the household and soon the whole village was alerted to the presence of the thieves. They were chased and eventually one was caught and beaten. The UP chairman was called and he said nothing could be done with the thief until the morning. He left the thief in the village and went home. As news of the thief's capture spread, more villagers came and joined in beating the thief. By morning, he was dead. Suphol, a Santal elder of the village, informed the thana police and under the chairman's instructions they arrested a number of people from the village. Young male villagers I interviewed told me there were no witnesses to the murder from outside the village and the list of people arrested included some who had not even been present on the night. They said those arrested were all people who had had confrontations with the chairman in the past. Most of those initially arrested were released due to lack of evidence, some went to court and were found not guilty.

Only two adivasis remained in jail when I visited the village. They were young men with families and they were the only people in the village who had jobs in the town (working in the missionary hospital) and had previously fought and won cases against dikus (on one occasion winning 3000 taka). Those involved seemed adamant that the thief had died as a result of a whole night of beating, involving many people and that no one person could be held responsible. Pondic, who had been arrested and released on bail pending appeal to the High Court, said that the police had arrested people who had past disputes with the dikus. He said 13 false witnesses (all non-adivasis) gave evidence against them during the trial and none of them had been present at the beating. One witness told him they had bribed the judge. Luke and Suphol – who had also challenged dikus in the past and were also arrested for the killing – said the two who remained in prison were chosen because they had made something of themselves, had jobs, money and would educate their children, and were a threat to the local non-adivasi elite – as evidenced by their previous successes. Putting them in prison had the effect of lowering morale in the village and severing connections to possible allies outside the village.

Non-adivasis regularly used violence, threats and false criminal cases to intimidate the Santal in Bangladesh. In both Thakurban and Dhanban villagers told me they had been taken to court by non-adivasis for land disputes that they were not a party to or for crimes they had not committed. In Dhanban the manjhi, the parganait and a village elder had been included as respondents in a land dispute between a Bengali, Ansar, and a Santal landowner. Despite the fact they were unconnected with the dispute, they were obliged to attend court and pay towards lawyers' fees until the judge pronounced that they had no interest in the case. They said Ansar was punishing them because they had won a case to prevent him taking over *khas* (government) land the villagers used to bury their dead. A legal aid NGO (BLAST)[11] had supported a Santal man who had been accused in several criminal cases on charges of unlawful assembly, trespass and theft. According to BLAST the charges had been fabricated to intimidate him into dropping a case he had brought against a Bengali who was trying to take his

---

11 BLAST is the only NGO that administers legal aid in Rajshahi and it has a mostly gender-oriented agenda – influenced by the global donor's focus on women's rights in Bangladesh. Most of its work is on domestic violence and honour crimes and it does very little on land rights in Rajshahi, which mostly affect the Santal. As such it has had a very marginal impact on the Santal's struggles for justice in Rajshahi.

land. Even high-profile Santal were at risk. During the Pakistan period, there had been a Santal MP in Rajshahi. Attempts were made on his life and a false criminal case was brought against him and he was eventually imprisoned. He was accused of stealing a large quantity of wheat, which he was given by the government to distribute, which he said had been taken from him by a local influential Bengali.

These types of cases were more prevalent in Bangladesh than in India, possibly because there are fewer Santal in government posts and the Santal have little land security there. The Santal have longer and firmer roots in India, having established themselves in the Santal Parganas from the late eighteenth century, and number approximately 6 million nationally as compared with 200,000 in Bangladesh. Santal villagers in Bangladesh kept ties with relatives in India and saw it as a second home, somewhere to escape to when they were in trouble. The family I was staying with used a wind-up radio I had brought with me to tune into a radio station in Santali broadcasting in the Santal Parganas. Villagers made references to migration to India and I was shown half-empty villages where families had already migrated to India for a better life.

Conclusion

In Bangladesh, disadvantage has been rooted in processes of differentiation that are historically validated and re-enforced through the Santal's determination to maintain their cultural distinctiveness. In India, efforts of the state to improve the position of STs through reservations in local and national representative bodies, local development plans and targeted legislation have had limited effect. The interplay of macro- and micro-factors that have contributed to the Santal's socio-economic and political status subordination demonstrate the difficulty of challenging inequalities in the context of status-based societies. These processes, characterized by discrimination and unequal distribution of resources, permeate social relations and recourse to state institutions. Lack of access to land as a critical resource is one of the most enduring and troubling aspects of this.

While the main purpose of this chapter has been to highlight the complex and endemic nature of subordination of the Santal cultural minority, the history of their subordination does also provide an indication of the possibility for the Santal themselves to push against their disadvantage. Although direct participation in representative bodies is problematic, manjhis have organized themselves as political brokers to gain leverage in demanding benefits for their people. We will see later, in Chapter 6, that in their local relationships with non-adivasis the Santal find multiple ways to aggravate the latter's privileged position. The Santal's historic demonstration of their capacity for open revolt, the uprising against the local traders and Mahajans in the mid-nineteenth century which resulted in the creation of the Santal Parganas, has been instrumental in maintaining unity amongst the Santal, nurturing political leadership there and providing a 'homeland' to which all Santal feel they can 'return'. Exit back across the border to the Santel Parganas, particularly to avoid state sanctions in Bangladesh, while not altering the status quo, has also been one part of an arsenal of responses, It is to these that I dedicate this book.

4
The Primary Construction of Inequality: Kinship, Law and Ritual in the Santal Family and Village

Every morning during my fieldwork I arose, tidied up my sleeping area, dressed and greeted the family I was staying with. I walked with the other women down to the village water source to collect water for the day and participated in cooking the morning meal of boiled or puffed rice and hot water. I had brought only two *salwar kameez* (trouser and tunic typically worn by unmarried South-Asian women), knowing this would mean I would, like the other women, have to wash my clothes each day and dry them ready for the next morning. Sharing in their daily routines helped me to immerse myself in the village, adopting the rhythmic pattern of movement, the unhurried but unceasing flow of tasks that characterized daily life. Days flowed into one another and the circular movements of people, cattle and the comings and goings of the men and women from the field, the gentle chatter of villagers as they met in the street, gave a pace to life that seemed perfectly in tune with the nature surrounding us. But this rhythm masked an underlying pressure for conformity. Looking down the village street shortly after sunrise each morning I remember seeing clouds of dust engulfing the stooped figure of a woman, brush in hand, in front of each house, moving almost in synchronicity as they swept the dust from their main courtyard ready for a new day. The women seemed to adopt a ritual of housework, its schedule enforced by collective acquiescence. This compliance was not enforced but was a manifestation of their belonging. It was also a tie that bound them, restricted their movements, and set their place within the family and wider community.

On my first day in Thakurban village I approached a woman sitting by one of the larger village ponds. She saw me and moved away. I stopped and waited. She spoke from across the pond: 'It is because you are educated that you can come and go freely.' Her statement struck me, not only because of the force with which it differentiated me, and possibly excluded me, but also because of the striking perception that while we shared womanhood, my education made me a different sort of woman, had won me freedom that she had not experienced, not only the freedom to move but to enter *their* village, to cross cultural boundaries. It also intimated a deep understanding of the injustice of class inequality and reminded me that I had not earned my right to be there in her eyes. The woman, whom I got to know well during my stay, was Mary, an energetic and thoughtful woman in her fifties. She worked hard, not only carrying out daily chores for her family of cooking, cleaning, washing, collecting firewood, making small repairs to the house, but also processing cultivated rice for sale. I rarely saw her husband who had tuberculosis and was quiet and withdrawn compared to Mary.

Their situation was unusual: in most households the husband is a visible authority in the family and the wife, busy with chores, brings little attention to herself. I remember the first time I visited the family of Luke, my assistant, whose family I lived with in Thakurban, and we sat in his courtyard waiting for his father and the village manjhi. I was introduced to his father and his brother and it was only when I enquired after his mother that he pointed out the lady who had been busily doing tasks around us the whole time! I had barely realized she was there and, embarrassed, I apologized to her as I greeted her. Her invisibility continued throughout my stay, she ate separately after feeding the rest of the family, and denied herself any small luxury such as meat or eggs the family afforded with the modest sum I had given them for food. I do not want to give the impression that she was unhappy or badly treated. Her husband was a kind and gentle man and she was very loved by her three children, but she had grown to assume very little importance for herself.

The Santal family

Family has ever been a site of inequalities (see Weber, 1978, pp. 356–69). Globally, societal resources are unevenly redistributed within households through familial power structures (Curtis, 1986). Authority, and its construction, is one factor that explains the persistence of power structures and, in particular, differences between men and women, children and adults. In status-based societies, men tend to organize themselves on a large scale to control resources, manipulate interests, strategize but also influence, coerce, intimidate. Authority translates this power into an ability to occupy a dominant position or make decisions for others. Patriarchy is the manifestation of this authority in the family, and men occupy a specific position of advantage as they bring resources into the family unit. Roles in the family develop as internal power structures but also set a prototype for relations within society, so the two are related. Men tend to become experts in authority both within and outside the family whereas women's influence tends to be isolated, impermanent and non-transferable (Cohen and MacCartney, 2004).

Internalizing inequality through the life cycle

The Santal family, as the fundamental social unit of village life, provides for all the basic needs of individuals and is foremost responsible for the socialization of children. Santal families are patrilocal (the woman moves to live in the man's village) and partriarchal and, although extended family members often live near to each other, Santal households tend to be formed around a nuclear family. Unlike Bengali and Indian families, who often take elderly parents to live with them, in Santal society older women and men whose children have married live alone, keeping contact with sons living in the same village and making seasonal visits to their daughters.

In Santal society the eldest male in the household has the highest authority over the family members and is treated as master of the house (Das, 1967, p. 8; Saha, 1969, p. 98). He is in charge of making economic and political decisions, usually in consultation with other male adults in the family. He manages kinship relations and is the leader of the family during rituals and festivals. He is also the main representative of the household before the village council. Despite this, the mother plays the most important role in ensuring that the children internalize the different roles of men and women in the family. She is responsible for the children for most of their childhood and will not only ensure that they are fed and kept in good health but will also be the main influence on their primary socialization (Das, 1967, p. 7; Saha, 1969, p. 100). As the children reach puberty a distinction is made between them, and the boy begins to spend more time with the father, learning agricultural work, while the girl remains in the house with the mother to learn to cook and manage the house. Perhaps because of the division of tasks along gender lines, the mother becomes the main disciplinarian for her daughters (rewarding behaviour with affection or redirecting behaviour through subtle humiliations, tellings-off, punishments), teaching them their role in the family and preparing them for married life: and the father becomes the main disciplinarian for his sons.

Marriage during early adolescence is common amongst the Santal. As marriage is patrilocal, daughters often leave the house in early puberty to join the household of their husbands and are initially in the charge of their husband's mother, unmarried sisters and sisters-in-law. Before settling with her in-laws, the girl visits the village headman with her father to thank him as representative of the ancestors for teaching her to be a good wife (Somers, 1977, p. 85). She continues to undergo a process of socialization in the context of relations of inequality with her female in-laws and learns from them the virtue of self-discipline. It is here that she progresses from childhood to adulthood and finds her place in the unequal power relations in the family. Once she becomes a mother, she is considered to have reached maturity and may move into her own house with her husband and the cycle of discipline and socialization of the next generation begins. Of course, not every family conforms to this and I did find some households where the women were in charge (see discussion in Chapter 6).

The rules relating to marriage provide another important indication of the distinct roles and powers of men and women in the family. Marriage is an essential part of life, linked to survival and status for women, and a daughter's marriage is also a means of expanding family ties and can be a tool for managing property. Santal marriages are mostly monogamous and patrilocal. The most common form of marriage is the *dol bapla.* Young women marrying in this way are in theory free to choose their spouse (Risley, 1891, p. 228). But in most situations the parents arrange the marriage and a marriage-broker (*raibar*) is used to introduce families who are looking to marry their children. The girl is shown off to the boy's family, and the boy to the girl's, and the two families communicate through the broker and the *jog manjhi* (Santal village official responsible for moral conduct of adolescents) as to whether they find the match suitable. The girl is unlikely to make an independent choice, and the degree to which she is consulted will differ between families: it is the mother and other female relatives who examine the prospective groom. The Santal marriage involves payment of a bride-price to the family of the bride – a bridewealth transaction. The bride-price is given in the form of a small payment along with clothes and other gifts to the parents of the bride and is negotiated between the parents prior to the marriage. She is given over to the care of the husband's family but she maintains links with her own family, and they are given much respect in the new relationship formed between the two families.

If a woman becomes a widow or divorcee, she is expected to remarry if she is young enough. But, as in many South-Asian societies, what Bina Agarwal (1997, p. 17) refers to as her 'worth in the marriage market' is diminished. There is a separate name for this marriage in Santal custom – *sangha*. A Santal elder, Kolean, interviewed by a missionary, the Reverend Lars Skrefsrud in 1871 (Bodding, 1942, p. 79), said '[t]his is no real marriage, we call it a temporary hire'. There is no exchange of gifts or feast, nor the usual bathing and other ceremonies associated with marriage. *Sindur* (vermillion) is not applied to the bride's head as in other Santal marriage ceremonies but to a flower placed in the bride's hair. Her second husband pays half the bride-price as it is thought that the woman will have to be returned to her first husband in the afterlife. This is further evidence of the perception that a woman is the property of her husband and her status in life and death is closely associated with her marriage status. According to Paul Bodding, a divorcee who does not remarry and is without parents 'becomes a piece of masterless property, utterly destitute except for what people may give her, or for what she may be able to earn through her own work' (Bodding, c. 1920, p. 242).

Perhaps because women are seen to depend on marriage for their survival, Santal law of marriage is pragmatic and recognizes many different circumstances in which people may choose to come together. Records of Santal law list up to 14 forms of marriage, or recognized situations of union.[1] Forms of ceremony provide flexibility for those with different financial circumstances – alongside the standard ceremony, or dol bapla, there is a poor man's wedding (*tunki dipil*) and dual wedding where brother and sister from one family marry a brother and sister from another (*golaeti*). While marriages which receive the consent of the village are the norm, Santal law also accommodates impulsive unions. Santal norms recognize a union where a couple sleep together and then agree to marry (*kundal napam*) or elope (*apangir*) where the ordinary rules do not allow them to be together because they are of the same clan or because the woman is already married. It even recognizes a union where a boy or girl forces the other to marry or they choose to marry but have not gained parental consent (*itut* and *nir bolok*).[2] But it does so while reinforcing certain principles. Couples who seek recognition of a marriage that breaches these principles do so at great cost. Marriage unions are normally required to have the village's prior consent, and those that do not, itut (forcing a woman to marry) and apangir (elopement), are accompanied by a trial of sorts and punishment. A boy who forces a woman to marry is likely to be beaten by the girl's family, have his house ransacked and some livestock seized. The village council then judges the extent of his infraction and fine the boy's father. If the family of the girl he has forced do not agree to the marriage, she becomes a divorcee, but as a divorcee any future marriage she has will be a half-marriage (sangha). Where a couple who are related or of the same clan

---

[1] Spellings differ: *sadai, golaeti, sangha, gharjawae, ghardi jawae, iputut, apaingir, kundal n'apam, tunki dipil, tikak' sindur, hirom cetan, kirin jawae, n'ir olo, or-ader* (Besra, 2002, p. 8). See also some definitions in: Risley, 1891, pp. 229–31; Bodding, 1942, pp. 40–82; Archer, 1984, pp. 227–307; Ali, 1998, pp. 137–9; Bodding, 2002, p. 197 – most have identified fewer forms than Besra.

[2] A Santal boy can force a girl to marry him simply by catching her and smearing vermilion or mud on her forehead and middle parting (Risley, 1891, p. 230). His motives for doing so may vary: he may have gained her consent but not that of her parents, he may wish to marry but be unsure if she will agree, or he may force her to marry out of anger. In nir bolok the girl goes to the boy's parents' house with a pot of rice-beer and must survive all attempts by his mother to get her to leave. If she persists with her claim to marry the boy, his parents must accept her, but she foregoes the traditional bride-price.

elope together, they are outcaste and disowned by their family who risk being outcaste also (Bodding, 1942, pp. 81 and 82). Unions that violate the principle of tribe endogamy or clan exogamy are considered serious crimes and lead to excommunication.

The law is designed to protect as far as possible the integrity of the whole while accommodating the exigencies of the few. *Kirom cetan*, the taking of a second wife due to infertility or illness of the first wife, ensures the family unit is multi-generational and functioning. Women who are unable to bear children or to carry out chores may be pressured to bring another co-wife into the family. This is not just a matter of custom but also necessity as a couple have little hope of alternative support if they are unable to work in later life. *Kirin jawae*, the marriage of a woman who has a child out of wedlock, prioritizes the establishment of a family unit over the woman's choice of partner. If the father of the child is not able to marry her, someone is chosen from the village to be the woman's husband and receives payment (livestock and paddy) in return for his agreement. *Ghar jawae,* a matrilocal marriage, allows a family with no sons to keep their daughter at home and to bring a house husband *permanently* into the house to assist the family. This form of marriage allows a father to ensure that the daughter retains possession of the family lands on the father's death – the couple inherit the father's land (Mardi, 1997, p. 55). In the *ghardi jawae* form a father may marry his daughter to a boy (often a poor boy or an orphan) who enters the house as a *temporary* house husband (he does not pay any bride-price) and is obliged to carry out certain tasks for the household for five years. At the end of this period he is given some goods to keep and he is free to go away with the wife or stay and receive wages for his work.

Marriage described above is a means of ensuring a woman will be provided for and have a place in society. However, it ultimately also brings into play considerations of the woman's fertility (kirom cetan), promiscuity (kirin jawae marriage), inability to inherit (ghar jawae) and lower worth as a source of labour (ghardi jawae) as important factors in her ability to found a family of her choice. The choice of partner is more likely to be based on the needs of her parents and adherence to Santal customs and she is the object of a transaction between two families.

Gendering labour's visible worth

Women are not only pivotal in the socialization and foundation of the family unit, they are also what George Somers (1977, p. 84) calls a 'working resource of importance to the household'. As well as household chores (washing clothes, repairing walls and floors, making dung cakes for fuel, childcare, collecting water, repairing and cleaning the house, foraging for wood, roots and leaves), women may join men in harvesting, animal husbandry and external agricultural and other work including working as migrant labour (particularly in India). There are some tasks that are reserved for men and which women are prohibited from: ploughing, negotiating with moneylenders and paying rent to the village headman.

Despite the fact that women often contribute more than their husbands to the household, their work is undervalued.[3] Perceptions about how much individuals contribute are critical to this undervaluing and correlate directly with the 'invisibility' of their work (see Sen, 1990, cited in Rao, 2005a, p. 357; and Agarwal, 1997, p. 10). This point is illustrated in the Santal folk tale 'A Quarrel between Husband and Wife' (Bodding, 1997, vol. III, p. 253). A husband returns home for his midday meal and scolds his wife for not having his meal ready. When the wife says she has been too busy to prepare the meal, he asks her to show proof of the work she has done. She protests that she cannot show proof but promises to keep an account of her work the following day so that they can compare tasks. The following day the man returns at noon and they count up the work he has done: letting out the buffaloes, spreading the paddy out and threshing it, winnowing the paddy, collecting it into a heap. The woman then produces her account of her morning's work: husking paddy, sweeping the courtyard, collecting water, cleaning the brass cups and plates, feeding the children, feeding the cowherds and adults in the house, cleaning the fire-place, making fire, boiling water, draining the cooked rice, plucking mustard leaves, cooking and serving the meal. She explains to her husband that every task she does is 'consumed' so that there is less physical evidence of her work and her tasks are varied so there is no one final product. This folk tale reflects the higher value given to men's work and associates the undervaluing of women's work with the absence of a tangible output.

The devaluing of housework globally is well recognized (Becker, 1981; Wills, 2001; Katz, 2010). The economist Amarta Sen described gender inequality in the household as exemplifying a 'false consciousness' that women experience in relation to their contribution to the household (see Rao, 2005a, p. 356). In status-based societies misperceptions about women's lesser contributions and therefore importance to the survival of the household translate into deprioritization of their needs (Agarwal, 1997). In Santal society, as in other patriarchal societies in Asia (Baxi, 1986), women do today and have historically eaten after men (Bodding, 1942, p. 92; Ali, 1998, p. 129). This reflects an underlying presumption that, since the man is her main provider, his welfare takes priority. The privileging of the man

---

3 This experience is not unique to the Santal or to South Asia, indeed it has only been acknowledged by economists in the West relatively recently (see Becker, 1981; Young et al., 1981).

and subordination of the woman become part of the logic of survival and are understood as part of a 'system of ... cooperation by means of which the household satisfies its material wants' (Saha, 1969, p. 98).

The link between contribution and needs extends further to affect the formulation of benefits and negative obligations. These are acted out in the context of the family unit in which the woman's needs are catered for, and her reliance on male members assured. According to William G Archer (1984), once married, a woman can expect: to be clothed, to share in the food and drink her husband enjoys – though he has priority – to be maintained in the absence of her husband, to get medical treatment, to see her family periodically, and to receive maintenance in the instance of separation or divorce for which she is not deemed to be responsible. When she marries she keeps her own clan name, although her children take the name of their father. In marriage all her needs are met and she gains respectability in the community. While giving her support, these teach a woman from a young age that the key to her survival is not her own resourcefulness but her ability to succeed in her marriage and conform to the duties and restrictions it demands.

As well as having access to benefits Santal women are the subject of negative obligations restricting their contribution to the running of the household. Archer (1984, p. 129) writes that a woman is not permitted to plough, thatch a roof or use a leveller, shoot arrows, use a razor, chisel holes, strike with an axe or fish with a line and hook, weave cloth or string a cot, sacrifice an animal or witness such a sacrifice, eat certain parts of a sacrificed animal or enter private shrines to *bongas* (spirits/deities) in some situations. One important outcome of the woman's lower worth is restrictions to her ability to inherit land. Landownership restrictions along gender lines affect women's power in and beyond the family. They contribute to women's dependence on men and limit a woman's ability to support herself outside the family. Where land-owning restrictions apply, this affects a woman's bargaining power by narrowing her fall-back options: 'the outside options which determine how well-off she/he would be if cooperation [within the household] failed' (Agarwal, 1997, p. 4). This means, as we will see in Chapter 6, that women are more likely to choose negotiation or cooperation for their greater benefits.

Under Santal law a woman may in some circumstances own property (movable and immovable). Although women may inherit their mother and mother-in-law's personal belongings (ornaments, clothes etc.), they are unlikely to obtain their father's property. During his lifetime a father may choose to divide up his land between his sons. At this time the daughter may get one cow, calf, sheep or goat. After his death, a daughter does not inherit land unless all male agnates and her mother are dead. The only exception to this is the *ghar jawae* form of marriage described above where a woman's husband makes a declaration on marriage to cultivate his wife's land and gives up claims to his own paternal property (Rao, 2005a, p. 359). A wife similarly does not inherit land if her husband dies leaving any male agnates. A widow gets only a calf, bundle of paddy, brass-cup and a cloth and should return to her father or brother's house unless she remarries. She could also go and live with a married daughter. It can be advantageous for a widow to marry a brother-in-law because she is able to remain living in her house with her children and continue her life almost as before. But she never gains more than customary *usufructuary* property rights over the land. If a man dies leaving only young sons, his wife keeps the property in the sons' name until they are old enough to inherit, and then shares it equally between them. She then lives with the youngest. If the wife remarries outside the family, however, male relatives take over the property and hold it for the sons in her place.

That is not to say that she may never own land: she may receive a gift of land (in the form of *taben jom* or maintenance) from her father, brothers or male agnates. She is also entitled to hold self-acquired land, which remains hers even after marriage. In practice, however, ownership of land, which is seen as pertaining to the community, by women is rare (Bodding, c. 1920, p. 242). Even where a woman does own land, her ability to profit from it is limited. The taboo on women ploughing means that she cannot cultivate the land herself. This fact legitimates man's priority over landownership and women's dependence on men. Where a woman does inherit, this can cause problems for her if male relatives feel that they should own the land and use physical intimidation to usurp it. In India there is increasing pressure from outside the Santal community to allow Santal women to inherit property in certain circumstances but the male tribal elite are resisting this (see, for example, Besra, 1995, p. 4). The state courts have been inclined not to undermine tribal custom, and apply the customary laws as they exist in a given region (Roy, 1997). Despite the disadvantage this creates for Santal women, a Supreme Court ruling confirmed that applying Santal inheritance law, which was less favourable for women than Hindu law, would not be deemed to offend articles of the Indian Constitution relating to equality before the law, prohibition of discrimination and protection of life and liberty, and each case would be examined on its merits (Roy, 1997). I discuss this further in Chapter 5.

The processes of inequality described above mean that many women experience their subordination in the family as part of a natural order, what I call relations of nature. Yet subtle renegotiations of this order are common. In relations between a husband and wife the division of labour creates opportunities for women to exert their own control over the benefits the man receives at the moment of delivery. Abandoning her husband at a critical moment in the agricultural cycle, or simply delaying timing or tampering with the quality of daily meals are but a few of the most common manifestations of this. Where disputes arise between husband and wife, the interplay of responsibilities of a woman's father, brothers and husband (and possibly also their sons in later life) to look after her wellbeing provide leverage for her to obtain support and assistance and to challenge overzealous domination. Recourse to male relatives in cases of domestic disputes exposes the man's actions to wider scrutiny. Although a woman's actions will doubtless also be examined, she has some control over how and when the matter is raised. These renegotiations of the microprocesses of inequality are important to understanding the evolution of change in Santal society and I examine them in detail in Chapter 6.

The village

If the family is the vital unit of village life, the village is its bloodline. The layout of the village, with houses positioned on either side of a main village road, facilitates a weblike interconnectedness between households through which all villagers travel. Archer describes the village street as the artery of village life:

> [w]ithin each village, it is the street that dominates the scene. Along its thoroughfare the crops and firewood come and bullock carts go off to market ... villagers share their feasts and collect for talk and councils ... The street is not merely a link between the houses. It is at once a dance floor, a council chamber and a court of justice. (1974, p. 19)

As well as being a symbol of their bond, the village street facilitates social control through visibility. The compulsion to walk or traverse the main street – anyone seen avoiding the main street, cutting through between houses, would be viewed with suspicion – makes each individual's movement subject to inspection. Open doorways into houses mean even the personal family space of the main courtyard of each house is subject to scrutiny at all times and visitors may enter without warning. Comings and goings and patterns of work are visible to all. This interconnectedness of village and family life is complemented and reinforced by the central importance of the village in each individual's life. Villagers actively seek social recognition, and participation of others is actively pursued in every matter, from house building to arranging a marriage (Kochar, 1966, p. 18). The village provides a community context in which each individual's progress through life is marked and recognized. It is a source of primary education, friendship, status and support. The importance of the village in life-cycle events, such as birth, initiation, marriage, death, divorce, and its potential to assist in cases of serious disease, as well as the compulsion to participate in festivals, the trial of serious crimes, such as adultery, murder, and incest, make community a central pillar of every individual's life.

Position, knowledge and experience

Santal society is often described by outsiders as egalitarian (between men) – all heads of household contribute equally to village decisions and all men are *mit' leka*, as one, and even the headman is considered 'first among equals' (Somers, 1977, p. 58). However, the organization of village life and subtle distinctions between individuals in Santal society by age, gender and capacity create social hierarchies. Seniority (in age or status) is marked by the customary low bow, *bodok' johar*, on the meeting of two people of unequal status. The gesture is distinguished between men and women: a junior male raises a cupped right hand to his head (left hand cups his right elbow) while lowering his head slightly, while a junior female bows deeply from the waist, arms hanging down until hands almost touch the ground. The senior person reciprocates: a senior man extends his right arm opening his palm to the sky and then turning it to the ground, a senior female extends both arms with palms facing the sky then draws them to her chest. Somers (1977, p. 60) says that the gendered differences signify different meanings: the junior male is asking for a blessing and the female offering her service to the senior person.

While age is a primary signifier of seniority, every village delegates important tasks and decisions to a selection of men designated as village officers, usually descendants of the men who founded the village. Each village has up to seven village officers. Each officer performs specific roles in the village. The manjhi, headman, and his deputy, the *paranik*, ensure harmony is maintained and that individuals respect Santal cultural norms and laws. The manjhi will hear disputes and correct deviant behaviour but he will also offer council in day-to-day matters, and is present for the naming of newborn babies and burying of the dead. Adolescents are watched over, in addition, by the jog manjhi (and in some villages his deputy, the *jog paranik*). He will in particular ensure that the young are not promiscuous and, if they are found to be, that they are punished. The Santal also have a spiritual leader, *naiki*, who principally is involved in overseeing all spiritual aspects of the life-cycle ceremonies. He is thought to be chosen by the spirits (bongas) as someone through whom they are able to express themselves (Kochar, 1966, p. 11). Finally, some villagers have a *godet*, messenger, who helps to gather the villagers together for council meetings and collects birds for sacrifice where required. Inter-village matters are dealt with by the *pargana* or parganait (regional Santal headman).

Traditionally, the manjhi's eldest son, who must have a wide knowledge of religious functions and folktales, legends, traditions and lores, and intelligence and the capacity to mediate between the villagers, inherits his post (Sinha, 1967, p. 222). However, the annual *mag* festival provides an opportunity for villagers to voice their concerns about a village official's performance and if an officeholder is found not to be carrying out his role properly he may be asked to stand down and another person selected in his place (Kochar, 1966, p. 11). An official may also resign during the festival if he wishes to terminate his position (Bandyopadhyay, 1999, p. 76). But selection of a candidate unrelated to the manjhi is permitted in some circumstances. In Thakurban village in Bangladesh, the headman had passed his title to his son after being manjhi for 18 years. But after only three years of service the son had stood down. The villagers selected another young agnate who was also the naike, but he also stood down after a short while claiming that managing the two posts was not realistic. A meeting of the village council was called and a number of candidates discussed. A few candidates (young men were preferred) were selected and once they agreed to be put forward for the post, the men of the village gathered to choose one candidate – a show of hands for each candidate indicated one candidate had the most supporters. Luke described this process as akin to an 'election' (a process the Santal are familiar with through NGO and state influences) rather than traditional 'selection' and it may have reflected a subtle change in practice.

The system of village officers is an important starting point for the allocation of power in the village. Clearly, those with recognized positions of responsibility (the manjhi, naike, paranik) have considerable powers in the village. Holding a village post suggests good character, knowledge of customs and conscientiousness. But selection is also thought to reflect the wishes of the ancestors and postholders act in a quasi-sacred capacity (Chaudhuri, 1987, p. 45). Postholders keep their posts by virtue of an informal village consensus and act as servants of the village (Archer, 1984, p. 3). If the manjhi's decision does not reflect the concerns of the villagers present at the council, it may not be followed. His authority depends on maintaining the respect of the community, or at least the majority of the men in the community. Despite this, however, the manjhi and other officeholders do have a greater say in village matters than other villagers.

While granting potential power to those with village officer posts, the system of village officers limits women's access to power. Women are not involved in selecting the village officers and are seen, at most, as having a supporting or secondary role in the duties of village officers. I asked villagers why there seemed to be no women manjhis and, in India, many people told me the manjhi's wife was the female manjhi. She plays some part in ceremonies, cleaning up and sometimes carrying out some of the rituals as instructed by the men. Also, interestingly, when I visited villages where the manjhi was away (usually working or simply visiting other villages), I would always be brought to see his wife to introduce myself to her in his absence. She seemed to be treated by male villagers as capable of representing him, although she was not considered to have any of his powers.

Archer (1984, p. 9) says that women *may* be appointed as manjhis, there is nothing in Santal law to prevent it (see also Mardi, 1997, p. 45). In his study of the political organization of the Santal, Somers (1977, p. 183) writes that the decision about who may become a manjhi is based on the *bos,* which, he describes as a link to a common male ancestry, However, he suggests a manjhi's daughter may also inherit the post if no male members of the manjhi's bos are suitable. However, Santal villagers whom I spoke to were vague about the 'possibility' of a woman taking the post. None knew of any villages with a woman manjhi. Some villagers suggested that women would not be given the post, claiming their argumentative nature made them unsuitable for the task of settling conflicts. Similar stereotypes appear in the literature. Kolean's testimony on Santal customs, taken down in 1871, states 'some women do not, like the men, talk what is blameless; their words may be aggravating, and therefore very noisy quarrels sometimes arise' (Bodding, 1942, p. 109). This stereotype appears to persist today and an NGO worker in Dumka who had visited a Santal village to set up a women's committee, aimed at starting up small-scale, income-earning projects and providing a forum to discuss women's problems, was warned by the men of the village not to let the women gather together. He was told they would argue and fight or practise witchcraft (I discuss witchcraft practices in Chapter 5).

Knowledge and experience, which also tends to be gendered, play a crucial role in access to power in the villages. These qualities are often linked to holding official village posts because villagers with knowledge and experience are more likely to become officers and because holding a village officer post allows a person to build on their knowledge and experience. A B Chaudhuri (1987, p. 45) says special knowledge is the resource that gives postholders power. This includes knowledge of Santal custom and tradition but also, possibly, knowledge gained through formal schooling and experience of the outside world – Somers (1977, p. 183) refers to manjhis in the villages where he researched having had 'training' through primary education in missionary and government schools which enhanced their suitability for the post. While such knowledge and experience is more available to men, it is not unique to village officers. Families with resources may send their children to school – I found one or two men in each village who had benefited from higher education. All villages also had a number of elderly men who assisted the village officers with decision-making. These men gain respect for their extensive knowledge of Santal customs and experience of carrying out ceremonies and resolving disputes. They were often considered to be as knowledgeable as the manjhi and sometimes more so. In some villages they were a more dominant presence than the manjhi and other postholders. Some were retired postholders, others had previously held government positions, such as UP or panchayat member, and others had gained valuable experience working outside the village.

As well as being associated with education, age and the holding of influential positions, access to knowledge and experience is also *controlled* to some extent by customary practices. Marilyn Strathern (1985) examines how customary rights in tribal society create power from knowledge and experience and then deny it to women through ritual control over access. Separating women from men during ceremonies, by distinguishing rites by gender or giving men more significant roles, enhances men's powers. This feeds into a social order that legitimates men's 'authority of experience' and subordinates women (Strathern, 1985, p. 61). In Santal society women are denied prominent roles in many of the rituals. Chaudhuri (1987, p. 45) writes that '[m]en have deliberately screened the kind of knowledge available to women within the society'. Women are, for example, not allowed to know the name of the *abge bongas* and *orak bongas* (house spirits), which are different for each clan. These are passed on from the father to his eldest son in a whisper before the father dies (Bodding, 1942, p. 133–4). Women are also excluded from offering sacrifices to the bongas. Chaudhuri (1987, p. 45) suggests that, while women play certain roles and have some awareness of mores in the society, they are not able to identify the symbolism that reflects particular goals of the tribe. They understand the need to defend certain behaviours or places but cannot explain this in terms of ideology.

Poverty, wealth, kinship and friendship

Although there is no acknowledged lower class amongst the village Santal, there are clear disparities of wealth between villagers, visible from the housing materials used to build their shelter and its condition and size, their physical appearance, food habits and health. Wealth is closely related to land holdings, and those with land or a bull or plough (which enables them to work as sharecroppers, getting a greater percentage of the harvest or to rent the bull/plough out to others) are likely to be better off and possibly even employ poorer villagers to work on their land.

Poverty has a direct effect on survival and with it access to influence and power in the village. The poorest villagers with no assets from which to earn or borrow money from moneylenders often rely on low-paid unskilled labouring work and have no surplus for periods of food shortage, costs of emergency medication and repairs to their houses. They are more likely to have a poor diet and are more susceptible to illness and, unless they can borrow money for medication, more likely to die. Although traditional medicines exist, these do not provide remedies for many serious common illnesses, such as malaria, and as a result of deforestation many of the ingredients used in traditional medicine are anyway no longer available. In Lahara, I noticed that there were many young families with only one parent. My assistant was young and had four children but no wife. He told me his wife had died of malaria, which affected the area regularly. I asked him what assistance the government gave and he said medical officers from the thana hospital visited the village once a year to take the names of those infected and provide free treatment. Poor villagers depended on this and one year when they did not come many poorer villagers of all ages died, children were orphaned and some couples were left childless.

In an environment of food insecurity and inadequate healthcare, a family is the greatest immediate asset. Small families with few or no children have no source of additional income and no security. One couple in Lahara who had lost all their children explained that they feared theft from non-adivasis more than others because their house was not secure and they both had to work, which meant being out of the village from morning to night. They felt more insecure and vulnerable to attacks because they had no one to protect them. In old age children are the only insurance against starvation, illness and insecurity. Government pensions are available in India but have to be applied for and collected in person, which means travelling, usually on foot, and often for several hours, making them difficult to access for those with impaired mobility.

The links between poverty and mortality affect kinship support, security, knowledge and experience and contribute to a resultant lack of power. But there is a less clear link between *wealth* and power in the village. The wealthiest villagers were often absent from the village or removed from village politics. This is because they usually lived near their place of work (factory, mine, government office). Their economic independence meant that they were less dependent on relationships with other villagers and therefore less likely to be involved in village customs and laws. The most wealthy, who were educated and lived outside the village, only returned to visit relatives, and were often considered to be 'dikuized' (having become non-adivasis) because of their dress, language and rejection of village customs. As a result wealth had little bearing on power and influence in the village.

Kinship and friendship were more important sources of influence. Although there is no agreed definition of kinship, the concept is associated with social organization of biological (consanguine) and marital (affined) relationships. Anthropologists study kinship by looking at forms of nomenclature and classification, such as relationship terminology, by looking at the rules that affect kinship behaviour and at what people do on a collective and individual basis in the context of kinship rules. There are few studies of the Santal kinship system and their kinship system does not correspond in all its features with studies of societies in South Asia generally. While Claude Levi-Strauss (1969) found that in Asia kinship systems are often based on an alliance system where lineages are linked through cross-cousin marriage, cross-cousin marriage has not been a feature of Santal marriage customs. The Santal system of marriage is more akin to the descent systems found in Africa where marriage occurs more or less at random outside an individual's lineage – more typical of Levi-Strauss's 'intermediate kinship systems' where society is divided into a number of lineages which are not linked by a regular pattern of marriage alliances.[4]

Santal kinship nomenclature – the way people refer to members of the kin group – gives us information about a person's status and position within kin groups. According to V K Kochar (1963), Santal kinship terms are taken from the Mundari and Sanskritic languages and distinguish fellow kin in relation to their sex, age and marital or blood relationship. A K Das (1967, p. 9) says that the kinship terminology amongst the Santal is descriptive or derivative in nature: *bifurcate collateral avuncular* terms used distinguish maternal from paternal uncles, cousins and so on. Santal kinship is based on patrilineal descent – a child's social status is acquired from the father (Tuck, 1976, p. 221). Kinship terminology helps to distinguish relations along the male descent line.

Kinship relationships among the Santal include the *gharonj* and *oaris* (family-related ties) and *paris* and *gutia*[5] (clan-related ties). Membership of the family and clan group are two of the most important attributes of social status (Kochar, 1964, p. 25). Family plays an important role in access to power in the village, and kinship ties may combine with other factors such as proximity of households or clan group to strengthen bonds between certain groups. The link between kinship support and survival means that these groups form an important part of status in the village. The unit of the gharonj includes several households that make up an extended family (Somers, 1977, p. 80; Ali, 1998, p. 130; Bodding, 2002, p. 518). In the Santal village, the gharonj functions as not only a social but also a political unit

---

4 See Furer-Haimendorf (1985, p. 113) on South-Asian kinship and, for background on different classifications in general, see Layton, 1997, pp. 70 and 75.
5 Gutias are religious rites carried out by a particular group. Each gutia observes rites of a special bonga or spirit, which are carried out once a year.

(Somers, 1977, pp. 80 and 85). No child is left without one. A child born out of wedlock will be given a clan name by a man who agrees to marry the mother or by the jog manjhi or jog paranaik or an elderly man in the village. Until the naming and initiation ceremony is conducted, the whole village is considered impure and cannot perform any ceremonies. If they fail to initiate the child, it is said that he or she will not have a normal marriage or cremation and his/her spirit will not reach full spirit status (bonga) but will remain a *bhut*, ghost (Kochar, 1964, p. 24). Thus the whole village has an interest in ensuring all its members are integrated into a family.

Extending a gharonj through marriage is an important way of building on the family's success in society. The Santali word for marriage, *bapla*, means the mutual strengthening of two families (Bodding, 2002, vol. I, p. 198). Because marriage is usually between individuals from different villages, it is also considered to be a joining of two villages in a new relationship (Troisi, 1979, p. 301). It creates a new alliance, an extended group of contacts and some actual entitlements, such as the oaris, which is a continuing interest in goods, that binds family members – such as the bride-price paid by the groom's family, which they have a continuing interest in (Somers, 1977, p. 87).

However, family relations may provide a more consistent source of power in the village for men than women. At this point it might be useful to distinguish relations of consanguinity (blood) and affinity (marriage). Because women leave the village where their blood relations reside when they marry, whereas men continue to live with their blood relations after marriage, men seem to benefit from stronger and more consistent kinship ties in the village. Besides having common lineage, blood relations share emotional and semi-legal obligations, for example, the oaris (bond of interest) between brothers who co-own an interest in their father's land (Somers, 1977, p. 87). Marital ties seem to create weaker links and women continue to rely on their own, physically distant, parents or brothers in times of trouble rather than in-laws (see my discussion of domestic disputes in Chapters 5 and 6).

As well as creating gendered disparities in power, I found that kinship also has an impact on individual power. When a son marries, a new house is built near to the parents, so relatives tend to live together, allowing large families to dominate an area of the village (see also Somers, 1977, p. 82). This intensifies intra-familial interdependence but also isolates those with no extended family. The extent of kinship support is mapped physically onto the layout of the village. The bigger the kin group, the greater the pool of resources that its members can access, and this improves their ability to cope with crisis. Belonging to a larger and more powerful kin group can also mean getting greater support from the institutions of village organization and justice.

While a clan group may not constitute kin ties, this category of inclusivity also has repercussions for power in the village. A Santal clan, called a paris, is a subgroup made up of 'all persons unilineally descended from a common ancestor of fictive or mythological character rather than through a known ancestor' (Somers, 1977, p. 74). Each clan has many sub-clans (*khuts*). The khut signifies the identity of the family meaning that where the khut is identical there is a blood relation (Baskey, 2002, p. 193). The exact names and number of the subclans is being amended as anthropologists register names they come across (Sattar, 1983, p. 75). Johannes Gausdal (1960) has found records of 188 subclans in total. There are 12 Santal clans: Hasdak, Murmu, Kisku, Hembrom, Marndi, Soren, Tudu (the original seven clans named after the first seven sons of the race) and Baske, Besre, Pauria, Core and Bedea. These clans are patrilineal kinship groups, which also serve as surnames in the context of the modern state. Families of the same clan share taboos and a common totem (for example, Hasdak – duck, Kisku – seagull: Ghosh and Ghosh, 2000, p. 153), and each clan also has a sign (such as Marandi →, Tudu ⊗, Besra +) which used to be used to mark their cattle's bodies (Baskey, 2002, p. 193). They are usually cited in a hierarchy (see also Biswas, 1956, p. 62; Gautam, 1977; Chattopadhyay, 1979, p. 34; Bouez, 1985, p. 87).

The clan was at one time associated with class and occupation,[6] and the two clans described as 'poor', Paurea and Core, seem to have disappeared – I found no one of those clans in any of the villages where I stayed and Somers found only nine of the original clans in the villages he studied (1977). These class distinctions have now disappeared and there is no longer any social distinction between the clans (Archer, 1974, pp. 24–5). There was no evidence in the villages where I stayed of division between the clans, nor did they constitute formal subgroups of the village or tribe. However, there does seem to be some evidence that clan can act as a factor for organizing kinship and power in the village. For example, clan title *may* play a role in choosing a spouse and thus in creating kinship alliances between clans. Serge Bouez (1985, p. 106) found a clear preference for some clans to marry mainly one or two specific clans, often a clan which is below it in the historic 'hierarchy'. Other authors have noted patterns of specific preferences (Archer, 1974, pp. 24–5) and dislikes (Das, 1967, p. 6) in the choice of clan of a

---

6 Kisku (Raja), Soren (military), Murmu (religious), Mardi (landowner), Hasdak (Raja's servant), Hembrom (day labourer), Baske (religious assistant), Besra (ironmonger), Tudu (musician), Core (poor), Powrea (poor). Interview with manjhi (Thakurban). Similar divisions are given by Somers (referring to a folk tale), 1977, p. 76; Bouez, 1985, p. 87; Ali, 1998, p. 123; Baskey, 2002, p. 192; Ghosh and Ghosh, 2000, p. 153. A 12th clan, Bedea is said to have been lost when its members refused to migrate with other Santal (Somers, 1977, p. 75).

prospective spouse. Das (1967, p. 6) and K P Chattopadhyay (1979, p. 37) both attribute these preferences to historical relations and liaisons between the clans, which stereotype relations as blessed or doomed. However, none found clear patterns for all clans – although Chattopadhyay (1979, p. 38) developed a complicated formula for calculating the frequency of marriages between different clans in the villages where he carried out his research. Ahsan Ali (1998, p. 126) says that in Bangladesh preference for a particular clan for marriage is no longer practised.

The importance of the clan as a basis for kin-based solidarity in the village seemed to differ from India to Bangladesh. Although in Bangladesh no one clan dominated any part of the village, in Lahara and Madhura there was a clear separation of clans, which tended to be concentrated in one or two areas in the village. This separation took place on the basis of clan and not extended family links – families sharing no immediate common ancestry but having a head of household with the same clan title tended to live close to each other. Proximity between households belonging to the same clan may have been intentional and strengthened the influence of that clan within the village. V K Kochar (1966) finds that vicinage (the link between a house and the houses on either side of it) is the most effective co-operating group in the Santal village. If this is so, in India, family ties, clan ties and vicinage ties may combine to create strong social units around a particular clan identity. This may mean that clan is a more effective basis of power in the villages in India than in Bangladesh.

Which clans are likely to be strong may not be a co-incidence. According to Chattopadhyay (1979, p. 35), research in Santal villages showed that the original group of men who established each Santal village were likely to have been from the same clan, and this gave one clan a superior position in the village from its inception because the founders took the official posts and passed them on to their children. Over generations, village officer posts will likely have been transferred through non-hereditary selection, however, the unity and size of the founding clan is a factor in its ability to maintain influence. Examining historic fluctuations in one village, Kochar (1966) found that positions of influence and power held by certain clans related to the ability of the clan to constitute a unified group and exert its influence over others. Clans that had been most successful in gaining power in the village had a greater number of original settler families and had some blood ties among households of the same clan. The age of members of the clan as well as the personal characteristics of their male household heads was also important. Too many young heads of households and no individuals who were influential and popular made a clan less likely to gain power. Clans that had lost most power in the village were constituted by only a small number of original settler families, with most current day members of the clan joining the village later as newcomers.

While the size and influence of consanguineous connections within the village seem to be a marker for power, this is not to say that those with fewer connections of this type will perish. Kolean's treatise on Santal customs suggests that, while there is a distinction between 'real relationships', relationship by birth and by marriage, and friendships, intimate friendships are an important part of Santal life: '[i]ntimate friends will give even their life to help each other in calamity and danger' (Bodding, 1942, p. 109). These intimate relationships start from youth. Girls can have a childhood friendship eternalized during a *karam* festival, through a ritual that ties them as *karam-branch* friends. Bouez (1985, p. 97) talks also about close friendships between either two women or two men which are formalized through the flower (*baha*) ceremony. The two friends become like siblings with the effect that their children cannot marry.

Having intimate or long-established friendships depends on longevity of stay in the village. Santal families or individuals sometimes move to a new village. They may leave their own village because they cannot get work there, because their relations with the villagers has deteriorated or to avoid disease or accusations of witchcraft. Santal villagers usually welcome newcomers but the newcomers are likely to live further away from the hub of village activity, thus making it more difficult for them to establish intimate friendships quickly. The repercussions of having neither intimate friends nor blood relations became clear during a case heard in one of the villages. While I was staying in Thakurban, a dispute arose between two men in the village, Bolanath and Paulus. Bolanath was at a disadvantage in the village. He married in ghar jawae form moving to live with his wife in her village and so had no blood relations there. Bolanath was of the Kisku clan and he and his wife were the only family of that clan group in the village. Also the people in Thakurban were descended from four couples, and Bolanath's wife's family was the smallest of the families. By contrast Paulus was part of the largest extended family in the village. Two of Paulus' brothers were village officers and, although poor, his family had much support. Bolanath and his wife, however, were not well integrated into the village. They both worked outside the village during the day and I noticed their house had a secure door, one of the few in the village, which they locked whenever they were out. I was surprised when I first saw their house locked up – in many villages houses do not even have doors and trust amongst the villagers is strong. The only reason for locking your door would be to stop theft by outsiders if there was no one to watch your house.

Paulus had accused Bolanath of stealing one of his ducks. It was harvest time, the busiest season of the year, and a meeting of the village council had to be arranged a week in advance on an evening when most villagers were able to attend. The council was held under a tree at the edge of the village and a mound of dirt was dug out of the soil to provide a 'seat' for Bolanath, the accused. Bolanath received very little support from the villagers who attended the meeting and made no attempt to defend himself. The only witness who appeared in his defence was his own cousin who lived in an adjacent village. Bolanath's lack of blood ties in the village or intimate friendships seemed to exacerbate his inability to defend himself. Rumours had it that Bolanath had been ordered to kill the ducks by a Muslim landlord of the area, Ahmed, and had acted without telling Paulus or consulting the village. The village council was convened to hear the case. There were 16 men at the council meeting. The accused had just two supporters sitting on his side, while Paulus had seven who were all sitting close to the manjhi and thus had a bigger part in the discussion and decision-making. There were four men who were not related to either family. Some women stood further back, watching, but made little or no contribution. Ahmed, who was said to have given the order to kill the ducks, stood near the manjhi and left halfway through when he felt his contribution was over.

Ahmed said he had instructed Bolanath – who worked for him occasionally – to kill two ducks that had wandered onto his land and were eating his crops. He could not say whether Bolanath had acted on this or what he had done with the ducks. No one had seen Bolanath kill the ducks and Bolanath did not admit to eating them. A witness gave evidence that he had seen Bolanath and his brother-in-law in a neighbouring village eating meat on the night the ducks went missing. Meat such as duck was a rare luxury in the village. Bolanath's brother-in-law – the only person at the meeting to speak out in his favour – said they were eating wild rat. There was heated discussion mostly between Paulus' supporters. Luke, who was not supporting either party, asked questions to both parties and Ahmed to try and ascertain the facts. The manjhi recounted the outcome of a previous similar case. Most of the discussion took place near the manjhi.

After this the manjhi announced the conclusion of the meeting. Bolanath was most at fault, not for killing the ducks on Ahmed's order, but for consuming the ducks and going to another village to do so deceitfully without telling anyone. He received a fine that would cover the cost of replacing the two ducks. Paulus demanded compensation for the two weeks' worth of potential additional eggs he had lost because he would be without the ducks for this period. At this point the manjhi reminded Paulus that he was partly responsible because he had allowed his ducks to consume crops on another's land. Because of this he would forfeit the extra compensation for the loss of potential eggs.

Although the decision attributed some blame to Paulus (he forfeited his extra compensation), the process struck me as heavily weighted against Bolanath. The numerical weakness of people defending him and his own reluctance to defend his actions made the discussions quite one-sided. This seemed not just to be a question of his having poorer support on the day but seemed to mirror his weaker position in society. He had fewer kinship ties in the village and was less well integrated. His alleged act of following the orders of a Muslim to the detriment of a fellow villager and then hiding his act and enriching himself in the process further disassociated him from the villagers. The judgment seemed to me to be punishing him not just for eating the ducks but for his general lack of integration.

Conclusion

Differentiation in terms of entitlements and perceived ability permeate social relations in the family and village in a way that, I have shown, is given cultural meaning. Forms of marriage and division of labour feed into distribution of responsibilities and benefits and facilitate the privileging of men over women. Gendered roles are re-enforced through socialization in the family and endorsed through life-cycle events and customary prohibitions. In the village, conformity is maintained through visibility and the social desire for recognition and support amongst villagers. Maintaining kinship and friendship ties is critical to survival. Nevertheless, we will see in Chapter 6 that some do challenge the prevailing order of social relations of the family and village. These challenges have the potential to create subtle alterations in the development of cultural practices.

5
Resisting from Without: The Illusive Promise of the Alternative Legal Order

The micro-processes of power in the state, village and family represented in Chapters 3 and 4 permeate social relations. I relied heavily in those chapters on historical, colonial and ethnographic studies of the Santal. But my own fieldwork presented a more complex picture of power and reveals the family, village and state as points of intersection. In this and the following chapter, I explore the dynamism of power: its multidimensional nature in the context of ordinary life experiences and the reality of intersections between village, family and state. Each social space functions as a semi-autonomous social field through which outside influences are attracted and repelled, used and remodelled to a specific purpose. I use disputing as a springboard to examine the complex ways in which law facilitates, with limits, this process. In turning to disputing, I reframe the spaces of the state, village and family as 'legal' orders, which offer solutions through processes of dispute resolution and alternative ways of viewing the grievances that underlie them.

There is a rich literature on how disadvantaged individuals navigate plural legal orders in search of justice, a practice known as forum-shopping (see Benda-Beckmann, 1981; Abrahams, 1996; Bouysse-Cassagne, 1996; Day, 1996). These illustrate, in particular, the external obstacles disputants face when seeking to use an alternative legal order in pursuit of a desired outcome: the need for alternative legal orders to offer a separate idiom (free from class or gendered prejudice, for example) in which their rights are recognized (Griffiths, 1990; Wanitzek, 1990); the social and economic cost of recourse especially to national courts (Griffiths, 1990); and the fact that (in legally plural states) forums themselves manipulate disputes to get political advantage (Benda-Beckmann, 1981). Using the examples of domestic disputes, women's inheritance claims and witchcraft amongst the Santal, I demonstrate that alongside these external obstacles are internal pressures that force individuals to mitigate their use of alternative legal orders.

I found that recourse to an alternative legal order, such as the state, is so fraught with difficulties that this is not considered a primary solution for many Santal men, and even less so for women. In reality, the community is the main source of livelihood, status, emotional, spiritual and physical support and a familiar way of life. Recourse to an alternative legal order such as the state strains this connection. The length of time it takes to get a decision from the state and the difficulty of enforcing the decision locally mean that state courts are at best an ancillary forum. Use of an alternative legal order such as the state is more likely to be part of ongoing negotiations internally. We turn in Chapter 6 to look more closely at those negotiations.

The individual: disputing across legal orders

The Santal have customs governing order and discipline, marriage, divorce, clan exogamy, tribal endogamy, trespass, preservation of water channels, animal grazing, trespass by pigs, theft, disturbing the peace, acts of violence and abuse, and respecting the authority of village officials. These customs are not written but passed on from one generation to another and between villages and the manjhi is considered the 'living book of law' and past precedents (Bandopadhyay, 1999, p. 73). In his ethnographic study of the Santal political structure, George Somers (1977) reveals the fluid process of customs that prioritize *ato sagai*, or village oneness, over strict application of rules (for a discussion, see Shariff, 2013, pp. 125–8). William G Archer (1984, p. 3), a colonial officer who recorded a detailed treatise of Santal law in the 1940s, acknowledged the organic and versatile nature of the law, and noted small differences in rules between geographic regions.

This flexibility is facilitated through a three-level structure of councils: each forum providing opportunity for the people involved in the dispute to voice their grievances and hear the views of fellow villagers. As well as these courts, and distinct from them, there are diviners (*ojhas*) and witchfinders (*jangurus*), described by the Santal elder Kolean in the 1870s as 'our High-court in connexion with witchcraft' (sic) (Bodding, 1942, p. 166). I say more about this below. Outside of witchcraft the resolution of disputes is not a matter of applying rules to facts but of measured analysis of wrongdoing. Blame is often attributed indirectly through the payment of a fine between the parties without naming their infractions. The aim of the adjudication is to re-establish peace in the village and reset the balance in village relations. To do so, it is important that all those who attend the meeting feel blame has been evenly attributed and the wrong corrected.

While most disputes, both relating to family and village matters, are resolved through the village council, there is no obligation for Santal villagers to take family disputes there. The family constitutes a distinct arena for disputing. The paths to dispute resolution are less visible but commonly reflect the tendency to favour senior over junior members of the family and reserve decision-making to men. Santal law relating to marriage, inheritance and so on, discussed in Chapter 4, along with the privileging of men in village councils, contributes to the bias towards men's greater ability to adjudicate. However, despite this, the family and the village do constitute separate arenas with some important differences. Those differences mean the village and family can be considered distinct legal orders for the purposes of dispute resolution.

The state law, though distant, also provides a separate and potentially rewarding avenue for disputes arising within the family or village context. The use of state law, which has its roots in colonial times, has been popular amongst the Santal for over a century. As far back as 1887 Santali domestic disputes were being referred to the colonial courts (Bodding, 1942, p. 129). In India and Bangladesh, criminal and family courts provide fertile forums for resolving a range of domestic disputes. Despite the many obstacles of using these courts (financial, geographic, social), during my fieldwork I came across a number of examples of women individually using the state legal order to contest a disadvantage in the family or village.

Domestic disputes

Domestic violence has been defined in various ways but relates to violence or emotional, psychological or sexual abuse perpetrated within a domestic context. It often involves control and subordination of one person by another, used to provoke fear and obedience, and takes place over a period of time (McCue, 2008, pp. 2–3). There is no reference to abuse within marital relations in Santal records relating to their laws and customs, most of which were written down during colonial rule, or in Santal folk tales which provide a rich source of information on role expectation.

While open arguments seemed to be conspicuous by their absence during my time living in the villages, there were occasional heated domestic disputes – family members could be heard shouting and sometimes screaming and crying. Sitting in the manjhi's courtyard one day I heard a crash and a woman's voice shouting, followed by a man's voice. I ran to the manjhi and he came out onto the main street and hurried down to the doorway of the house, looking a little nervous. He stopped, listened for a moment, and then turned back to me. '*Galmarow*' (discussion/argument) he said, shrugging his shoulders and looking a little relieved that he would not have to intervene. I pressed him further, 'Should we not go in'? 'It's just an argument' he said. This response was repeated in other villages. Unsolicited intrusion of the village into the family is rare. This seems to be not just a matter of practicality but of protocol – a Santal folk tale ('Two Brothers Who Quarrelled', Bodding, 1997, vol. II, pp. 338–45) demonstrates that disputes taking place in the context of the family are only addressed by the village on request of the parties. This creates a particular problem for women in the context of domestic violence as it means that the village will not intervene and it is left to the woman to raise concerns.

This reticence to intervene also hides a subtle acceptance of domestic violence. Domestic violence was not openly acknowledged in the villages, yet discussions I participated in during my fieldwork revealed chastisement of women was considered acceptable. A new bride had been welcomed to a village adjacent to Thakurban. She was older than most, in her late teens, but seemed shy. A small group of women had gathered and we chatted about married life. I asked the new bride how she was enjoying her new life and if her husband treated her well. She giggled and said 'ok'. I asked did she ever get told off, and gestured a hit. Shyly she said, 'Only if I don't do my work properly, if I am good then he will not hit me.' Her tone reflected her desire to fit in in her new village and suggested that this was what was expected of her. I asked would she hit back if he hit her. The women all laughed and one older woman said, lifting her hands in resignation, 'What can we do?' – her voice betrayed a sense of frustration at women's inability to prevent violence.

In fact, women are not completely helpless in these cases and the village headman (manjhi) will, when asked, intervene and if necessary punish those who use violence arbitrarily. However, a finding of fault on the part of the husband is conditional on an assessment of the woman's behaviour. The manjhi makes a judgment in each case and may accept a man's defence that he used violence only to correct deviant behaviour. Waiting for my assistant one morning in Dhanban, I spoke to Mala, a young woman who had been designated the leader of the village women's committee (set up by a local NGO to help families save money for future emergencies). She repeated the established rule as an unproblematic statement of Santal practices – that the manjhi would help a woman if the woman had given no cause for the beating – adding that if the husband got drunk and beat his wife then this was not allowed. Mala's acceptance of violence as a means of discipline was part of the logic of gendered relations. A woman who did not carry out her work in the house was accepted as being at risk of being hit.

In the focus group with women in Thakurban, I asked what advice they would give to a woman who was being beaten by her husband. The responses relayed the different possible outcomes of a case and one woman gave her own intimate feelings about what should happen.

A1: We'd tell her to go to the manjhi. He'll call the village people and hear the case. He'll say if you keep hitting your wife we'll fine you. So the husband will become afraid (he's just a day labourer so has no money). Pondic's wife left because she was afraid but the manjhi will hear the case.

A2: If the husband says 'I only hit her when she's bad' the manjhi will say 'You should behave. Should listen to your husband.'

A3: (Older woman): It is never ok to hit a wife, it hurts. If I do wrong then my husband should tell me what I've done.

Older women seemed less accepting of village authority and more likely to question men's use of violence. Watching women interacting and talking to them, I noticed younger women seemed more eager to fit within the parameters of conventional practices. In the interviews, women aged 46–70 tended to be more assertive about the facilities they had in the village whereas younger women (aged 30–45) were more likely to be unsure. Older women also tended to list positive material benefits owed to them as women (food from family, gifts from villagers at marriage time, welfare for themselves and their children, being able to inherit their parent's property). Younger women mentioned emotional benefits such as love from the family. The absence of women manjhis was attributed by younger women, euphemistically, to tradition. Older women were more likely to mention reasons why women were not manjhis: *men* do not allow it; women are not able to travel out of the village safely; women do not know how to do the work or have other roles to play; it is socially not accepted for women to have group discussions. Older women seemed more likely to be able to demystify Santal practices and this seemed to positively affect their ability to take recourse to law.

A neighbour in Thakurban village, Mary, a Christian Santal in her fifties, who had not moved villages on marriage, had brought cases to the village council and to the state court to stop domestic violence. Mary, whose own brother lived in the same village, had turned to the village council when her own family had failed to provide an effective check against her husband's violence. Mary was a small, slim lady in her fifties and wore an old thin sari. She was a hard worker, looking after the house and family as well as working as a day-labourer. When she had a moment free from working, she would launch into angry monologue about the poverty and misfortune she and her family had suffered. Near the end of my stay she invited me to her house for dinner and we chatted about her husband, Jogonath, and about their life. I had rarely seen Jogonath during my stay and when he did appear he rarely spoke. He was tall and well-built but in poor health and had been recovering from tuberculosis for many years and had been unable to work. Jogonath's father had been a landowner with a substantial area of land (54 bigas) but in 1947 Jogonath was orphaned and the land was appropriated by non-Santal who began to pay taxes on the land and drafted false ownership papers. Mary told me that when his tuberculosis was at its worst he had been depressed and drank heavily. He used to beat her and she would run away to her brother's house in the same village for protection. The village people were supportive of her and the manjhi warned her husband he would be fined 5000 taka (six months' wages) if the beating continued. She said he took this seriously because they had no money to pay such a big fine and for the next nine months the drinking and beating stopped. Since then he had recovered a little from the tuberculosis and things had been better.

Mary had also been involved in bringing a case to the state courts, this time against her son-in-law. Her daughter, Sara, married young to a well-off Christian Santal who had a job in the town working in a hospital. Mary told me the husband used to beat Sara badly, she had been hospitalized three times, and eventually left her. He was now living with his mistress, who also worked in the town. In the village where Sara lived, Rajbhan, the people asked the manjhi to look after her while they tried to persuade the husband to take her back. After two months the manjhi was unable to continue to maintain her and she returned to her natal village. Women from Rajbhan told Mary to take a case to court against Sara's husband. Mary told me she was unsure how to take a case to court and at first was afraid of going to the police but the villagers promised to support her and an NGO helped her file a case. The case was ongoing and Mary told me they were struggling to find the money to continue with it. During my fieldwork, Sara was living in a separate house in Thakurban with her children and seemed to be settled there.

Mary was able to use the village council and state court as forums to challenge violence by a husband but with potentially significant limits. The village council provided an effective solution – Mary's husband was threatened with a fine and this was enough to change his behaviour. The village council's resolution was final and could not easily be ignored since Jogonath and Mary lived in the centre of the village and any dispute would be easily heard. Jogonath's actions had now become a village matter. But, of course, recourse to the village council only helps if women are considered not to be at fault. How this is measured is then critical to its effectiveness. Given that the village is a tight-knit community, this seemed to depend at least in part on the quality of the relationship of the individuals involved with other families in the village, and past experiences of their actions. Mary was well integrated into the village and her brother lived in the village and, although not holding any position of authority, was well respected. As discussed in Chapter 4, the ability of individual villagers to gain support in the village council can be affected by the extent of their own integration in the village – quality of friendships and blood relations. The council, being a gathering of the male heads of household of the village, is more likely to be supportive where a woman is well regarded in the village.

The state law courts were offering Mary a remedy in the case against her son-in-law but required financial support (she was getting support from her brother and an external charity). State courts often take a long time to reach a decision as well as requiring what Michael Anderson (2003, p. 16) calls 'institutional skill' (the ability to understand and use the system). Their decision can also be very difficult to implement in remote villages. There was some worrying evidence also that the state courts viewed Santal women with suspicion. Interviews I had in Dumka with members of the senior judiciary revealed a negative perception of women's motives in turning to the court in domestic matters. One senior judge told me that Santal women took advantage of the state law to claim benefits from men in a way that abused the legislation. He used the example of cases filed under s. 493 Indian Penal Code (enticing a woman to intercourse) where a couple engage in intercourse on the promise of a future marriage, but the man then refuses to marry. He told me that open sexual relationships were prevalent amongst the Santal but some women used the courts to sue men they had slept with. His comments pointed to a perception that Santal are comparatively promiscuous and that the men in the cases that came to court were victims of women's manipulation. He saw these cases as a ruse by Santal women to make a claim for compensation under the law and noted many such cases were settled out of court. This experience led to mistrust of Santal women in other cases of abuse. In witchcraft cases, where men were accused of committing violent acts against women on the basis of witchcraft accusations, he said there was often a lack of evidence of actual violence against the woman filing the claim. He attributed the use of state law to a misuse of the legislation by women with other grievances against men. I was not able to substantiate these claims but, clearly, it was evidence that Santal women bringing a case to the state courts would find their own motives and actions being questioned.

Inheritance

Another area of disputing where women take recourse to the village council and state courts is inheritance. Women may, in limited circumstances, inherit their father's land. The village council and state courts may enforce the woman's customary right to inherit, for example, when women who *do* qualify to inherit land (e.g. married in ghar jawae form) are denied it by family members. The customary right to inherit is a Santal community matter but its application and interpretation takes place initially in the family. Decision-making power in the family is in the hands of male relatives and a woman's interests are unlikely to be represented there unless they coincide with the interests of men. Male relatives may have an interest in denying a daughter her exceptional customary right to inherit land if they are next in line to inherit the property. Using the village to address an inheritance dispute allows the woman to make her grievances known in a forum where people other than her male relatives have decision-making power. Despite the gender bias of the village council, I found that women placed great faith in the village system to support their interests in such cases.

The fact that women themselves, generally, and women parties to a case play little part in the discussions of the village council does not necessarily preclude it from acting as an alternative forum giving relief to women. Women also find their own way to secure support within the council. Nitya Rao (2008, p. 241) gives the example of a Santal woman, Noni, who has a dispute with her husband when he takes a second wife without her permission. He refuses to share his assets between the wives and she turns to the village council for help. Knowing that she will not be able to make her claim in full before the village council on the day of the trial (women are not always allowed to speak at will during the trial), she visits the houses of the male elders in advance to tell them her story, securing their support. During the trial itself she manages to negotiate a share of her husband's land and assets.

Rao notes that the presumption that other women are a woman's best defence has little foundation as it is unlikely to be other women who are best placed, or even willing, to challenge male relatives who abuse their powers. Rao tells us that the tendency to override Santal law on inheritance to take land away from women is endorsed not only by male relatives who stand to gain but their wives also. While women in similar subject positions within kinship groups (daughter, wife, sister, widow) may offer support, there is no general support along gendered lines (Rao, 2005a, p. 356). Contrarily, men may actively support a woman's customary right to inherit where they identify with her circumstances. Rao (2005a, p. 358) notes that women's interest in land is intimately connected with men's interest in land. Land is often viewed as a joint resource – even though women's entitlement to land and ability to profit from it is not equal to men's. Taboos on ploughing mean women cannot cultivate land without assistance from men. Rao (2005a, p. 361) says men in the village who identify with a woman's position, for example, if they themselves were married in ghar jamae form, will also support them. Those holding a position of influence, such as the village officers and elders, may also see supporting disputing women as important to maintain their own authority and further their prestige as impartial interlocutors.

Women themselves will go to great lengths to make their claim to land where they feel they are entitled to inherit. In Lahara, I lived with Magli and her husband. Magli, a woman in her forties, was a shrewd businesswoman. Her family owned more land than most and she cultivated chilli and mustard seeds. She was one of the few in the village to own cattle, which she kept in her relatively large house. The villagers told me that her husband was mentally ill and she ran the house and managed the land on her own. She not only looked after her own household but also kept a keen interest in her married daughter's livelihood. Her daughter had been married to Jonus just a few years previously and had borne a son. Magli told me the marriage was going well but Jonus' father was trying to get a divorce for his son to remarry. Magli was worried that she would be left to support her daughter and grandson and told Jonus' father that if he pursued the divorce she would apply to the state courts for declaration of her grandson's interest in his land. Jonus' father refused. Magli asked the manjhi and panchayat for help but they were not able to influence him. With the help of her father and brother, Magli then started a case in the state court in Dumka for declaration of the grandson's interest in Jonus' father's land. The case was ongoing.

There were legal precedents relating to inheritance under Santal customs and the Supreme Court requested the state of Bihar to consider changing provisions in state law which allow for exclusively male succession of property by Scheduled Tribes. In 1992 the Bihar Tribal Consultative Council (BTCC) met to reconsider the restrictions on women inheriting under tribal law and concluded that letting women inherit would cause unrest in the area among Scheduled Tribes. In 1996 the Supreme Court directed the state of Bihar to 'comprehensively examine the question' (see *Madhu Kishwar and Others vs State of Bihar and Others* 1996 All India Reporter 1864; 1996 Supreme Court Cases (5) 125). The numbers claiming inheritance are, however, modest: at Deoghar court in the Santal Parganas the sub-judge (first instance for civil cases) told me of the 300 cases he hears a year, between six and nine are Santal cases and four or five of these are inheritance cases involving women. Rao (2008, Annexure 4, p. 320) found in the Sub-Divisional Court in Dumka that, of the 200–250 land-related cases (demarcation, tenancy and inheritance) each year, between five and nine were brought by adivasi women.

What happens when these cases get to court is by no means straightforward. The personal law system in India means that state courts will seek to apply Santal law or its equivalent to cases brought before it. The transformation of Santal law through the state law process means that these courts still perform the role of an alternative forum of sorts, though it also means their outcome is always uncertain. In the Santal Parganas in India, the courts apply Santal inheritance law as set out in the *Gantzer Land Settlement Report* (1936) – a British survey of the customs regarding land laws amongst the Santal. *Gantzer* sets out some basic principles of Santal inheritance law but adds 'if a change in custom has been well established and generally accepted it will of course be treated as the customary law of the locality ...'. This principle was confirmed by the Supreme Court, which has stated that, where a tribal party is governed by custom, their custom, which varies from people to people and from region to region, should be applied. Each case has to be examined based on its own facts (Roy, 1997). According to the Santal lawyer and activist Basu Deo Besra (1995, p. 15), lawyers use this to assert unverifiable variations in custom to their advantage and this has led to confusion and contradictions in the case law.

In Santal Parganas, where the case relates to a transfer of land to a daughter married in ghar jamae form, the *Gantzer* report has also to be read in light of the SPTA 1949, put in place to limit the transfer of land away from adivasis. Together they misinterpret Santal customs such that it is the son-in-law and not the daughter who is deemed to have inherited the property (Rao, 2008, p. 245). Rao says this has left space for male natal kin to object to a woman's claim of inheritance under ghar jamae, for example, where she is widowed or divorced.

A further complication is that Santal tribal customs relating to inheritance apply only to individuals deemed to be non-Hinduized. The *Gantzer* report states that Hinduized tribals, who worship Hindu gods, are considered to be guided by Hindu law (*Gantzer* report, s. 46). This creates a considerable grey area as many Santal live in close proximity to Hindu families. It was not uncommon in the villages where I stayed for Santal to attend some of the many festivals and pujas hosted by those families. They did so without any real sense of identity conflict and I never met any Santal who described themselves as Hindus. Nevertheless, one sub-judge told me he routinely asked whether parties wanted Santal or Hindu law to be applied, and I was shown case files where lawyers had argued that their Santal clients followed Hindu festivals and customs sufficiently to be considered Hinduized for the purposes of inheritance law. This can make a significant difference where inheritance is being claimed through ghar jamae marriage. Hindu law differs from Santal law on the matter of when a son-in law may inherit land. Under the *Gantzer* report, where a Santal woman is married in ghar jamae, her husband is regarded as an adopted son for the purposes of inheritance and it is he who is deemed to inherit the wife's land. Under

Hindu law, however, a son-in-law proves his entitlement to his father-in-law's land through a deed of adoption. In other words, while the state courts need proof of marriage in ghar jamae form to certify a son-in-law's right to property, under Hindu law a deed of adoption is required. I was told that this provision can be used by others wishing to take the land, who use evidence of the Santal woman worshiping Hindu gods to persuade the court to apply Hindu law and, when the woman is unable to produce adoption papers to show her husband's right to the property, they launch their own claim to the land.

In Bangladesh, Hindu law is anyway applied in all Santal cases – the laws are misunderstood to be equivalent but the interpretation of them differs from India. A leading Santal lawyer and activist in Rajshahi, told me that the interpretation of Hindu law in Bangladesh gives women greater rights than they would have under Santal law. He recounted the case of a woman, Budrea, with no brothers, who inherited her father's land. Her father's nephew protested and claimed she could not inherit the land because she was a widow and could not plough the land. She took the case to the state court. Budrea was able to show that she had sons who could plough the land and won the case. The law seems to be interpreted and applied differently in Bangladesh and judgments may be influenced by the long-term debate about the introduction of a uniform family code there based on universal human rights to give women the same inheritance rights as men. The significant international NGO presence in Bangladesh, which has increased awareness of women's rights over several decades, has also raised the profile of issues such as inheritance, so there is more awareness of this as a human rights issue.

Bringing a case, even winning one in the state courts, is however, no guarantee of a resolution. Rao (2005a, p. 359) mentions a case of a woman, Baha, who, while entitled to her father's land (she married in ghar jawae form), is forced to leave her village with her husband due to threats on her life by her male cousin who takes over cultivation of the land. Despite taking a case to the state courts where her entitlement is recognized, and despite the land registry recording her as the lawful heir, she is unable to cultivate the land. Her cousin only finally agrees to give her a share of the land after a village hearing of the dispute. We will see further below that disputes that have their locus in the village need primarily to be resolved there, and state law, even when it does reach an enforceable decision, will not necessarily signal an end to the dispute.

The disputed nature of inheritance in both countries also meant that outcomes were uncertain. Usually, considerable time and money was involved in bringing these cases to state courts. Rao (2008, p. 245) notes that many Santal with land disputes in India file cases as government suits which means that legal fees are waived. While this facilitates some in initiating cases they would otherwise not have the financial means to take on, Rao says lawyers taking such cases have no motivation to resolve the case and they often drag on for many years. Villagers I met referred to land-dispute cases taking 10–20 years.

Auto-subversion in the use of alternative legal orders

While the challenges of using the state system described above make it more difficult for women to use those forums to achieve a final enforceable resolution to the dispute through state law, those who approach state law often do so as only one aspect of a disputing strategy. The challenges (time, cost, uncertainty of outcome, enforceability) of achieving a resolution through the state courts make it practical to look concurrently at alternative processes. But, for some, the instigation of the state apparatus is a backdrop to primary dispute resolution elsewhere. Where the resolution that the state law offers clashes with principles of village justice, those taking cases to the state may nevertheless purposefully avoid a state-based resolution of the dispute.

As Mary recounted to me her attempts to stop her son-in-law from abandoning his responsibilities to her daughter, she explained that she did not want to see him imprisoned:

M: If my son-in-law says that [the separation] was a mistake, he wants to take his wife and children back and if he abandons his second woman then they would be willing to withdraw the case. We have filed the case to give him punishment. I think if he does not take his wife back and the case continues he may be convicted for the offence and he would go to jail and lose his government job, so we want peace.
F: You want your daughter to once again go back to her husband?
M: If he takes her ok. If he does not and goes to jail, the children will suffer. But if he does not lose his job it will be good for him. We are threatening him with jail so that he may come back to his wife and children and keep his job and his focus comes back to them.

Her view of what the state law offers fits with other anthropological findings that disadvantaged people using state courts experience a lack of control over the process (see, for example, Benda-Beckmann, 1981, p. 143). But there may be more to this. Firstly, her grammar suggests that she herself disassociates from the process, which has a separate identity of its own – stopping the case is a decision taken by others. Not only does she distance herself from the process but also the outcome (prison for Jogonath), which is at odds with her own sense of a good outcome in the case. The trial has an intermediary role for Mary which subverts its own intention. While the state sees its role as sanctioning the violence he has committed against his wife through incarceration, Mary sees it as important that he is not incarcerated and uses it to pressurize Jogonath to return to his wife and children, thus conforming with his duties as conceived through village customs. Forcing him to attend court, pay fees and so on, is not a means to an end but an end in itself – his punishment for not conforming to Santal law. The domestic violence Sara has suffered seems not to be taken into account here and the priority seems to be that Sara is financially supported. Mary ends by telling me that, being Christians, there is no system of divorce (although divorce is allowed in Santal law) and if Sara's husband does not take her back she will live in great hardship. She spends much time emphasizing that if the state court process comes to its natural conclusion, imprisonment, this would not be in anyone's interest.

In the 1980s, Marc Galanter's (1981) paper 'Justice in Many Rooms' highlighted the fact that participants in disputing processes were often able to devise better solutions to their disputes than the courts. The courts, however, play a critical role by producing a sort of 'bargaining endowment', which adds weight to different stages of bargaining between disputants. In a later paper, Galanter (1984, p. 268) coined the phrase 'litigotiation' to describe the situation in America whereby much of the negotiation taking place in legal disputes happens alongside litigation. Mobilizing the court is part of the strategy of settlement and the possibility of the trial provides a compelling presence. One difference here is that, for the Santal, the 'settlement' of the dispute is not a private matter between two parties but often involves others in the village and community dispute resolution councils are given additional importance.

An elderly man, Sapha, told me that, when a village dispute ended in murder, although the state was informed, it was the village that those involved turned to for a resolution. The incidence began with an attack on his village. Non-adivasi men from another village had come late at night to steal cattle. The sound of the animals moving woke one family and they alerted the villagers. The Santal men tried to catch the intruders and Sapha's nephew, Basu, hit one of the intruders with a stick. One blow hit him on the back of the head and he died of his injuries. Basu fled to India. Sapha said he reported the robbery to the police asking them to file a First Information Report (FIR) – he said it was better to report it and have them record *his* account of the robbery and resultant death. Because Basu had fled (and the villagers claimed not to know where he was), the police were not able to prosecute. State law had been engaged and subverted.

However, Sapha ended by telling me: 'We found the case was disturbing everyone's life so we decided to settle it amicably by giving the murdered person's family three bigas of land.' – the custom for resolving a murder charge under Santal laws. The failure of the state seemed to bolster the power of the local dispute resolution forum. Sapha's story seemed to be relaying to me his sense of power, the fact that he was able to manage the police, and ultimately resolve the case through his own and his fellow village elder's authority. Despite the criminal nature of the case, meaning that the state claimed sole jurisdiction, it was the village that finally settled the dispute on terms that were conducive to re-establishing harmony. This story tells of the perceived impotence of state law – that the village is conceived locally as the more influential site of dispute resolution even in more serious criminal cases. There are examples elsewhere of the village's ability to resolve criminal matters more efficiently than the state (Archer, 1984, p. 457; Rao, 2005a, p. 359).

Critical tensions in cultural meanings: witchcraft-related crimes

The complex relationship between customary law and state law has been the subject of decades of studies in legal anthropology. John Griffiths (1990) shows that forums are not isolated but function as part of a whole system of dispute management. Ethnographic studies illustrate that state law can at times be overridden locally by customary law and at other times customary law will defer to state law, albeit to defend its own decisions. Customary courts borrow, sift and ultimately reinvent, sometimes subverting as they go, to bend state law to their will (Santos, 1977). However, where state law clashes fundamentally with customary law, the latter may find ways to avoid the imposition of state norms. I have suggested above that individuals use forum-shopping in their disputes as a tool for resisting pressures and biases within their own customary norms. But this practice of individual resistance through disputing confronts the individual with critical tensions and obstacles, in a context of cultural clashes. An individual who seeks to use state law to escape or challenge a belief that is entrenched within the cultural minority may fail to gain protection from the state.

My assistant in Thakurban, Luke, told me that two years before I visited Thakurban two men in the village died suddenly. Some of the villagers believed a woman in the village had cast a spell on them, that she was a witch. They threatened her and she and her husband left the village. Luke told me there were occasional witchcraft accusations but he said he rarely heard what happened. Luke's own grandfather was a diviner called an ojha (able to identify and cure witches) and witchcraft accusations were common in his day. Luke's father, Shyam, explained that his father would tell the suspected witch that if she wanted to cure herself of the evil spirit inside her then he could help her, but if she denied she was a witch then he could not help her. Once she admitted she was a witch, he would perform a ceremony to rid her of the evil spirit.

In Santal mythology, all women and girls in the village are at risk of being abducted by spirits and given powers of witchcraft. Older witches are thought to teach the girls to invoke bongas (spirits) using mantras and songs and to become possessed. Men can assist by playing drums for the witches during their gatherings at night as 'witch boys' (Archer, 1984, pp. 488, 491). Pradip Kumar Bhattacharya (c. 1991) also found that some men were accused of witchcraft in the villages he studied in West Bengal. Archer (1984, p. 487) was told witches gathered at night and could be seen as faint lights and closer up in their naked full human form.

Witches are thought to be the cause of all fractured relationships, illness, disease and death in the village (Bodding, 1942, p. 160). Once she has become a witch, a woman is thought to be able to induce sickness and cause death of close male relatives. Witches are also thought to be capable of causing epidemics amongst cattle (Chaudhuri, 1987, p. 109). It is believed witches can kill using a number of methods. It is believed the witch can ask a bonga to arrange the killing directly or through an agent such as a tiger, dog or snake. Bongas can transform into a buried stone, which once stepped on brings the trespasser disease, or into 'seeds of sickness', which are sprinkled in wells or on the lanes of the village causing people there to become ill (Archer, 1984, pp. 494–5). They are also thought to cause illness or death by cutting out a person's spirit organs (liver, heart or lungs) and cooking and eating them (see accounts in Bodding, 1942, p. 160; Archer, 1984, p. 490; Chaudhuri, 1987, p. 105). The damage eventually affects the physical body of the victim. If an entire spirit 'organ' is consumed then the victim will die and nothing can save him, but if only part is extracted or eaten it may be regrafted onto the body and the man saved (Archer, 1984, p. 492). This possibility of reversing the witch's deed provides the basis for an elaborate system of witch-hunting.

Paul O Bodding (1942, pp. 164–6) and Archer (1984, p. 497–8) describe the process for identifying a witch as practised at the end of the nineteenth century and beginning of the twentieth century. Where death or illness occurs in the village, the Manjhi calls out to all the houses in the village that a person is ill and if he does not recover the witch responsible will be found. If the person does not get better then ojhas (witchdoctors) are called to divine what the cause of the illness is. If the cause of illness is found to be an unhappy house bonga or god, disease or poison, then steps are taken to appease the bongas or gods, to cure the disease and so on. However, if three different ojhas find the illness is the work of a witch, then the manjhi of the village carries out a divination placing fresh-cut branches into the soil to see which person or household is responsible. If one branch consistently dies, the household/person represented by that branch will be presumed to be responsible. The relatives of the ill man may then take the matter to a janguru (witchfinder).

The husband and male relatives of the woman suspected, men representing the ill man, and other villagers acting as witnesses visit the janguru, who should be far enough from the village to have no personal knowledge of the matter. The janguru becomes possessed by spirits and tells them information about their village and the names of the ill person and his family to show he has spiritual sources of knowledge. Once this is shown, he demands his fee and tells them the names of the witches or bongas responsible (Bodding, 1942, p. 166; Archer, 1984, pp. 498–9). Archer (1984, p. 501) says that a second and possibly third or fourth janguru will be visited to confirm the divination. If there is inconsistency, the woman may deny the charge of witchcraft and can even interrogate the janguru to discredit his opinion. But, if a second janguru confirms the divination of the first, the woman is proved to be a witch. Once a witch is identified, the villagers gather to decide what punishment should be given to her (Bhattacharya, c. 1991, p. 29). The action depends on the state of the ill person. As long as the person remains alive but unwell, pressure is put on the witch to confess and make him well. The ritual varies according to how the illness was caused but may involve making sacrifices to the bongas and giving the victim a replacement organ to swallow (possibly of a sacrificed animal).

While this represents the normative position, Archer (1984, pp. 501–02 and 504) records a woman being beaten into confessing and being forced to drink a mixture of human excrement and urine to prevent her from further communications with the bongas. Bodding (1942, p. 162) describes women being beheaded. As far back as 1871, Kolean acknowledged that jangurus were no longer truly spiritual diviners, they were learning the trade rather than being possessed by bongas and were becoming more deceitful (Bodding, 1942, p. 168). In a study carried out between 1984 and 1989, Bhattacharya (c. 1991) recorded and analysed 50 cases of witch-hunting handled by jangurus in 46 Santal villages across three districts of West Bengal. He found that most depended on hired agents to collect information about the victim and their illness. Others used agents to find out about existing convicted witches in the village and conflicts between the ill person (and his family members) and other relatives or neighbours. Kolean similarly mentions the use of 'secret informers' and where there are none he says the jangurus 'feel their way' changing their findings according to how the villagers respond (Bodding, 1942, p. 168; see also Bhattacharya, c. 1991, p. 29). Bhattacharya (c. 1991, p. 18) says sometimes the ojha and villagers or relatives of the victim connive with the janguru to fix who will be named in his divination. A B Chaudhuri (1987, p. 97) writes that women who have characteristics of greed and jealousy and are prone to break codes of Santal behaviour may be seen as potential witches. Being unable to control anger, being argumentative, having a physical deformity or suffering from fits of hysteria or epilepsy can be taken as signs that a woman may have associations with bongas.

Despite all this, the belief in witchcraft is strong. Bhattacharya found in his study that witchcraft accusations did result from a strongly held belief in witchcraft. In 14 per cent of cases those making the witchcraft accusation had suffered disease themselves or within their family, which they believed the accused to be responsible for. In 56 per cent of cases the accusation was in response to death in the village resulting from disease, snake-bite, childbirth, drowning and burning. In other cases the accusation resulted from death of cattle or other causes and in only two cases there was no particular cause for the accusation (Bhattacharya, c. 1991).

The repercussions of an accusation of witchcraft are serious. Punishments given to witches range from fines and degrading cleansing rituals to excommunication and even death. Bhattacharya's research showed that in 42 out of 50 cases he studied in India the witch was fined. The women in Thakurban told me that if a witch was found out she would be fined and beaten. A Santal lawyer in Rajshahi confirmed that he was referred cases where women accused of witchcraft had been killed. According to Bhattacharya (c. 1991, p. 30), if a witch refuses to pay the fine, and sometimes even if she does pay it, her house may be burnt down or she may be beaten or killed. In nine cases, the accused witch or her family members were threatened with death, three ended fatally. Although people in the villages were reluctant to talk about witchcraft, in India particularly cases of attacks on women and murder on grounds of witchcraft were well known outside the community (Chaudhuri, 1987; Kumar, 1997; Awasthi, 2002). S M Naqavi (1979, p. 178) found that witchcraft was the highest motivating factor for murder in Santal villages in his research area in the Santal Parganas.

Although there was little recognition outside the Santal community of witch-hunting in Bangladesh, in India witch-hunting is a criminal offence under the Prevention of Witch (Daain) Practices Act 1999. Under s. 4 of the Act, a person who causes physical or mental torture to a woman by identifying her as a witch may be imprisoned for up to six months or fined. The legislation is well used. A senior magistrate in Dumka and a member of the senior judiciary in Deoghar said witch-hunting represented the most common basis for criminal cases brought before them involving the Santal. The magistrate received one or two cases a month (I was shown five case files of cases that were ongoing) and in Deoghar witchcraft cases represented 30–40 per cent of all criminal cases. However, a senior member of the judiciary in Deoghar said that of all the cases alleged to have a witchcraft dimension only 10–15 per cent are actually found to be motivated by accusations of witchcraft, the rest fail or fall under the Indian Penal Code.

This caused suspicion on the part of the judiciary that women used the witch-hunting legislation to gain advantages even where witchcraft was not a factor in the dispute. It is possible that lawyers are using the witchcraft legislation where a witchcraft accusation is tangential to a dispute or is made by a single individual, rather than in cases where there is a village-wide accusation of witchcraft. The magistrate in Dumka said 30 per cent of cases he heard were settled out of court and dropped, which indicates a village-level dispute resolution process at work. I was shown a number of case files in Dumka court which involved assaults on women and men by individuals accusing them of practising witchcraft and which had ended with an out-of-court settlement – the accused promising not to carry out any further assaults. Reports in the press suggested witchcraft accusations were used as a front for disputes over land. A newspaper article in a local paper in Dumka reported land disputes were responsible for 20 deaths of women who had also been accused of witchcraft, noting that landed widows were particularly targeted for witchcraft accusations (see the newspaper *Dainik Hjagren*, 27 February 2003). Lawyers and judges in Chaibasa and Deoghar confirmed that many of the cases they received involved women who had disputes over land with their accusers.

However, the low success rate of cases brought under the Act may also reflect the difficulties of proving witchcraft accusations given the need for corroboration from members of the village community to support the prosecution. Out of the 50 cases Bhattacharya found in the villages, only three were brought to court and none resulted in prosecution at the time of his study – one ended through lack of witnesses and other evidence, two were ongoing (c. 1991). A lawyer practising in Chaibasa told me that only 5 per cent of the witchcraft cases he represented actually made it to court and few ended in convictions. Although initially a member of the accused witch's family or a friend would support an FIR and assist the prosecution, in most cases they were put under pressure from the villagers to withdraw their support. Judges whom I interviewed in Doeghar told me that in most cases the villagers did not cooperate with investigations into alleged witch-hunting. A Santal lawyer in Bangladesh confirmed that, once a village had decided someone was a witch, no one would question the decision or inform the police or UP chairman.

Disputing in the context of group survival

During the first half of the twentieth century the influential anthropologist Bronislaw Malinowski (1939) recognized that the success of the group was dependent on each individual playing their part and culture, in turn, meeting the biological needs (and other imperatives derived from them) of the individual. He demonstrated that the needs of individuals shape the emergence of the group but, as time passes, the needs of the group and its integrity and unity become increasingly important. The group becomes not just a container for physical survival but also for a specific way of life that permeates everything from role expectation, timing and significance of life-cycle events, to beliefs, modes of expression and thought and even the development of the human organism itself. These lessons are still relevant to our study of individual–group dynamics in the twenty-first century. Protecting the group can become more important for the individual than realizing externally cultivated ideas such as equality and rights – this may also explain the lack of solidarity amongst women within the Santal discussed below. The collective drive for group survival may also mean that individuals who seek to challenge that integrity may find themselves threatened with punishment and expulsion.

The drive for group survival permeates all aspects of Santal village life and disputing is an important aspect of this. In the 1990s, Laura Nader, reflecting on her study of the Zapotec people of Mexico, demonstrated that disputing within a community that has historically experienced macro-process of domination (such as colonialism, state formation, religious missionary activities) takes on not only a legal but also a political significance. She found that the Zapotec dispute resolution, which had the function of containing disputes within the village and promoting internal harmony, was not merely keeping disputes in, but also keeping external powers out (1990). I discuss elsewhere (Shariff, 2013) the ways in which the Santal engage in inward and sometimes outward-facing disputing practices as part of their strategies of resistance against non-adivasis and the state.

Evidence of an inward-looking strategy of dispute resolution can be seen in the case of the stolen ducks discussed in Chapter 4. The dispute, which took place while I was staying in Thakurban village, was between two Santal villagers, Paulus and Bolanath but involved a local non-adivasi landlord, Ahmed. Ahmed, who occasionally employed Bolanath to work on his land, had instructed Bolanath to remove and dispose of ducks belonging to Paulus, which had encroached on his land adjacent to the village and were eating his crops. Paulus accused Bolanath of stealing and eating the ducks. A meeting of the village council was arranged to hear the case. The resolution of the dispute acted not only to apply Santal law within the village but to assert its authority over the dispute more widely and exclude Ahmed in the process. Ahmed was present at the trial. He stood at the periphery of the gathering and was invited to give evidence. When invited to speak he stated without apology that he had indeed instructed Bolanath to remove the ducks, which had been eating his crops. He said he did not know what Bolanath had done with the ducks and then continued that he had his own grievances: the ducks had encroached on his land and eaten his crops, adding, who would compensate him for that? He swiped the air with the back of his hand as he said this as a gesture of frustration and his question seemed knowingly not to anticipate a response.

The villagers' silence after Ahmed's outburst confirmed that his grievances were not a matter that concerned them and his frustration was clear. At the time, I had been surprised that the council had not included Ahmed more centrally in the dispute. He was a wealthy landlord who had money and had arguably played a part in the loss of Paulus' ducks. Luke, my assistant, told me if he had been a Santal he would have been fined for ordering the ducks to be killed. But including him in the trial would also have necessitated a fuller recognition of his grievances and the council's silence gave a clear message that he was not their concern – they were there to serve the Santal only. Later in the trial, after Ahmed had left, when deciding the level of Paulus' compensation, the manjhi reminded Paulus of the responsibility of villagers under Santal customs to prevent animal trespass on others' land, without making any reference to Ahmed. It was clear that Ahmed was no more than a witness. The inward-looking resolution of this dispute and focus on re-establishing harmony by both fining Bolanath and limiting Paulus' compensation sought to strengthen the villagers' sense of unity and shared responsibility. But it also was a clear assertion of their own power both to ensure conformity and respect to the rules internally and to draw the boundaries of inclusion and exclusion.

It was common, in Bangladesh, for villagers to opt themselves to contain and resolve disputes internally. In interviews I carried out in the villages I asked about how various types of infraction would be dealt with. A theft, whether by a Santal or a diku, would likely be resolved within the village – some said they would administer the punishment themselves without even involving the village. Land disputes were an exception given the state's authority in registering land title and almost half of respondents said land cases were always a matter for the state (UP, chairman or state court). State law was not something they willingly engaged, but pragmatism was key. The counter-hegemonic strategy here was to deal with whatever matters they could but engage with their oppressors head on where this was needed – a matter not of choice but of necessity given the immediate and present positioning of their adversaries.

The Santal in India were also likely to keep disputes with fellow Santal in the village. Following their own law over state law was closely associated with their sense of identity and unity. Their approach to dispute resolution fitted with a harmony ideology model – internal disputes were contained to keep outsiders out, and respecting Santal law was used as a political identifier. This was so regardless of the type of dispute. In land and minor theft disputes with other Santal almost all respondents said they would turn to the Santal village manjhi. Maintaining disputes between Santal within the village performed a counter-hegemonic role. This was made possible by the fact that they perceived their struggle to be situated in a nationalized movement for resources and power. The distant sources of their disadvantage gave them the space to build unity through commitment to their own group.

Resolving disputes internally was also a tool for nurturing unity within the village. Including fellow villagers in the decision and ensuring that both parties to the dispute acknowledged their responsibilities to the village meant that dispute resolution reinforced commitment to the integrity of the whole (see further Shariff, 2013). Its role was not only counter-hegemonic against power performed by outsiders and the state but also hegemonic as it supported and enhanced the power of those in positions of authority within the village. The disadvantage of this was that it militated against claims made internally against the status quo. It re-enforced inequality within the tribe. Research shows that Santal women, for example, are unlikely to make claims as a sub-group to have the same inheritance rights under customary law as men. Rao (2005a) carried out fieldwork in the Santal Parganas in 1999–2000 and found that, while Santal women would stake their claims to land based on kinship relations, marital status and education, they were not willing to mobilize for women's land claims per se. Part of this was attributed to the fact that, while individually male agnates may support a female relative's attempts to acquire land in some circumstances, men were not in favour of women obtaining greater customary entitlements to land. There is evidence elsewhere that women will support better recognition and assistance for the group over efforts to improve their position as women vis-à-vis men. Sherry Ortner (1995, p. 178) points out elsewhere that asking women to raise questions of gendered inequality within a subordinate group opens them up to accusations of undermining subaltern solidarity and plays into the hands of the oppressors (see also Madhok and Rai, 2012).

Conclusion

Disputes have long been regarded as an important area of study by anthropologists seeking to understand law in minority groupings. In the context of legal pluralism, it has been shown that dispute resolution can also be an arsenal of sorts as people cross between legal orders to challenge disadvantage. I have discussed above how using an alternative legal order can give some small advantage. But the limits on these are considerable. In disputes involving domestic violence, whether a man is deemed to have used violence in an inappropriate way is a calculation made case by case and may depend on the woman's ability to elicit support within the village. In inheritance disputes, a daughter's ability to take possession of land she is entitled to depends on her success in navigating the uncertain terrain of state law and its interpretation of customs, and implementing a favourable decision often depends on her own village council enforcing it through its own judgment. In witchcraft cases, men and women who experience threats and assault rely heavily on members of their own village acting as witnesses and providing evidence to the state courts. Mistrust by the state about women's motives for bringing cases and the difficulty of the state and authorities in enforcing their decisions only exacerbate these problems. In all these cases, it is support within the village that is critical. The auto-subversion of recourse to the state courts and tendency to find final resolution in the village confirms this.

This context poses some important questions for the use of state law to assist individuals within minority communities. The use of an alternative legal order, such as a state forum, also engages a critical tension between pursuing individual needs and protecting group identity. Use of forums outside their community to fight adversaries from within the community creates distinct challenges because the group seeks to control internal disputes to re-enforce its autonomy and keep the state out. The fact that these individuals depend on the group for their basic needs puts additional pressure on individuals to involve community where possible and most consult internally before having recourse to an alternative legal order. State law, in particular, is then likely to be an adjunct to village negotiations rather than an alternative. Because of this it is critical to develop a better picture of how those negotiations in the village, and family, develop and what utility they serve, rather than focusing, as policy tends to do, on state law as the ultimate resource. I turn to this next.

6
The Realization of Needs from Within: The Power Product and Non-compliance

As illustrated in the previous chapter, while the state tends to focus on providing assistance to disadvantaged individuals in minority communities through law, for the individual concerned, internal pressures and external obstacles make recourse to an alternative legal order prohibitive. We saw that, while people may nevertheless engage with alternative forums outside the immediate social field of the dispute, the need to resolve matters within the social field where the dispute arose is prioritized. In this chapter I turn to this aspect of social relations to examine how individuals seek to have their individual needs met from within power relations. Whereas I refer to the use of alternative legal orders as 'resistance', I use the term 'renegotiation' to refer to the attempts to make changes from within.

While, as discussed in Chapter 2, micro-power is a force that directs people's actions in a way that primarily restricts, it is simultaneously *productive* and its productive force provides an important context for facilitating the individual in satisfying their needs within prevailing power relations. Here, I look at two dimensions of this productive force, counterpower and non-compliance. Firstly, in the process of creating forces that make individuals accept their status position, power also provides benefits for the individual, the power product. If we understand the individual's motivation as primarily related to their drive for biological survival and social acceptance, then benefits within power relations that meet this need might be significant. If these benefits meet most people's individual needs and the corresponding burdens of the power relation do not interfere with this, disputes are less likely and renegotiation may be less frequent. If, however, an individual's assessment of their needs suggests that the benefits are insufficient, or if the burden of the power relation limits the ability of the individual to satisfy their needs, they may become more assertive about the benefits due to them, even to the point of claiming benefits that the dominator did not intend them to have. This facilitates adjustments to the relationship and has the potential to create new meanings. I have borrowed the term 'counter-power' from Michel Foucault's work to describe the latter possibility, although I use it to refer specifically to the ability to use the benefits produced within power relations to negotiate advantages to the individual, rather than a more general idea of struggles inherent in power relationships that he explores (Foucault, 1977, pp. 219–20).

Secondly, in situations where individuals occupy dichotomous status positions (dominator-subjugated),[1] power creates oppositional forces in relation to those positions. Through non-compliance, the individual may seek to limit the full force of domination, to push back against it. Whereas counter-power seeks to extend the benefits emanating from the power relation, non-compliance seeks to reduce the domain of the dominator's control. This does not make the dichotomy of domination and subordination disappear; it rather puts it under stress. This resonates with Foucault's concept of an 'agonism' within power relations in which forces 'are not superimposed, do not lose their specific nature' (1994b, p. 346) but 'each constitutes for the other a kind of permanent limit, a point of possible reversal'. While reversal itself is rare, these strategies play a role in limiting the negative effects of domination.

Counter-power and non-compliance are both ways of adjusting the power relation to alter, in subtle ways, the meanings of existing practices and lay the foundations for new practices to emerge. However, they do not constitute a rejection of the power relation, but rather function within a paradigm of acceptance. They are therefore not 'resisting' power so much as working through it to achieve, moment to moment, the best possible outcome for the individual. The basis of acceptance means, however, that, where a balance is achieved between the burden of the power relation on the individual and its ability to meet their needs, renegotiations may be less assertive. Some individuals will also be more willing than others to accept a weighty burden of the power relation in some contexts. I illustrate below, in the context of village relations, how mutuality creates an environment where there is little recourse to counter-power or non-compliance. Change is still possible but more likely to result from a process of consensus, such as changes to the process for selecting the manjhi discussed in Chapter 4.

---

1 Political anthropologists claim the non-fixity of power and everyday nature of resistance means it is hard to conceive of a ridged opposition of dominator-subjugated (see, for example, Ortner, 1995, p. 174). But Weber (1978, p. 54) states that this problematic association of domination with command depends on how domination is legitimized, and domination is often found in relation to a ruling organization.

The power product

While we think of the provision of facilities or benefits today as the domain of the state, these have a long history that runs parallel to and predates the state as a form of governance, for example, British colonizers' politics of 'improvement' in the Indian subcontinent and duties of the Raja Dharma (Indian caste elite) to protect, foster, support and promote the subordinate (Guha, 1997, p. 35). These benefits have served as a vital ingredient of success for the ruling elite, a matter of efficiency, but were also revealed as a platform for the subordinate to ascertain unintended advantages. E P Thompson (1963) notes that the courts in eighteenth-century England, despite being part of the class structure, were used as a genuine forum for struggles of class conflict. Courts were also a forum for challenging the rulers in a study by Genovese of the slave–master relationship. He notes that the need for the law to validate itself ethically meant that the courts began to recognize the slaves not as mere property of their masters but as human beings with rights. Although essentially the law gave slaves no protection, it enforced agreements made between the master and slave, for example, for the use of certain areas of land, such as garden plots (Genovese, 1976, p. 31).

While these examples attempted to demonstrate counter-power as a positive tool of resistance, elsewhere the integration of these benefits into the system of domination was shown to be too comprehensive for them to be treated seriously as capable of supporting the interests of the subordinate. In the Indian context, Guha (1997) wrote that providing benefits reduced the likelihood of revolt and produced a necessary counterweight to successful and efficient domination. Pierre Bourdieu revealed elsewhere that efficient domination required the subordinate to misunderstand the role of these benefits in perpetuating inequality. Benefits were delivered through what appeared to be socially legitimate exchanges of gifts or debts, which had the effect of euphemizing the force of domination, what he called 'symbolic violence' (see also Bailey, 1971, p. 24):

> the gentle, invisible form of violence, which is never recognized as such, and is not so much undergone as chosen, the violence of credit, confidence, obligation, personal loyalty, hospitality, gifts, gratitude, piety ... (Bourdieu, 1977, p. 192)

Using the power product as a form of resistance was seen to fail, ideologically, because it was performed within the power relations that created and sustained the subordination.

However, I found in my research that it was not the measure of how or whether the individual was subject to power that was paramount in the individual's experience, but their assessment of their ability to see their individual needs met. As identified in Chapter 5, individuals valued social inclusion and sought primarily to have their individual needs met in the context of ongoing relationships. This was so despite the fact that those relationships were imperfect: benefits were sometimes in the form of promises, never quite met, or given then taken away. The relationships provided a context in which individuals felt able to realize their individual needs. This dynamic varied a great deal between the legal orders, however. Where inequalities were at their greatest and benefits were harder to come by, in the state, efforts to realize benefits from the relationship were more difficult, and individuals sought to push the limits of the benefits due to them. Conversely, where inequalities were less pronounced and benefits flowed more easily between individuals, in the village, there was very little evidence of counter-power or non-compliance.

The power product in context

For the Santali people, rights and benefits of different kinds were identifiable in the socio-legal orders of the state, family and village. Under state law the Santal enjoy various rights both generally available to all citizens, and additional rights for STs. These were easy to identify, and in the Santal family there were also clear lines of responsibility and benefits due. I discuss these in detail below. Nevertheless, the nature of the benefits in the state and family differed. While rights language is a common feature of relations with the state, it is not transferable to relations within Santal society, a lesson I learnt early on in my fieldwork.

My fieldwork combined participant observation with focus groups and one-to-one interviews. One of my first jobs when I arrived in Thakurban was to translate my interview schedule into Santali with the help of my assistant, Luke. I had taught myself basic Santal grammar and sentence structure before I arrived, and had a reasonable vocabulary. But I was wary of the misunderstandings that can occur through shallow translation. I discussed with Luke what I was aiming for and listened to how he made sense of it through concepts within the Santal language. One of my questions related to the villagers' own perceptions of the rights they had within Santal society. Luke questioned my use of the term 'rights' to describe these and we debated for some time over the best translation for the term. Luke finally suggested the Santali word *bhloi*, meaning facilities.

But I discovered even this was not a good match for the more fluid exchange of benefits within Santal village society. One of my first interviews was with Katarina. In the context of a series of questions relating to Santal identity I asked the question '*Chit chit bhloi nyamda* [What facilities do you receive]'? Katarina looked puzzled. She asked me to explain further

– facilities from whom? I replied 'from Santal society'. She looked away again. 'Do you mean from the family?' I acquiesced and she seemed comfortable in talking about what a woman could expect after her marriage from her husband and parents. I changed the question to be more specific. In fact, I later found that it was no coincidence that it was in the family and not in the village community that she saw opportunities of benefits. The benefits of village membership were less proscribed, for women and men. The concept of benefits was not one that easily fitted the dynamics of village relations.

When I asked people in the villages about what facilities they could expect within Santal society many were unsure or vague in their response. Most responses referred to the family: respective rights of men and women to get land and goods from their parents on marriage or after the parents' death, often mentioning women's lesser rights. Others mentioned that children and women get love, support, food and clothing. References to benefits from the village were of mutual assistance: that villagers worked together and gave each other gifts on marriage. The village represented a complex of relationships in which people simultaneously pursued their individual and family interests while engaging in patterns of mutual assistance without, for the most part, treating these as conflicting.

While villagers were very unprepared to answer my questions about the facilities they enjoyed in the context of Santal village life, they were able more easily to identify with this type of question when I asked what they were due, or wanted, from the state. Santali people used the Bengali term *odhikar* when speaking of rights in relation to the state. I remember being struck when I first piloted the interview questionnaire and a villager, in response to my question 'What rights do you have in national law?', began to recount the civil and political rights set out in the Universal Declaration of Human Rights! I later learned that these were used by local NGOs as a basis for seminars it held in the villages to give villagers information about their civic rights and duties. I found during the course of my fieldwork that people had become very used to talking about the state in terms of rights. When I asked people what rights they wanted from the state for the Santal, they were very detailed: scholarships; medical facilities; food relief; housing; livestock for an income; irrigation; land for the landless; a return of land taken by the government; an end to land-grabbing; reforestation; roads; non-monetary and monetary welfare; protection from non-adivasis; positive discrimination and equal treatment ('the same as what the non-adivasis get'). They also seemed aware of who could provide the things that they needed. They were easily able to differentiate the various types of assistance they would get from a local official, a court or a politician, for example.

Below I examine the different ways in which rights and benefits were used in the context of the state, family and village. I will use the term 'rights' to refer to those benefits emanating from the state, and 'benefits' to refer to facilities provided from within Santal family and village. The difference between these rights and benefits is not to do with the sense of entitlement felt by those able to avail themselves of the beneficial outcome, but the means of realizing it. People may have strong feelings of entitlement when they attach importance to what they feel is 'right', 'correct', regardless of whether they have 'a right' to it. The difference between 'rights' provided by the state and 'benefits' accrued from within Santal society is the means by which they are realized. Whereas rights provided by the state limit the state's power – create a duty the state takes upon itself and which it may be challenged to enforce against itself – benefits in Santal society are not enforceable in this way. They are more likely to emerge and evolve in response to immediate needs, rather than ideals of the dominant. Realizing them depends on the quality of the relationships through which they are performed. The better the quality of the relationship the more effective the ability to realize the benefit. This in turn means that the practice of counter-power takes on a very different form in relation to the state where enforcing rights and challenging wide margins of inequality are clear and visible, compared with the family and village.

State law and the restitution of land

Litigation, particularly in relation to land disputes, was a lived reality in all the villages I visited, and the Santal have become much more aware of state courts as a possible platform to enforce their rights against non-Santal. In India in particular, the Santal are beginning to actively pursue their rights through recourse to state infrastructure. Where the law does provide certain rights, the Santal are zealous in claiming the benefits of these and directly challenging those who fail to respect those rights. I explained in Chapter 3 that land rights are at the root of the Santal's economic and political disadvantage and, historically, there has been a net decline in land holdings by adivasis. After the Santal Hul, legislation fixed rents and land titles and, between 1872 and 1879, many Santal tenants and headmen were reinstated and given security of tenure and raiyati land was made non-transferable under the Santal Pargana Rent Regulation II of 1886, and III of 1908. When the British left and Santal Parganas fell under the governance of the new state of India, the SPTA 1949 was passed to incorporate and strengthen these provisions and outlaw the transfer of tribal land to non-tribals.

In spite of the legislation, extra-legal means have evolved that have seen land being transferred away from adivasi landowners. Nitya Rao (2005b, pp. 4439–40), in her study of land displacement in Dumka and Deoghar, found several tenancy and sharecropping arrangements that are widespread in the region. Firstly, land mortgages (*bhorna* or *miyad*) were common in the region and usually followed a loan of grain or money to the adivasi landowner. Secondly, a form of sharecropping (*bhag*) exists whereby the adivasi loans the land to a tenant who uses his own seeds and labour to cultivate the crops which are split equally between landowner and sharecropper. This is commonly used by women-headed households who cannot plough the land themselves and use the arrangement to allow male kin to cultivate the land without risking loss of ownership. Another sharecropping arrangement, known as *krishani*, commonly used in paddy-growing lowlands, requires the crops to be split less equitably with the landowner taking two-thirds of the output. These are described by Rao as creating a social relationship between the landowner and tenant sharecropper in which the landowner is in a dominant position due to the high rent paid. Finally, a legal (registered) lease of land (*bhugatbandha*) for a maximum of six years is permitted under SPTA 1949. This is more commonly used amongst Hindu landlords who are not permitted in law to acquire land in the region through other means.

While these forms of transfer seem to work within the requirements of the SPTA 1949, and some seem to benefit adivasi landowners, in reality they are rarely monitored and Rao (2005b) notes that land leased as bhugatbandha is in fact rarely registered and possession remains for decades with the leasee. Over time it becomes increasingly difficult for the original owners to regain ownership. A survey carried out for the Ministry of Rural Development acknowledged that there has been considerable land loss by tribals in the Santal Parganas despite the prohibition on the transfer of land under the SPTA 1949. S L Batra (1999, p. 115) notes that in the region's capital leases and mortgages have been partly responsible for this, but also forced sales, in the form of gifts and direct encroachment, and forced eviction have also been prevalent. The vast majority of mortgage agreements that have resulted in land-loss have been taken out to cover medical and household costs. The government has also played a part in land alienation in the region with 52,600 acres of land in Dumka taken for public use between 1950 and 1995. More recently, the introduction of quarrying near Dumka and Deoghar has also led to foreign companies circumventing the SPTA 1949 to acquire the land there (Rao, 2005b, p. 4440).

We know little about the personal circumstances surrounding these land transfers, however, small benefits such as compensation for state-acquired land and the promise of future assistance in times of sickness or other need from money lenders, coupled with a perception that they have no choice, may have made villagers reluctant to claim their rights. Ronald J Herring

(1981, p. 140), writing about land reform in South Asia, notes that peasants often do not avail themselves of legislation in their favour and many accept the legitimation of landed patrons' privileged position. It is feasible that many of those who lost their land from the 1900s onwards did not conceive that they could achieve restitution of land through the courts. However, attitudes seem to have been changing. When I visited the Deoghar and Dumka courts in 2002–2003, judges told me that they had had an influx of cases from Santal who claimed the right to full restitution of their land, registered in their ancestor's name at the time of or before the passing of the SPTA 1949. Because the Act prohibits any transfer of land title in any form, they are using the legislation to claim back their right to ownership. Many of those whose ancestors acquired the land through extra-legal means fight these cases on the basis that their ancestors did pay money or give other benefits in return for the land and that it is they and not the original Santal owners who have paid tax on the land ever since. However, the law provides no legal means for a change of ownership between private individuals. The SPTA 1949 gives no protection to non-adivasis who took over tribal land after 1937.[2] Whereas the legislation was devised as a shield against land alienation, it is now being used as a sword against the descendants of those who originally gained the land through mortgage, lease or other extra-legal means.

It is not only through the restitution of previously owned land that the adivasis are managing to use the courts to their advantage. Rao (2005b, p. 4441) notes also that, under a programme of land reforms in Santal Parganas, surplus land and wastelands are being distributed to the landless. However, in two forested blocks she studied (Kathikund and Gopikandar), no land distribution has taken place. Rather than waiting for the administrative system to run its course, adivasis in the area have taken the initiative of reclaiming land from the forests (ostensibly in contravention of the law protecting the use of forest land) and then registered it in their own names. She notes that the government has not only facilitated this by allowing the land to be registered but also paid out material assistance for cultivation. When I carried out my fieldwork in 2001–2004, landownership amongst villagers in India was high: 97 per cent of the Santal households in the villages where I stayed had some land which they cultivated as part of their livelihood.

Despite the comparative weakness of land rights legislation in Bangladesh, a similar pattern is emerging there. Under tenancy laws inher-

---

2 Any sales that occurred before 1933 (the date of the last land survey in the region) were recorded in that survey. However, sales between 1933 and 1937 supported by a forged '*kulfa*' (land title document) are accepted as legal transfers.

ited from the British period, adivasis who wish to sell their land must go through the Assistant District Commissioner (ADC) Revenue. This process was created as a check against land-grabbing and forced land transfers. The sale is not permitted if the ADC finds the reason for selling is frivolous or if the sale leaves the adivasi with less than two acres. Any sale that has been made without going through this procedure is void. The Rajshahi court receives ten cases a year of declaration of ownership of land by adivasis, disputed by non-adivasis who claim their ancestors bought the land from the adivasis. Most of these cases relate to illegal transfer of land between 1969 and 1974, when Bangladesh gained its independence from Pakistan, and many Santal fled in inter-faith riots. But transfers are still being made today that do not go through the ADC. Non-adivasis who wish to buy the land convince adivasis who have converted to Christianity (the vast majority of Santal in the villages where I stayed in Bangladesh had) that the law no longer applies to them, or adivasis themselves chose not to involve the ADC's office because of the additional cost and time involved. As in India, where the ownership papers of the non-tribal party are found to be false or the sale was not authorized by the ADC Revenue, the title returns to the adivasi without any compensation being owed to the non-adivasis. These cases have been celebrated as correcting a past wrong and they are an example of the Santal using law's counter-power to their advantage. Non-adivasi landowners who had taken land from adivasis without going through the ADC Revenue quickly learnt of these cases, however, and in 2002 there was an increase in applications to the ADC to recognize previous sales to non-tribals as legitimate. The Santal's use of state courts to try to alter practices of land alienation has not been a perfect solution but has affected the way people approach land sales and provided a fertile starting point for land reclamation.

Interestingly, this escalation of cases has permeated the Santal's sense of entitlement to land more broadly. While in Thakurban, I was called in a hurry to join Luke just outside the village where an argument was developing with some non-adivasis. Between Thakurban and an adjacent Santal village there was an acre of land on which the Santal were beginning to build temporary houses. It was an area – of khas land belonging to the government – which they had habitually cultivated for 30 years. Before that it had been barren. One of the Santal families in the village needed houses for their family as their sons had married. As the family did not own any other land in the village, they began to build on the khas land. However, non-adivasi families who had recently migrated to the area claimed the land for themselves. Overnight they had erected tall bamboo sticks on the plot where the Santal were planning to build and had ripped down the structures that the Santal had put up, claiming the land would be theirs.

The Santal called for the UP chairman and he told the non-adivasis that the land was not theirs. He promised to help the Santal to get papers for the land. The Santal said they had gone to the chairman because they knew him well and knew he would help. Luke said that elections were imminent. The non-Santal were a minority in the area and therefore less important when it came to re-election. A dispute like this would be heard about by all Santal villages in the region. The UP chairman was making a politically expedient decision in siding with the Santal. It seemed the Santal were also making good use of the timing to elicit his support and, as a majority in the area, felt they had priority over the land.

The logic of rights has also developed outside the context of land disputes. Santal now also push for what they regard as just treatment even if there is no specific law giving them entitlement. The local government schools in Lahara and Madhura, India, employed Hindu teachers. In Madhura, villagers had written to the block development officer (BDO) in charge of education) asking him to replace the Hindu teacher with a Santal. They had heard that the Hindu teacher had bribed the BDO at the time of his appointment but they were adamant that if he did not respond positively to their demands they would take the matter further to the deputy commissioner and then the member of the Legislative Assembly. Lahara was in a predominantly Santal area and there were a number of educated Santal (who had attended university) living in the villages who worked as day-labourers. The village men of several villages in the area met regularly and were adamant that, since the school was in a Santal village and there were qualified Santal men available for work, a Santal teacher should have been appointed. They had also demanded that the block level administration should appoint a Santal teacher. Since no law required the appointment of a Santal teacher, they appealed to the administrators' sense of justice. Although there was no legal foundation to their request, the logic of the demand meant it was difficult for the administration to deny them outright and negotiations were ongoing.

Domestic disputes revisited

According to Santal customs, within the family women have their welfare and interests looked after by their fathers, husbands, brothers and male relatives. In marriage, they can expect to be clothed, fed and sheltered by their husbands and to be brought to visit their own families from time to time. Their brothers, fathers and, later, sons remain their guardians and this gives them an insurance against becoming destitute, which is exclusive to them (there is no equivalent provision for men). Once married, a woman is dependent on her husband and his family. But her father and brothers still have some responsibility for her and the husband must keep good relations with her family and take her once a year to see them. If any of her brothers visit her they are treated as privileged guests.

In the discussion of domestic violence in the previous chapter, we saw that, while women took recourse to the village council to stop physical abuse within the family, the village did not intervene in domestic disputes unless asked, and some disputes were resolved without village intervention. The village and family offer something different to the woman. Primarily, the village seeks to provide a 'judgment' of guilt. The village council will scrutinize the evidence to verify whether the woman has provoked the husband's violence, or whether he has been reckless and deserves a punishment. The finding of fault depends partly on her support within the village, and whether she is viewed as a good wife. In the family, however, she has more space to voice her own grievances amongst people who have known her from birth (her husband's village will only know her from her marriage onwards) and have a personal commitment to her well-being. A resolution takes place as part of a process that has as its aim the re-establishing of marital relations, but serves also a therapeutic role in which the woman is central.

In the cases of domestic violence I came across, women tended to turn to their families for immediate assistance: Mary turned to her brother for protection from her husband; Mary's daughter turned to her parents and returned to live with them. There was another incidence of domestic violence that was being resolved while I was staying in Thakurban village. Pondic's wife had left him because of domestic violence. No one talked about it. A young child of four years came to the house where I was staying to eat one evening and I asked whose child he was. Luke's mother told me in a mumbled voice with her head lowered that his mother was away from the village. It was only after persistent enquiry that I learnt that he was Pondic's son and that each of the villagers were taking it in turns to give him food. Pondic himself had to eat in his brother's house and depend on friends for other support. Luke's wife, Suru, told me Pondic's wife had just left one day without warning. She had not gone to the manjhi, as was the custom, she had just left. Her parents lived nearby so she was able to go alone. Perhaps pre-empting my curiosity about whether she would be safe travelling alone, Suru said it was not uncommon for a woman to make the journey to her parent's house alone if necessary, even if the parents lived many hours' walk away. She said nothing about the domestic violence and instead explained that Pondic had been one of the men arrested after the controversial incident when the non-adivasi thief had died after being beaten by the villagers (discussed in Chapter 3). Although there was no evidence he had been directly responsible, he had spent six months in jail before he was released on bail. Suru told me that after his release Pondic had been depressed and he and his wife argued regularly. Her narrative seemed to reflect on the mitigating circumstances in light of which Pondic's behaviour would be judged, putting it in the context of his own life events. But there was a sense that Pondic's wife would get all the support she needed through the family and, if necessary, from the village council.

The Santal elder, Kolean, whose treatise on Santal customs and traditions was taken down verbatim by Reverend Lars Olsen Skrefsrud in 1871, explains that it is expected that a woman's father and male relatives will look after her best interests if the husband fails to do so:

> [W]hat women have really to rely on, is their father and male relatives. When husband and wife do not live in harmony, or when the husband worries and beats his wife, or somebody calls her a witch, then she will cry out to her father and male relatives, and they will stand up for her. This is their right, because on the day of her marriage they have stipulated for this ... Because of this the women have great trust in their father and male relatives. [sic] (Bodding, 1942, p. 98)

However, despite the inference that the male relatives are there to protect the woman, it is unlikely they will act as mere agents of her wishes. My experience was that there was an expectation that women would return to their husband. In the focus groups, I asked what the parents would say if a woman left her husband and returned to them. An elderly lady in Dhanban told me that the parents will tell her: 'You have to go home, you have to eat your husband's rice.' Another woman in Lahara was adamant that the women of the parental village would tell the girl to return to her husband, even if she was being beaten, because the parents paid a bride-price at the time of the marriage. We saw in the previous chapter that, while Mary's daughter, Sara, had been hospitalized by her husband, Mary still felt that persuading the husband to take her daughter back would give her the best future.

The pressure on women to remain in a marriage means that the woman has to use recourse to her relatives with care. But the intervention of the parents may in itself be a powerful gesture to the husband that his actions will be scrutinized. Her parents are likely to defend her, at least in the first instance, and, if there is real fault on the part of the man, to put pressure on him to change his behaviour and seek the intervention of the manjhi if he is uncooperative. Anne Griffiths (1990), in her study of the Kwena women of Botswana, shows that the very act of speaking out about domestic disputes has the effect of publicly censuring the man, subjecting him to humiliation and enlisting social support.

Parents are also not the only source of support. Once the woman has grown-up children, she may seek protection from her sons. I asked the women in the focus groups if it is ever acceptable for a man to hit his wife.

A middle-aged woman in Lahara told me that, if a woman has an adult son, then her husband will not hit her because her son would question his behaviour. If the son is married and established in the village, it is his responsibility to look after his mother. All this is not to say that the woman herself remains silent, leaving the men to argue over her fate. As Bodding (c. 1920, p. 242) points out in his discussion of female inheritance claims: '[i]t goes without saying that the women themselves, when occasion arises, will push their own case, or at least their own individual case'. Women do also manage to live independently in the village – elderly widows and divorced women, for example – although they tend to remain in villages where they have some family and friends.

Recourse to family members in cases of domestic disputes is complex and is likely to prioritize the re-establishment of marital relations between the woman and her husband. Despite this, women seemed to prefer to resolve these matters internally in the first instance. The local UP chairman near Thakurban said that, despite the fact that most of the cases he handled for the area were cases of domestic violence, he had never had any such cases referred to him from within the Santal community. Having recourse to their own family members, in the knowledge of the limitations of their intervention, may seem a more effective means of challenging men. I talk more about how we should understand the impact of these efforts later.

Mutual assistance in the village

In the village the greatest threat comes not from other villagers but from the struggle to maintain basic living needs (food, water, shelter, security, companionship). The village provides a safety net of sorts in this respect. There are several groups who are subordinated within the village: outsiders who do not participate in village society; newcomers with no contacts in the village; those without kinship ties; the poorest with no relatives for support; and women. The relationship between subjugated and dominating groups is less explicit and the benefits gained for those dominating less overt in the villages than in the family or state, and consequently the benefits less emphatic.

Assistance given to villagers by others is not a question of right of one over another, it is part of a bond between individuals motivated by the need to survive. It is described by Timotheus Hembrom (1996, p. 74) as solidarity and fellowship between rich and poor. Kolean describes a pattern of mutual assistance in the village:

> .. when building a house, when ploughing, planting, making ricefield, ridges, and harvesting they help each other, and those who ask for help have only to give rice and curry ... (Bodding, 1942, pp. 108–09).

Villagers celebrate festivals together, and carry out all important ceremonies for birth, adolescence, marriage and death together. Newcomers and the poorest villagers who participate in these communal rituals are a part of village life and contribute to its unity. Integration and conformity are important if a village is to protect itself against outsiders and also work to reinforce internal power relations (Shariff, 2013). While the demands of integration may seem burdensome, those demands are suggested rather than imposed. If conformity is the norm, it is because individuals do see the benefits of inclusion. If a person has no food or job, his or her only means of support is the village people. Kolean said that poor Santal never beg, they are always supported. The wealthier villagers give them jobs and employ their children to collect water and leaves and 'people give them more than what they have a right to get' (Bodding, 1942, p. 108). But this system of support depends on commitment to relationships within the village and acceptance of and participation in village life, and the power relations that are prevalent there. Outsiders who do not participate in village society, and in fact any villagers who do not participate in the society, do not gain the benefits of this interrelationship. Kolean says that many people have become greedy and selfish, not helping others, and they suffer the consequences: 'if they themselves fall into difficulties, no one will look at them; they rather say: Thakur [god] is punishing this man in retribution' (Bodding, 1942, p. 109).

Women in the villages, while also benefiting from the practices of mutual assistance, have fewer privileges. However, as childbearers and mothers responsible for primary socialization and as nurturers of the family unit, they play a crucial role in village unity and survival. As such, their willingness to participate is crucial and, if they have a strong interest in a village decision, it is unlikely that the men could afford to simply ignore their input. They have certain roles to play during rituals and ceremonies. This means that ceremonies cannot take place without them and ensures their inclusion. However, the women rarely conceive of their gender as a subordinating identity in the village and, even where women's committees had been established by NGOs (as in Bangladesh), there was no evidence of the women making demands against the men (see further my discussion of disputing in the context of group struggles in Chapter 5).

Village life did not impose too much on the individual but offered support and structure for those who wanted it. There was a sense that belonging, being part of the village, was a benefit to the individual and many men I spoke to said that without the village to support them they would be destitute. As with the family, the ability to benefit from the power relations in the village depended on the quality of the relationships there and a degree of acceptance of and investment in those relationships.

Non-compliance

Everyday resistance appears in many ethnographic studies and was particularly popular in studies of power from the 1980s onwards (Comaroff, 1985; Scott, 1985; Risseeuw, 1988), though it was heavily critiqued in the 1990s (Mitchell, 1990; Ortner, 1995). Non-compliance was a principal focus of James Scott's (1985) study of everyday forms of peasant resistance in a rural village in Malaysia, *Weapons of the Weak*. He identified everyday resistance in the form of 'foot-dragging, dissimulation, desertion, false compliance, pilfering, feigning ignorance, slander, arson, sabotage and so on' which the peasant cultivators of Sedaka used to challenge the social order. Lila Abu-Lughod (1990), while seeking to critique this approach, found many examples of Bedouin women expressing their non-compliance with the privileging of men, through songs, folk tales and jokes that belittle men or assert women's strengths. In these studies, everyday resistance seemed to act as an integral component of relations of domination and Abu-Lughod (1990, p. 47) conceded that their existence poses analytic problems for theorists of power. Feminist literature has preoccupied itself with the dilemma that recognizing women's everyday resistances may attribute them with forms of consciousness or politics that the women themselves do not recognize, while ignoring resistance plays into gendered prejudices. These problems are exacerbated when faced with evidence that women often both resist and support the prevailing social system. Explaining this in terms of false consciousness on the part of the women is inadequate.[3]

Rather than tackle these, Abu-Lughod diverts the question through a 'shift in perspective', suggesting that we overcome these dilemmas by limiting our theorizing of resistance to a diagnostic tool for understanding strategies of power (to understand the forms power takes). However, this does not necessarily mean demoting individual renegotiations of power to a benign element of power: it can actually help to uncover how, and how far, renegotiations can affect power. An examination of trajectories of renegotiation that reveals power's different forms can contribute to the discovery of what Sherry Ortner (1995, p. 180) calls an 'authentic, and not merely reactive, politics' of resistance. Below I examine examples of the way men and women's non-compliance within Santal society *sets limits* to the dominator's power. I use these in the next chapter to show that individual renegotiations can be important features in the evolution of power relations.

---

3 There is a whole literature on problems associated with attributing intentionality to resistance and Ortner (1995, p. 175) puts this in perspective when she notes that intentions anyway often shift and evolve as resistance is played out.

Family as a site of intimate struggles

Renegotiations between husband and wife in the context of the family are probably the most intense because they take place at the most intimate level of personal relations. In order to limit excesses of domination by the husband, the wife may hold back a little of what she is capable of giving, exercising control over his domination by denying him some aspects of control over her and the duties she performs. The acts of non-compliance through which limits to the husband's domination are established may seem small but they have a significant impact because they strike at the man's dominance in his most private space and the most acute site of his survival, the family. They threaten the most basic unit of survival in which all parties must play their part.

Although men are primarily responsible for building a house and ensuring the family has food, the woman is responsible for the final delivery of these necessities. She is the one who carries out daily repairs and maintenance (sweeping the dust from the mud floors, reinforcing the ground and walls with mud and dung as they deteriorate in the heat) and who delivers the meals (collecting firewood and foods from nearby forests, trading with neighbours, walking to market and preparing the meals). These tasks she performs are vital to the smooth running of the family but also constitute a potential counter-point of pressure that can be used against her husband. Women's power over provision of meals is exemplified by the Santal folk tale 'A Quarrel between Husband and Wife'. A man comes home for his midday food and his wife has not prepared it. She says she has been too busy. While the man suggests her failure to provide the meal is due to laziness or lack of effort, the woman persists with her argument and goes on to prove that she does more work than him and thus he must conform to her timing for meals rather than the other way around. This final control of the woman over mealtimes is strikingly summed up by the storyteller:

> You see, we call a dog: then only he will get food. In such manner we men are the women's dogs. When they tell us to wash our hands, then only we get food. (Bodding, 1997, vol. III, p. 259)

This control over the provision of food is not only a token gesture of her power in the household, it can, if the need arises, be a means for her to inflict a punishment of sorts. In the cases of domestic violence discussed earlier, Pondic's wife and Mary withdrew to their families and left their husbands with no one to cook for them or collect food or run and maintain the house. Pondic had to rely on help from relatives and friends in the village until she returned. This was not a mere inconvenience but a public shaming and he had to call in favours from friends and relatives that would have to be repaid. Rao (2005a, p. 357) gives another example of a woman, Nirmala, whose husband planned to lease some land and hire labour to cultivate it. The arrangement would have required Nirmala to provide cooked lunch and dinner for the labourers every day (it is customary for agricultural workers in rural areas to be provided with meals as part of their payment). She warned him against taking the land saying she could not manage the additional work. He ignored her and at the critical time of paddy transplantation she left the village, returning to her parent's home and leaving him without support and unable to feed his labourers. Rao calls this agency reflected in 'passivity and withdrawal'.

A woman's non-compliance with her perceived subordinate position in the family may affect not only her relationship with her husband but also with in-laws. A newly wed girl in a Santal family is in a seemingly powerless position, living with her in-laws and under their control and guidance. She has little recourse to her own family, initially, she is at the mercy of her in-laws. George Somers (1977, p. 84) writes that the 'role of a subordinate woman in a household often results in frustration and deprivation'. However, she is not altogether powerless: if she does not conform to her role, or if she cannot live harmoniously in the family, she can significantly affect the unity of the family. Somers notes conflict amongst sons' wives in an extended family can lead to the nuclear unit withdrawing from the family. Given the importance of family unity in strengthening the position of its members in the village, this threat can be significant.

Once a Santal woman becomes a mother, her position becomes stronger and N K Saha (1969, p. 98) says women may 'manage' their husbands tactically, or even openly control the affairs of the household. In Thakurban and Lahara, I came across women who seemed to have taken over control of the running of the family, pushing the limits of domination right back so that the men had very little power at all. I met three women, Sama, Magli and Mary, who were all accepted in the village as being in charge of their family's affairs. Sama, in her thirties, was bright, assertive, confident and had experienced interactions with officials and lawyers when she was young. Her father, who owned land, had many cases brought against him by non-adivasis and, unusually, had shared his experiences and knowledge with her. Through his management of the land she had also gained greater experience in business and dealing with officials than her husband. Magli, in her late forties, was intelligent and business-minded, while her husband, who was taking medication for a mental illness, was quiet and subdued. She ran the house and brought in an income by managing the family land and cultivating and selling mustard seeds and chillies. Mary, in her fifties, had taken over the family for her own and her family's survival when her husband all but stopped work due to long-term illness. She had a son and two daughters. The husband of one of her daughters had died and the other daughter's husband had sent her back to the village and taken a mistress. Her son, Mary told me, was a good student (she showed me stacks of books in their modest house) but had no time for study as he had to work to support the family. Mary herself worked to process what little rice her husband cultivated during the day. She had taken a loan of 5000 taka to carry out repairs to her house.

These three women were exceptions but showed that a restructuring of power relations was possible. In these instances, the women's determination to ensure the family's survival in light of the man's inability to do so led to an expansion of their domains of control within the families. Although the change did not constitute an actual reversal – the man, of course, did not assume the woman's responsibilities in the family – it did change the power dynamics of the relationship.

State and local elite: avoidance and non-compliance

I discussed in Chapter 3 the multiple layers of the Santal's subordination within the state, visible in the allocation of resources and social control nationally and at the local level in relations with non-tribals. State law in India seeks to regulate some aspects of Santal cultural practices, such as witch-hunting (discussed in Chapter 5), home-brewing of alcohol and *bitlaha* that nevertheless continue to be accepted practices in Santal culture. Bitlaha is a ritual that involves the banishment of a couple who have been found to have entered into an illicit relationship (breaching the codes of tribal endogamy or clan exogamy) and is treated under state law as contravening the Indian Penal Code. The ritual involves a gathering of armed Santal men from the village (bows, arrows and other traditional weapons are used), and sometimes neighbouring villages, who force the couple and their family to flee the village, destroying the house and soiling its courtyard (see Sachchidananda, 1955; Chaudhury 1961; Sachchidananda, 1969). During a personal communication in January 2003, a professor of Kolkata university told me that he had been visiting a village in the Santal populated area of Jhargram (West Bengal) in 1998 and had seen adivasi men gathering with bows and arrows. He learnt that they were going to excommunicate a couple who had broken the code of tribal endogamy. There were police informants in the village who should have reported the incident to the police, but the authorities were told nothing and the attack went ahead. The Santal do not admit that bitlaha still takes place, but, like witch-hunting, it is a part of Santal culture that goes to the heart of their belief system.

While direct conflict between Santal customs and state law tended to result in secrecy and a closing of ranks to frustrate state attempts at prosecution, preventing the abuse of power by those in dominant positions locally was more difficult and was bound into ongoing relationships. Nevertheless, I was struck throughout my fieldwork by the confidence with which Santal men and women challenged and refused to comply with expectations of conformity in relations with non-Santali interlocutors. In Lahara, my assistant, Chunu, a very poor man in his forties with three young children, had lost his wife to malaria. He had no land or education and had borrowed money from a Hindu low-caste landowner, Adithio, in a neighbouring village. Adithio, who had introduced me to Chunu at the start of my stay in Lahara, described Chunu as his childhood friend. Chunu had no regular work and no assets to pay back the debt and Adithio made him work in his house doing odd jobs to repay it. A day of work in harvest time would have earned Chunu 40–60 rupees, but his work in the Hindu's house was worth only 20 rupees per day against the debt (different rates of pay for different work may have accounted for this but 20 rupees was the lowest possible remuneration for work). It was not clear how this arrangement had been agreed but Chunu seemed to do all he could to avoid it. He would regularly not turn up to work or work very slowly taking rest breaks or leaving early, saying he felt unwell or had some other duties to attend. In this way he created as much inconvenience as possible for Adithio and did as little work as possible. While he could not avoid the work completely, he was able to exercise control over the quality and timing of the work. Ultimately, Adithio got very little output for his 20 rupees-worth of labour. During my time in Lahara, I paid Chunu directly for the work he did for me – an average wage for skilled labour of 100 rupees per day for helping me arrange interviews and answering questions about the village. As I said, it was Adithio who had set up the introduction, telling me nothing of the debt Chunu owed him, but I later discovered he hoped Chunu would use his income to pay part of his debt back. Although I paid Chunu at the end of each day, I heard that Chunu had told Adithio that he hadn't been paid and, it seemed, he had no intention of using the money towards the debt.

Another young Santal man, Joglal, in Madhura was employed on an ad hoc basis by the dominant local NGO. This was one of the few opportunities for income in the area and the NGO hired only a few local people on its staff. However, Joglal seemed to resent the fact that the NGO was not doing more to support local Santal families and, although the NGO warned him that it would not employ him unless he was reliable, he regularly did not turn up to work or came late (giving family chores priority). When I spoke to the head of the NGO, she seemed not to want to sack him because he was otherwise a good worker, but his non-compliance had the effect of reducing the NGO's de facto ability to make demands on him to conform to its work schedule. A relationship in which he should have been subordinated was being managed in accordance with his preferences and he showed little deference to the NGO as his employer.

This propensity to challenge the wider domination of non-adivasis in the context of individual relations was starkly evident in my experience with an elderly lady, Hara, in Mohara, a village adjacent to Lahara. I had carried out a pilot research trip six months before my principal fieldtrip and had interviewed a number of villagers in Mohara. Compared to Lahara, Mohara seemed quite hostile to non-adivasi outsiders. At the time of the pilot visit I had taken photos of many villagers and their families and promised to bring them copies when I next came. The first day I arrived in the area to begin my principal fieldwork I returned to Mohara to distribute the photos. Adithio accompanied me on a borrowed motorbike. He was on good terms with the manjhi of Lahara, a relaxed and chatty headman, who seemed keen to keep good relations with non-Santal neighbours. Adithio's predominantly Hindu village was the hub of activity in the area, housing the post office, local shop and relief store (where government subsidized food was distributed). Lahara and Mohara, both less than a mile away, were poorer with no brick houses. There was some tension in the area between adivasis and land-owning Hindus and, although I lived in Lahara, I was not able to distance myself from Adithio during my stay. Lahara was over three hours on foot, across featureless scorpion and cobra-ridden plains, from the nearest road, with no transport links. My only means of leaving the village was through Adithio's contacts outside the area. For safety reasons, he remained in the neighbouring Hindu village during my stay and made frequent (unsolicited) contact with me. I had underestimated the division between adivasi and land-owning Hindus in the region.

When we arrived in Mohara we approached the headman to seek permission to distribute the photos. He was busy and uninterested and said it was fine, without paying too much attention to us or the photos. I met some of the villagers whom I had interviewed six months previously on the main street and gave them their photos and we sat and made conversation. Other villagers passed by and stopped to claim their photos. After about half an hour I had passed on most of the photos and we were preparing to leave when an elderly woman, Hara, whom I had interviewed during the pilot fieldtrip, approached.

Hara was a woman in her late sixties. She did not have a privileged life in the village (land, schooling) but she was a respected person in the community and was quick-witted and confident. She was short and slim, with short hair, and wore an old sari with no blouse and carried a walking stick. As she approached I gave her my *johar* (the customary Santal deep bow to a senior). She greeted me in return and received her photo. Her immediate reaction took me by surprise: she took the photo and, looking displeased, asked for a photo frame, saying, what good was the photo without a frame! I said that was true and apologized for not having brought any, thinking that it would be left at that. But she was not happy with the answer and said if I had no frame, I could at least give her some food or money. We had brought neither with us. By this time Hara positioned herself in front of the motorbike, which Adithio sat astride. She continued her questions, finally asking us to leave the motorbike! I thought this was a joke and looked around for confirmation from the other villagers, but everyone was silent.

Clearly, alone she posed no threat but, as our exchange continued, other villagers began to gather and I was aware of a young group of men standing in the shadows of a nearby house watching us. I felt intimidated and helpless as all my efforts to lighten the conversation or change to a new subject failed. I was also concerned that the discussion could be perceived by the villagers as a confrontation. I remember being struck by the way the image of Hara's position with her frail aged legs astride and almost touching the hard black mass of the front wheel of the motorbike – symbolizing her weakness and our strength – took on another meaning. We were on her territory and she had the power at any moment to call on the other villagers who would at once perceive the sight as proof of *our* aggression against *her*. Hara's fearlessness may have been linked to the fact that we were in her village, and that as outsiders with some wealth there was a presumption that we were there to exploit rather than assist – this despite the fact we had parted amicably after my previous visit and that I had returned as promised with her photo. She was clearly not afraid of us and my association with Adithio seemed to override any attempts at befriending her. Eventually, she relinquished her position and we left immediately. These examples from India suggest that non-compliance, far from being a benign and trivial nuisance, could manifest itself in powerful assertions that pushed back and altered the dynamics of power relations.

Optimization and the rational subject

In theory at least every relationship, with a given set of variables, has an optimal point at which the assertion of domination by one is tolerated by the other. In the context of counter-power, the dominator allows the subjugated to benefit from the relationship up to the point where the dominator's interests are maintained. Where there is interdependency, the ultimate purpose of appeasing the subjugated is to keep them in the relationship and allow the benefits of domination to continue without the relationship being fractured. Conversely, if the person in the dominant position takes this too far, they increase the chances of counter-power and non-compliance and, the further they push their dominance, the more assertive this becomes. Non-Compliance, like counter-power, takes place as part of a balancing act between conforming to and renegotiating (while remaining within) the power relation. Like counter-power, non-compliance, in theory at least, aims for an optimum point at which an individual can alter the effect of domination without inciting counter-strategies that would be to his/her detriment. Where this optimal point lies will vary depending on the circumstance and on how much each individual depends on maintaining the relationship. Acts of non-compliance and counter-power are themselves tools that help the subordinated test where this point lies, while simultaneously pushing it to its limits.

This process of optimization is endlessly imperfect and affected by complex and multiple variables that intersect at the level of individual psychology and human interactions. However, it does come up against some theoretical entanglements. Firstly, it seems to have at its base the presumption of the rational thinker making choices based on an objective calculation of the odds. This idea of the rational thinker in resistance studies has been critiqued for its failure to take into account the way the dominant ideology permeates and sets the limits to individual conceptions of what is possible (Mitchell, 1990). In Foucault's early work the subject's knowledge and modes of knowledge are effects of power/knowledge and their transformations. Raymond Caldwell (2007, p. 774) notes that this blurring of the distinction between power, knowledge and the subject seeks to 'destroy the optimism of Enlightenment reason – its faith in individual autonomy and self-identity through rational knowledge of the self and the world'. However, Foucault's later work (1981; 1988) on the self, and particularly his formulation of the free subject, clearly counters this, returning to us the (semi)autonomous individual.

But the correlation between rationality, freedom and Enlightenment is revealing. The transference of Foucault's ideal of the free subject, born out of his research in the West, to status-based societies in the Global South is seen as problematic. There is a danger that we extrapolate from this that no person acting within a cultural setting that has not embraced 'Enlightenment' can think rationally or be free as long as they remain within their culture. In development and human rights discourse, the idea that the 'rational thinker' must be constructed from the outside is deeply problematic. Feminist scholars demonstrate that disadvantaged women designated 'third world' are forced to conform to neoliberal ideals of rationality to be worthy of development aid assistance (Madhok and Rai, 2012).

In development policy, the new focus on self-management of poverty has promoted the ideal of the developing-country woman as a 'hyper-rational' subject, 'self-affirming, self-reliant, self-sufficient, responsible, capable of authoring and executing her own actions' (Madhok and Rai, 2012, p. 648). Sumi Madhok and Shirin Rai's study of the Sathins in Rajasthan, poor low-caste women who were trained in women's rights, showed this creates serious shortcomings and puts women at risk as they are made to re-enter their cultural setting as ambassadors for liberal individualist ideals of choice. Sally Engle Merry (2009) notes that, in human rights discourse, women from cultures in Africa and Asia are denied agency unless they conform to Western liberal stereotypes. A woman who chooses cultural practices – such as veiling, arranged marriage under pressure, female genital mutilation – which are deemed by modern secular and liberal standards to contravene her human rights, are seen as lacking agency.

In reality, the realization of individual needs will not always conform to Western liberal ideals of freedom. Culture itself intervenes to determine the character of renegotiations because this takes its meaning within the cultural context. An act of defiance, such as leaving a husband to cook for himself in retribution, may by Western standards seem petty because it does not fundamentally alter her subordinate position, but in a cultivator society, where each person fulfilling their (gendered) allocated tasks is fundamental to familial survival, it may provide considerable leverage to the woman to get her needs recognized. This may be a significant act to the woman, her husband and others in that society. It has the function of what Claudia Strauss and Naomi Quinn (1997) call embedded agency – which seeks not to undermine power but to actively engage in shaping the individual's life through it.

This has its complications. Many factors, including their own individual character, personal circumstances and past experiences, may either reduce the likelihood of attempting renegotiations or act as motivators. Also people's beliefs about the fruitfulness of renegotiating moments in relationships are not only learned within relationships but through group experiences. Power relations are not always clear, linear relations between identifiable individuals. Patterns of abuse can create presumptions about the limited productiveness of negotiating a change. As we saw in Chapter 3, the Santal in Bangladesh have a genuine fear of attacks and reprisals from non-adivasis whose abuse of power they attempt to challenge. This affects their experience of power relations with non-adivasis and affects how some respond.

Fear of retaliation is a common theme in peasant studies of land disputes throughout South Asia (Herring, 1981) and was common in the villages where I stayed. In Dhanban the village elite (manjhi, parganait, elders and others) had successfully challenged a local influential Muslim man, Ansar.

Ansar had claimed rights over a small area of land that the Santal used to bury their dead. The land was government khas land. Ansar tried to take the land by force but the Santal got help from the local UP chairman and were able to get permission to continue using the land as their burial area. Possibly because the case was well known in the area and the UP was supporting the Santal's application to get title to the land, Ansar accepted defeat. However, according to the parganait, he soon took his revenge. A little while after this dispute, he took a case against another Santal man, Noresh, from a different village. The case concerned a dispute over the title of land owned by Noresh's forefathers. Noresh cultivated the land but Ansar claimed that he had gained rights to the land when Noresh's grandfather fled to India in the 1940s. When he filed the case against Noresh, he also included the names of the men from Dhanban who had fought with him over the burial land. Despite the fact that these men had nothing to do with Noresh's case, they were obliged to go to court and pay towards lawyers' fees and court costs before the judge ruled that they in fact had no interest in the case.

One evening in Dhanban village I was chatting to a young man about his recent experience of selling his house through the District Commissioner (DC). He was reasonably well off in the village with some land and good family support. I asked him if he had ever been to court and he told me that he had once acted as a witness in a land case involving a Santal neighbour of his and a non-adivasi. The non-adivasi claimed to own land belonging to the Santal. He told me that when he went to court to act as a witness he was afraid that the non-adivasi would take revenge on him, but at the time nothing happened. I asked if he was still now afraid that some action would be taken against him and he replied *'eta o asse, amader adivasi bhoi'* (that is always there, our adivasi fear).

This fear was well justified. A legal aid NGO in Rajshahi had been involved in a case which had ended in the killing of a prominent Santal leader, Alfred Soren, in August 2000. He was a well-known Santal who headed an adivasi political group seeking recognition for the Santal under the Bangladesh Constitution and, as such, had some influence in the area. His home village, inhabited by 19 families, was under attack from local influential Bengalis. The land they lived on and cultivated was government land which they were entitled to apply for ownership of – because they had occupied it for 15 years – but which they had as yet not gained rights to. A non-adivasi landowner in the area took support from the local UP chairman to try to evict the Santal families from the land in order to take possession of it. When the Santal families would not leave, they were threatened. False criminal and civil cases were taken against several of them individually and the landowner carried out a campaign of harassment. On 18 August 2000 a group of men entered the village and attacked the villagers. In the attack Alfred Soren was hit with an axe and died. The day before the attack he had sent a letter to the police listing the false cases brought against his village people and violence by non-adivasis against them, naming the landowner and others involved and asking for them to be arrested. One hundred people were arrested for Alfred Soren's murder but most absconded or were released.

As I explained earlier, the Santal in India did not have this same fear. Their longer history of settlement and sheer numbers (6 million as compared with approximately 200,000 in Bangladesh), and perhaps also their greater rights as a minority, contributed to this. But this difference did not make the Santal in Bangladesh less likely to respond. It did, however, impact on the way they did so. Whereas in India I saw more examples of non-compliance, in Bangladesh I saw more recourse to the courts – i.e. counter-power. Their weaker status and greater vulnerability meant that they did not feel able to use non-compliance in the same way. But it also gave them more incentive to push further, using means that would be more likely to challenge the relationship. I discuss in the next chapter in greater detail how use of an alternative legal order, counter-power and non-compliance impact on power relations and how the nature of the relation of power affects responses.

Conclusion

Feminist readers of Foucault's early work on disciplinary power often point to the absence of resistance or agency in his concept of power. While this is remedied to some degree in his later work on the self, we are still left with an incomplete notion of agentic potential (McNay, 2000, p. 9). Indeed, in one passage, where Foucault seems to talk directly of internal renegotiations, he dismisses it without interrogation. In *The Ethic of Care for the Self as a Practice of Freedom*, Foucault (1988, p. 12), talking about conjugal relations in the eighteenth and nineteenth centuries, says:

> [W]e cannot say that there was only male power; the woman herself could do a lot of things: be unfaithful to him, extract money from him, refuse him sexually. She was, however, subject to a state of domination, in the measure where all that was finally no more than a certain number of tricks which never brought about a reversal of the situation.

The ineffectiveness of the woman's denials here is associated with a failure to '*reverse* the situation' of domination. What real reversal would mean, and whether it is possible in conjugal relations, is not explored. Foucault probably did not intend to infer that renegotiation must always reverse the inequality. The narrative of reversal of power presumes power is something ordinarily unitary and fixed, which goes against Foucault's notion of power as fluid and 'never in anyone's hands' (Foucault, 1980, p. 98).

However, it is implied that the circulatory nature of power is such that, as long as she remains in the relationship, the woman will always assume a position of subordination. What is inferred in the woman's failed attempts at countering 'male power' is that there can be no 'female power' in the true sense because male power ultimately dominates. The idea that 'female power' may manifest other than through overall domination, that it may exist alongside male power, is not entertained. This uses male power as a measure of the quality of power, then denies it to women.

In her discussion of Santal women's land rights, Rao (2005a) questions the assumption that the patriarchal nature of Santal custom makes it difficult to give women land. She notes that the variability of conjugal relations and intra-household dynamics throughout the life-cycle provide a moving feast of sources of support and opposition for women. Men may support a woman's land claim if this boosts their own sense of authority. Conversely, women may internalize what Rao refers to as their subject-positions as wife or mother and identify with male prioritization of land interests because, the household being a site of shared interests, they receive the benefits. The family or village are themselves sites in which the woman invests and takes certain benefits. The family or village's success permeates her life experience and many women and men invest in these social fields in order to benefit their own situation.

The importance of the relationship as a source of benefits means that the realization of needs is unlikely to take place as a battle for a fundamental change in the relationship itself. It is more likely to aim at an incremental, and possibly momentary or isolated, adjustment to some element of the experience of the relationship. Homi Bhabha (1990, p. 216) acknowledges that in any political struggle new sites are opened up and continual negotiation should be a primary aim. Negotiating allows the subjugated to work through and test new possibilities, to optimize their ability to realize their individual needs through the relationship. As Strauss and Quinn (1997) put it, people will not always seek to undermine power, they may rather seek to actively shape their individual experience of power.

7
A Tripartite Theory: Power Practices and Embedded Change

In previous chapters I have examined three ways in which resistance external to the relationship and renegotiations within the relationship take place: recourse to an alternative legal order, counter-power and non-compliance. Although I did not set out to use these as a diagnostic tool of power (Abu-Lughod, 1990) when I sought to understand why people took recourse to these, it became apparent that different forms of power relation were in play. Earlier in the book I introduced the concept of power conceptualized by the French philosopher Michel Foucault as a micro-force. Micro-power organizes individuals within the state, Santal village and family to act in certain ways that privilege some over others. I found that resisting and renegotiating this organizing force did not only take place through recourse to an alternative legal order – such as the state – but also occurred within the social field where the inequalities took shape. I highlighted the complications of this for individuals trying to improve their situation. In this chapter, I want to explore the links between forms of power and different responses to power's organizing force in more detail. In particular, I suggest that how individuals respond to domination is not random, but relates closely to the nature of the binding forces prevalent in the power relations.

These findings are important for social policy initiatives that aim to address cultural practices within minority communities that breach normative formulations of rights and equality. Such policies rely on individuals within these communities to seek help through recourse to state institutions. Such an approach is already criticized for relying on the vulnerable and subordinated within cultural minorities to take action against the cultural hegemony (see, for example, Shachar, 2008). Those offering such a critique advocate a tougher stance for the state in intervening to assist these individuals. I want to challenge the premise of this critique, which treats subordination as a human characteristic, attached to the individual rather than the power relation. Advocates of increased state intervention understand the failure of these women to help themselves in terms of incapacity and vulnerability. They presume the individual in such a position should not be tasked with challenging the cultural hegemony. While this may be true in some situations or for some individuals, taking this as the starting point for policy fails to recognize those subjects who are engaged in renegotiations. This denies them the opportunity to participate with the state in the development of the new reality to be worked towards. The subject is made the object of the discourse and the state replaces the cultural elite with its own ideals and pressures. The power relations in which the subject is subordinated therefore transfer onto the new relationship.

In ruling out the role of the subject actor, another assumption is made: that the only way to challenge the cultural hegemony of the minority community is through recourse to the state. However, I found that recourse to the state was part of a broader strategy of negotiations. It was also only one of several options. Far more prevalent was recourse to internal renegotiations. While everyday resistance has remained a valued preoccupation for scholars of peasant resistance and women's resistance (Scott, 1985; Manning, 1999), the failure to reconcile it with external standards of equality and rights has reduced its impact and it has been largely ignored in social policy. Given that everyday resistance often functions within the context of the normative order of a minority and therefore takes recourse to principles that also function to support the hegemony there, it is dismissed as a negotiating strategy with little real impact (Mihelich and Storrs, 2003). Agency that works within existing power relations is disregarded, seen as 'tricks', 'blinding people to the painful reality of the extent of their powerlessness and exploitation' (White cited in Mitchell, 1990, p. 555).

This chapter offers an alternative view. I found that counter-power and non-compliance correlate with two particular modes of power practice, which I call relations of nature and dependence. These involve the individual in accepting inequality in the context of ongoing relationships that they value. This acceptance is not absolute. It is an acceptance that nevertheless makes certain demands on the dominator and responds to fluctuations in power practices. Its instability means that it acts on these power practices, affecting changes, no matter how subtle. While the ebb and flow of power practices makes the direction of change uncertain, it provides a basis for social change. We need to take into account that a multiplicity of power relations may exist, and resistance through external forums is only one of several options. Internal renegotiations and also mutual support, solidarity and harmony, discussed in Chapter 6, are also accepted ways of living within power relations that fulfil individual needs.

The focus on external resistance through state assistance in policy responses, which relies on a third power practice that I call relations of force, fails to engage productively with this process. It ignores the diversity of power relations and presumes that change can be instigated from the outside. Importantly, the tendency to focus on external resistance is founded in the view that agency and resistance are only valid when they seek out equality in a manner and form prescribed by the state (Merry, 2009). Renegotiations within power practices are rejected because they work through existing relationships and are shaped by them. However, if internal renegotiation is to be properly factored into policy, then there needs to be an acceptance that change is an organic process that emerges from current practice.

This is not to say that there is no place for state law and its equality principles. All legal orders exist in relation to their others. But it is not the ability of state law to penetrate but the willingness of other legal orders to let it in that is critical. Amongst the Santal, as with other minority communities, the desire for the elite to maintain its position of dominance means that an encroaching state causes a determined response, either a turning inwards to maintain unity against the outsider state, or, if the aggression is near, an outward battle against it (Shariff, 2013). By contrast some studies of the impact of colonial rule show that new ways of thinking brought in by the European colonizers had their most profound impact where they put in place new forms of interaction which met emerging needs within those communities and transformed social relationships (Moore, 1973; Snyder, 1981). I consider below the nature of social transformation and the place of internal renegotiations within this.

Three forms of power practice

The many different manifestations of power have been a constant preoccupation of political anthropologists, not least the main distinction between power through domination and power through discipline (Weber, 1978, p. 53). It has been less common to find theories that attempt to identify differences within power practices at the level of social relations. Eric R Wolf (1990, p. 586) has distinguished four modalities of power, which are implicated in different kinds of relationships. He defines each with reference to a time and place: power as the attribute of a person on entering into play; power over others during exchanges; organizational power that allows one actor to control the operating unit in which the other functions; structural power that structures flows of power and organizes wider settings. He seems to recognize that power changes during the course of human interaction. This association of different forms of power with structural places is also visible in Boaventura de Souza Santos' (1995 and 2002) work mapping law and power in a globalized society. He distinguishes six structural places: the householdplace; the workplace; the marketplace; the communityplace; the citizenplace; and the worldplace – each with a kind of law that regulates, a kind of power relations and an epistemological form. His work distinguishes the differing sets of relationships which the individual inhabits (household, work, community and so on) as having their own form of regulation and power that produces social relations and forms of unequal exchange. He allows that the logic of regulation in each space, though specific, is not self-contained, given that social relations themselves are developed through their articulations with social relations in other structural locations (Santos, 2002, p. 374).

While these theories help us to view power as a structuring force and explain how power's mode of organization changes through different spaces of interaction, it does not help with understanding the dynamics of change. It identifies each form of power with a particular place or moment and does not recognize forms or modes of power that exist regardless of broader structural dynamics. I found that by examining power relations from the perspective of the subject, at the point at which power is put into practice, it was possible to identify three power practices that each functioned at the level of the family, village and state. These power practices provided a foundation for understanding the pressures put on the individual and the potential for change.

My data suggest that a critical factor in the use of resistance and renegotiation is the degree to which the individual accepts the inequality within the relationship. Also critical is how this acceptance functions within the relationship. The three forms of resistance and renegotiation discussed in Chapters 5 and 6 each present a different experience of power. There is a wide and varied body of social theory literature – designated cultural theories – concerned with power practices and performativity (see Reckwitz, 2002; Shove et al., 2012). These provide a basis for understanding norms and cultural practices as both routinized and shifting. Social practices reproduce social structures not as fixed but as temporal, flexible, materializing, unstable, leaving space for change (Butler, 2010). However, despite acknowledging the flexibility in this process and the possibility of change, these theories portray the subject's experience of power as constant. The culturally conditioned subject is condemned to act within the parameters set by culture, they understand the world according to particular cultural practice. Pierre Bourdieu (1977, p. 17) describes the starting point for cultural practice as pre-law customs held in the group's memory and reproduced by each member. Practice emanates from (sections of) society and makes demands on the individual. The agentic subject is dismissed because even when she or he exercises some break in the norm this is done based on past experiences (culturally bound) which shape his or her expectation of future experiences (Bourdieu, 1992, p. 54).

My own data suggest a more complex and varied subject experience of power. Given the context of legal pluralism, the unstable process through which cultural practices are (re)produced, reiterated (Butler, 2010) when social practices are put into action, facilitates the individual in constituting and reconstituting him or herself as a social subject. As the process of reiteration will sometimes take place in reaction to something new, whether coming from outside the social practice or resulting from 'deviant' acts within, it exposes the individual to multiple experiences. These variations may be constituted within a particular time or place, as with Santos and Wolf's modes of power above, but are not confined to them. Knowing that such variations exist raises the question of whether it is possible to distinguish experiences of power as typologies.

In my research on the Santal, I sought to understand resistance and renegotiation in the context of legal pluralist societies. Examining these proved a useful way into understanding variations in power practices. I found three power practices that capture different ways in which individuals experience power and affect how they respond. Where there was evidence of recourse to alternative legal orders, power practices that I have called relations of force seemed prominent. Where counter-power was used, those relations seemed to be characterized by qualities of dependency, what I have called relations of dependence. Where non-compliance arose, this seemed to be most suited to relations of inequality disguised as natural – I call these relations of nature. These three forms of power practice were all present in the socio-legal fields of the family, village and state.

We will see that, while each power practice encompasses domination and subordination, the cognizance of this differs. Understanding these helps to explain why individuals respond in different ways. It is not the 'level of repression' (Scott, 1986, p. 28) as much as how domination fits into the mechanics of the relationship that affects this. This cognizance of the domination, along with perceived opportunities for an alternative outcome, provide different conditions in which certain responses are more likely and others less so.

Relations of force and the use of alternative legal orders

Mary's recourse to the village council discussed in Chapter 5, when her husband drank heavily and beat her, showed an ability to view his actions, within the normative order of the family where men are privileged, as unacceptable and open to challenge. She took recourse to the village as a normative order outside the marital relationship that could nevertheless put pressure on the husband to change his behaviour. In the village, domestic violence is subject to scrutiny and a man's actions are assessed for fault. A husband who drinks and beats his wife is considered not to be exercising his power justly. When Mary took recourse to the village headman (manjhi) to get a decision against her husband, she therefore was transferring the power relation to an alternative forum that viewed her husband's actions not as an accepted part of married life, but as capable of being subject to conditions. To take this step she had had to reconceptualize this dimension of the inequality between her husband and herself in the family as unacceptable, a relation of force. Using the alternative forum meant she also recognized that she would not be able to alter the situation by making adjustments within the relationship itself.

Relations of force occur when the individual does not accept the inequality and feels they are being compelled to conform by force or fear, or that the dominant party's will is imposed on them. This is only a power relation if there is some scope for escape (Foucault, 1994b, p. 342). However, this type of power practice leaves very little room for negotiation *within* the power relation and is more likely to lead to a direct challenge of the relationship itself. Recourse is taken to an alternative normative order that views the responsibilities of the parties differently and recognizes the inequality as unjust. Although taking recourse to a forum outside the power relation risks rupturing or damaging the relationship, the examples suggest the primary intention is to renegotiate power inequalities rather than to exit.

Once an individual experiences a power relation as forcing an inequality or injustice on them, they will not necessarily rely on the ideology of the most obvious alternative forum for a solution. Once the transition has been made not to accept some part of the relationship, they are likely to use whatever external means possible to achieve their aim. In her study of Santal land disputes, Nitya Rao found some other good examples of this. Rao (2005a, p. 364) notes that usually a man will attempt to get the consent of his first wife before bringing a second wife into the household, and when she agrees will divide the customary rights to his land between her and the second wife, as security for her maintenance. If the first wife denies consent, the norm is for her to be thrown out or humiliated until she leaves – the allotment of land to the first wife is no longer necessary. However, Rao found examples of Santal women challenging this convention.

In one example a woman, Rani, whose husband takes a second wife without her consent, challenges him to give her a share of his assets, thus reconceptualizing their relationship from one where gendered differences provide a basis for unequal control over assets to one where she has a direct claim over his assets. She gains support from the village council to keep a portion of his land. However, reasserting his privilege within the family, he continues to clandestinely harvest her land (he sees this as justified as he has limited alternative resources) and denies access to labourers she has employed, exposing again the fragility of her position in the family. She turns again to the village council, but this time they support his plea to maintain some customary rights over the land and suggest that Rani share the land with her husband, which would be the common practice. She refuses and refers to another social field of norms that better suits her demands, her Christian identity, to argue another vision of the commitments between husband and wife (Rao, 2005a, p. 365). Her actions show an ability to recognize the inequality in distribution of assets in the family and re-imagine herself other than as prescribed by the relationship as viewed by the family (first wife with limited rights) or village (having limited conjugal rights to her husband's property).

In some exceptional cases using another socio-legal order may mean shifting to inhabit that alternative sphere (moving out of the family to live alone in a village or more exceptionally moving outside Santal society). Judith Butler (2010, p. 155) notes Masao Maruyama's conception that the individual who articulates ideals from outside breaks out of the framework and is him or herself transformed. If the transfer of the experience is radical, then the individual may leave the power relations completely. I do not believe, however, that every individual is equally disposed to this. Leaving the power relation completely, referred to by feminists as 'exit', has its own complications. I discuss in the following chapter how this plays out in the context of forced marriage cases where young men and women of South-Asian decent living in Britain turn to the state for protection against their families and find themselves having to start a new life away from family and friends (see also Shariff, 2012). Santal men and women I interviewed saw themselves as having very little chance of survival if they left their village communities. In most cases, however, an individual who seeks assistance from outside the power relation will not have exit as their primary aim. In societies where family and community are important for survival, individuals will tend, in the first instance, to find a solution that keeps in place their existing relationships.

Relations of dependence, non-compliance and counter-power

Relations of dependence occur when the individual recognizes their disadvantage but accepts it in part in order to gain some perceived advantage in a relationship of interdependence. Here, individuals are more likely to use counter-power, or in some situations non-compliance (discussed in Chapter 6), as this depends on a strong interdependency between the parties. This means that they use the benefits offered by the privileged party in the power relation to push for more advantages. Because most relationships are multiplex (meeting a variety of needs) rather than single-interest (Gluckman, 1955, p. 19), the subordinate may be highly dependent on the dominator: an employer may also provide loans or help in time of hardship and illness, advice or assistance in disputes with other non-adivasis. Relations of dependence can appear at first as relations of force – an individual sees their subordination as imposed – but the difference is that the individual does not wish to risk rupturing the relationship and has some scope for, and sees a possible benefit in, improving their position within the relationship.

Women who turn to their parents or brothers for support in situations of domestic violence provide an example of this. As discussed in Chapter 6, they accept their subordinate position in the family in part but the duty of relatives to support them improves their negotiating power against the husband. The fact that women turn first to their family members for a solution, and that the solution likely involves remaining within the marriage, suggests that they see themselves as dependent on the marriage in future. Divorce is acceptable in Santal customs, but the woman has to prove the man is at fault to receive any money in 'damages' and may find it difficult to remarry (Bodding, 1942, pp. 78 and 83). Also, in Bangladesh in particular, women who have converted to Christianity may not be able to divorce.

Dependency within multiplex relationships will vary according to the scope of needs met by the dominant party and the extent to which there is reciprocation. Where few needs are met through the relationship, or the dependency is higher for one party than the other, there may be fewer opportunities for counter-power and the individual may turn to non-compliance. We saw an example of this in Chapter 6 when Adithio, a local Hindu moneylender, asked Chunu, a quiet and subdued Santal man with few resources, to work in his house, for the lowest of wages, to repay his debt. Adithio was one of few moneylenders Chunu could turn to if he needed funds for medication or other emergencies so it was in his interest to maintain the relationship. He did not refuse Adithio's offer of doing work for him in lieu of repayment, but he made every attempt to frustrate Adithio's efforts to set the terms of that work. This non-compliance was just enough to frustrate Adithio's ability to control the conditions of repayment of debt without jeopardizing the relationship.

Examples of this were prevalent in social theory on everyday resistance that emerged in the 1980s. In James Scott's study of rice farmers in Malaysia, foot-dragging and evasion were used against the introduction of mechanized harvesting. Instead of open confrontation with the farmers, peasants employed in the process of paddy transplantation used non-compliance to communicate their dissatisfaction at the reduction in work that would result from the introduction of combine harvesters, letting it be known that they would be reluctant to transplant the fields of farmers who hired the combine (Scott, 1985, p. 251). This took place against a background of routine challenges over wages, tenancy rent and paddy distribution that were constantly testing and renegotiating production relations. Michael Adas (1986, p. 69) found peasant cultivators in colonial and pre-colonial south and south-east Asia used avoidance through calculated errors or incompetence to deny their exploiters their labour. He sees these as being aimed at achieving specific demands rather than reform, but also as integral to the process of exchange between elite and cultivators.

While non-compliance and counter-power are both options in relations of dependence, use of alternative legal orders is less likely because it seeks to override the authority of the dominant party, directly challenging the relationship on which the subordinate depends. Even where the alternative legal order offers rights that are actionable through the power relation, claiming these single-interest benefits is likely to displace the multiple benefits gained through the relationship. Landlord–tenant relations provide a good example of this. In his study of South-Asian land tenure reforms, Ronald J Herring (1981, p. 141 citing Nair) found that tenant farmers voluntarily forwent their statutory rights to a minimum wage because they valued the residual benefits (clothes, loans, gifts during festivals, birth and death) that were withdrawn by landlords when statutory rights were enforced. The alternative legal order of the state offered benefits that were less critical, or less flexible, than those experienced through the power relation itself.

Non-compliance and counter-power in relations of dependence rely on a commitment on the part of the dominant party to maintain the relationship, from which they stand to benefit. But if relationships change rapidly, interdependencies may be broken. If the dominant party ceases to rely on the other, for example, because she or he can get the same benefits elsewhere, then there is no reciprocation, no power relation in the Foucauldian sense. In Scott's (1986, p. 17) ethnography of the impact of mechanization of farming on women labourers in rural Malaysia, the women's attempt to use foot-dragging to stop landlords from bringing in machinery to replace them for some agricultural tasks, reducing the work available for the labourers, was not effective. The landlord simply threatened to bring in alternative workers to do the jobs that the women were still needed for and the women were given the choice of conforming under the landlord's terms or losing an important source of income. The new machinery reduced the landlord's dependence on the labourers and he was not committed to a continued relationship with them. This stark example shows how rapid change brought about by outside influence can break the pattern of social relationships to the detriment of the subordinate parties.

Relations of nature and non-compliance

Relations of nature exist when the individual recognizes their subordination as a natural state flowing from their gender, class or caste, for example. Relations of nature feature centrally in theories of social control, such as Bourdieu's theory of habitus. Bourdieu (1977) sees social structures as naturalizing a given social order, turning the arbitrary into the accepted. A certain ideology is portrayed as natural or as the 'truth' and is sustained as such by transforming itself into 'necessity'. From the subject perspective, however, while the inequality is normalized as a part of life and portrayed as permanent, individuals as parties to the relationship experience this as temporal, finite. The individual may not anticipate a reversal of their position, they nonetheless recognize the fact of the inequality – a worker in Foucault's workshop knows he or she is subordinate to the managers, the student to the teacher.

Where power is conceived in this way, renegotiations are most likely to take shape through recourse to non-compliance. In the context of relations of nature, this does not circumvent the power relation (as with use of alternative forums) or seek privileges within it (as with counter-power) but acts to stop misuse of privilege by the more dominant party or temporarily prevent them from enforcing their will. The individual uses his or her control over *how* he or she carries out obligations in the relationship to limit the impact of domination. Without challenging the more privileged individual directly, the subjugated prevents him or her from controlling certain aspects of the way he or she behaves within the relationship. This is the least rupturing of the three responses and may cause inconvenience to the dominator, which directly or indirectly challenges their authority.

This inconvenience may have a considerable effect on the more dominant party. In Chapter 6 I give the example of a man, Pondic, whose wife left him due to domestic violence. Her sudden departure to her parents' village left him to look after the house and their son alone. There is no electricity or running water in the village so preparing food involves a series of jobs, collecting green leaves to eat and deadwood to build a fire to cook on, fetching water from the tubewell to wash and cook the rice, taking pots and dishes to the pond to clean. Pondic's wife would also have carried out many daily tasks essential to maintaining the mud-built family home, such as small repairs to the walls, floor and roof, sweeping and cleaning the mud floor of the courtyard, feeding any goats and chickens the family has and bringing them to the pond for water and so on, washing clothes as well as looking after their son. Pondic was a day-labourer who worked away from home during the day and a sudden absence from work would have risked him losing his job. He had to rely on other villagers to feed him and look after his son. While villagers will support others in times of need, there is little spare food in any house and there is an expectation that assistance will be reciprocated. Non-compliance in the form of removal from the home by the wife therefore had lasting repercussions for Pondic. The timing of a woman's withdrawal from the home can maximize the impact of her non-compliance. Rao (2005a, p. 357) gave the example of Nirmala who left her husband to stay with her parents when he took on labourers against her wishes. The labourers working on her husband's land near their village needed to be fed (it is common for agricultural day-labourers working far from home to be fed a meal of cooked rice), a task he had asked Nirmala to perform. Without her assistance he was unable to continue with the paddy transplantation, jeopardizing his investment.

Culture as a dynamic context for change within

My study was not a longitudinal one and therefore was not designed to examine social change. However, theoretical literature on social practice provides some insight into how the internal renegotiations I examine here may be understood as integral to change. While I focus on the internal dynamics of relationships, much of what I discuss below does involve input from external social fields. Legal pluralism, the juxtaposing of semi-autonomous social and normative fields, provides a dynamic context for change. What is meant by change is critical here. I suggest our aim should be to value individual renegotiations, not in relation to paradigmatic change – change conceived from outside the cultural communities as progressive – but in relation to subtle changes in perceptions and practices that are part of an organic process of change, or have what is known elsewhere as the 'butterfly effect'.[1]

Power practices and social change

Andreas Reckwitz (2002, p. 250) notes that the individual acts as the carrier of a practice, a routinized way of knowing, but these are qualities of the practice, in which the individual participates, not of the individual him or herself. This allows us to imagine the individual as capable of being a carrier of multiple practices, or bodies of knowing, thinking and acting. In Carla Risseeuw's study of the female coir workers (who process the fibre from

---

1 This is a phenomena used in chaos theory, noted by a meteorologist, Edward Lorenz, that in complex systems, a very small event or change at one moment can result in a major change to the system sometime in the future (Silvester, 2003).

coconut husks to weave into rope) in Sri Lanka she found that the women acted differently in the way they related to those who dominated them inside and outside the home. While the women did not recognize their subordinate position in the household as exploitative, they did perceive exploitation in their relationship with the traders (Risseeuw, 1988). In terms of my power practices the women were experiencing relations of nature in the home and relations of dependence or force in their relations with the traders. This suggests that power practices are a feature of relationships and not a characteristic of the individual, so that a single individual may simultaneously engage in a variety of power practices.

How this difference occurs, and whether recognition of inequality in one relationship facilitates such awareness in other relationships, is critical to our understanding of power. In explaining the different experiences of inequality amongst the coir workers, Risseeuw (1988) refers to Bourdieu's (1977) concept of discourse. Bourdieu distinguishes three forms of discourse: orthodoxy (dominant opinion); heterodoxy (opposing opinion); and doxa (taken for granted). The doxa conditions without explicit instructions. Within the doxa practices are not debated or discussed. It is only when practices enter the realm of orthodoxy that they are revealed as arbitrary, subject to contestation through heterodoxy, or opposing views. Amongst the coir workers, the relationship between husband and wife falls under the doxa, that which is not discussed. The women are unable to view their relationship with their husbands as constructed. Their relationship with the traders, however, falls under orthodoxy, exposing it to challenge.

Discourses are capable of separation (some falling under the doxa while others fall under the orthodoxy) and each discourse relates to a domain of relationship (family or work in this case). The implication of this is that awareness of inequality in one relationship is characterized by the type of relationship, or field of relations, and does not necessarily transfer across to other types of relationship. Yet, historical texts are full of examples of traditions undergoing transformations, sometimes slowly over time, sometimes more rapidly (Snyder, 1981; Medeirost, 1984). For Bourdieu, discourse only shifts away from the doxa if it becomes part of orthodoxy, therefore subject to discussion, and opposed through heterodoxy. Bourdieu (1977, p. 169) associates this change with crisis and collective struggle, which is capable of lifting the censorship associated with the doxa and revealing the arbitrariness of imposed definitions.

But discourse itself is not static or, in most societies, isolated in the way that this suggests. Even Bourdieu acknowledges that different social groups have different experiences and therefore the habitus of each group will also be different. In my research the heterogeneity of fields of social experience provided a rich base on which to draw and greater opportunities for exposing discourse to opposition. Men and women in Santal villages have access to a variety of discourses relating to standard relationships such as marital relations, employer relations, neighbourly relations, state–citizen relations. Many aspects of Santal social organization facilitate this. Although all Santal villages subscribe to the same Santal customs that perpetuate standard relationships within the village legal order, Santal laws have regional variations (Archer, 1984). Kinship ties create links between people living in different villages and across internal state boundaries in India and national boundaries into Bangladesh, so that exposure to these variations is part of every Santal's life. At the basic level of interactions within and between Santal villages, individuals are exposed to multiple variations on standard-type relationships. To add to this, some villages are mixed (Santal live alongside other adivasis and non-adivasis) and in most villages government officials, missionaries, health workers and NGOs have, to varying degrees, introduced the language of gender equality, Christian duty and citizenship rights[2] into relationships.

Seasonal migration of Santal villagers to other states in India to find employment in the agricultural and industrial sectors is common, particularly in Jharkhand where work is often difficult to find. Such migration, where regular or prolonged, exposes Santal to an alternative lifestyle. S Banerjee's (1981, p. 75) study for the Anthropological Survey of India into the Santal working in the coal-mining complex in Jharia-Ranigauge found references to Hindu practices, such as aversion to eating beef, amongst the Santal there. Cooperative labour, where neighbours would offer services in times of need in exchange for assistance when they required it later, were abandoned in favour of cash payment for services: even traditional bonds between Santal and Hindu castes, such as the *doms* (drummers) who were traditionally paid with paddy for providing a service during Santal festivals, were transformed.

These transformations took the form of collective changes *in situ* but it was common for villagers in the areas where I stayed in India to migrate individually on a shorter-term basis for seasonal work in other internal states. Their return home was marked with an evening of drinking and music in which all the villagers gathered to hear stories from the returnee's travels. Such stories revealed to the villagers the customary practices of adivasis and non-adivasis in other regions, variations in how working relationships were managed, and how people related to one another in ordinary life (whether neighbours helped each other, how marital disputes were

---

2 Villagers were able to call on these in response to my questions about what assistance they wanted, using terms such as 'positive discrimination' and 'recognition'.

resolved, what financial support networks were available). Those listening intuitively compared what they heard with their own experiences of working relationships, neighbourly support and so on. This comparison involved relating experiences of one type of relationship (working relationships, neighbourly relations, conjugal relations) between two social settings.

Experiences of alternative ways of doing, and thinking, can alter an individual's conception of themselves and thus permeate how they relate to others in a variety of relationships. Luke, my assistant in Thakurban, was one of a handful of villagers to go to university (he was in his second year of a sociology degree at Rajshahi University). When the village met to consider the case of the stolen ducks discussed in earlier chapters, Luke took it upon himself to play a role of neutral intervener. Normally, the council would be formed only by the male heads of household of the village and, since Luke's father was still living, Luke would not normally have been required to attend and would not have been seen as having any particular authority to address the meeting. He did, however, attend and, though he stood on the periphery of the council meeting, he occasionally addressed the villagers with his own contributions, raising questions he felt needed attention.

When I asked him about the role that different villagers took in the process of hearing the case, he included in his description a 'third-party neutral' who may intervene to raise questions for discussion – the role he had himself played. I saw no record of this in any literature on Santal village council meetings nor did I hear of it in other villages I visited, so it seemed to be a role he had made for himself. His exposure to university life had impacted on how he approached his relations with the villagers. The role he occupied as student and the actions of his lecturers, contributing to and facilitating discussion, were transferred directly to the village. But as a junior in the village he had to position himself with care. He did not sit with the other villagers, thereby avoiding the awkwardness of the social positioning that would have been attributed to him as a junior in the gathering, but stood on the periphery. There were a number of people standing watching the hearing, all outsiders in one way or another: Ahmed, the Muslim landlord, who was asked to give evidence in the case; an NGO worker who happened to be visiting that day; Mary who, being a woman, was not entitled to participate as household representative; and myself. Standing put Luke in a position of exteriority to the council, yet he used his privilege as a village member to address the discussion without invitation and walked freely around the men gathered there. His experience of a university education did not only impact on his way of thinking and being in the university environment but also affected how he related in social practices with his village community. His interventions may not have been accepted by the council as a new form of engagement for junior, educated Santal but they were tolerated.

Sumi Madhok and Shirin Rai's study of *sathins*, low-caste village women in India, is another good example of this. Sathins (meaning female friend) were women who were co-opted to implement an NGO-run rural development project. They were themselves village women chosen because they would be able to interact with the village panchayats and other village women as 'friends'. During the project they took initiatives relating to water supply and sanitation, health, child marriage, girls' education, famine relief, and making the family the central unit of development as a way of challenging gender oppression. In preparation for taking up the post, the women were given extensive training, drawing on feminist theories of women's empowerment, and were familiarized with concepts such as self-reliance, self-expression, concerted action, internalization and team work (Madhok and Rai, 2012, p. 655). Madhok and Rai note that, while the programme itself was not successful, the process of training affected a transformation in how the women viewed their own social positioning in relations with villagers and with the state. For example, though the women were not government employees (they were volunteers, paid only through honorariums), they demanded salaries and the right to organize a workers' union to demand entitlements from the state.

These are stark examples of direct exposure to, or rather instruction in, alternative discourse or modes of thinking (Luke through the university and the sathins through NGO training), but such exposure may be more subtle. Although not as explicit as this, Sama, Magli and Mary (discussed in Chapter 6) all gained knowledge and experience from outside the village, which altered their outlook on village life. Sama had been included by her father and brothers in their interactions with state officials and lawyers over family land disputes and dealings with business contacts over the management of the land. Magli was a businesswoman in her own right managing cultivation and processing of a variety of crops such as chillies and mustard seeds to sell at market. She had also been involved in a court case against her son-in-law's father over land. Mary managed the household and worked to bring in an income when her husband became ill with tuberculosis. She liaised with NGO workers over the case against her son-in-law for domestic violence and seemed fully aware of the wider picture of her powerlessness, not just as a woman but as a Santal adivasi with no contacts in the town and no bargaining power in relations with landlords. Through business contacts outside the village, experiences with officials or contact with NGOs, these women had transformed their relationships within the family. This impacted on how they saw themselves in the village. Mary was one of the few women who represented her household by attending the hearing of the village council about the stolen ducks – although she stood on the periphery of the meeting. In the interviews, all three women were much more vocal about the problems the Santal faced in general and able to articulate their disadvantage more confidently than other women.

Embedding change

I showed in Chapters 5 and 6 that use of alternative legal orders is complex and that renegotiation within the social field of inequality through non-compliance and counter-power is prevalent. If we relate this to power practices described above, this suggests that individuals are experiencing inequality through relations of nature and dependence and not necessarily as forced. Yet, as outsiders, we perceive their inequality in clear terms – *we* experience them as relations of force, domination imposed on individuals. In our minds the pursuit of equality for the individual is an imperative goal and there is no value in the relationship without it. We demand of those individuals to see the relationship through *our* experience of it.

Sally Engle Merry (2009) has noted, in the context of human rights discourse, a tendency to force our own (liberal individualist) notion of agency on women in cultural fields and deny agency to those who choose cultural practices endorsed through familial and community relations. Merry explains that the rhetoric of human rights also seeks to foster a certain kind of personhood. Under human rights provisions, women have a right to individual freedom, but only where their decisions fit the profile of a 'rational', 'self-interested', 'responsible person' as defined by secular modernity. Consequently, women who accept, adopt or even enforce cultural practices that challenge this vision are seen as lacking in agency. An epistemological leap takes us from 'women cannot possibly want these experiences' to 'they cannot in fact really be exercising choice when they appear to accept them'. This type of presumption permeates feminist race literature and suggests all cultural codes are inherently gender-biased and part of a schema of control of men over women (Okin, 1998). Women then, in order to discover their true self, must free themselves of this culture.

Empirical evidence shows time and again that individuals do accept situations that clash with liberal ideals of what is right. Herring (1981) notes that legislative reform introducing a minimum wage for labourers and fair payment for sharecroppers in South Asia was voluntarily refused by some peasant farmers due to reliance on patron–client relations imbued with social, ritual and political imperatives. Farmers also opposed land reform legislation aimed at helping them on the grounds that it was immoral to take property from others (Herring, 1981, p. 140). In Bangladesh, employers regularly failed to pay wages of Santal day-labourers on time and, although inconvenient, this was accepted as part of an ongoing relationship in which reciprocal flexibility allowed them leverage when requesting a salary advance or loan in times of medical or other emergency. Accepting that the individual in these circumstances may value the relationship in spite of the inequality, necessitates a shift in our imaginary of the individual from one who strives for individual freedom, to one who seeks their freedom, albeit in a more limited sense, primarily within those relationships.

This does not have to negate social change. Some feminists and social scientists warn that deference by subordinates within cultural settings to the dominant ideology makes resistance futile (Mitchell, 1990, p. 555). But the dominant ideology is not fixed in the way this suggests. Customs exist moment to moment, they emerge, and internal renegotiations are integral to the process of ideology reformation. Butler (1993, p. 10) demonstrates that, although social structures are perceived as constant, the process of reiteration through which social norms materialize is inherently unstable. Gaps and fissures appear that cannot be fixed by the repetition of the norms in play, producing a destabilizing effect. This instability creates opportunities for new norms to develop. In Roy Wagner's *The Invention of Culture*, he demonstrates that it is the individuals within the social system who, through constant manipulations, shape the codes within society to create these new meanings. Meanings are attributed in a given context, and context is both a broader environment in which elements relate to each other and is itself formed by the act of relating (Wagner, 1981, p. 37).

Counter-power and non-compliance are unlikely to consciously aim to make paradigmatic shifts. They have the aim of facilitating adjustments to a particular relationship at a particular time. They work to create new meanings out of existing normative practices. John Mihelich and Debbie Storrs (2003) call this 'embedded agency'. Their study examines women of the Church of Latter Day Saints who pursue a university education in defiance of their fundamental role as caretaker of their children and household. Mihelich and Storrs see this as a different conceptualization of agency, one that does not seek directly to undermine hegemony but to actively engage in shaping the individual's experience of hegemony.

Despite their subordinated position within the church, these women have a positive experience of their place in society, considering themselves as having more freedom than the men because their missionary work is less structured. In terms of my power practices, the women experience their inequality within the church as relations of nature. The way they do so is revealing. While they recognize difference in what is expected of them compared to their male counterparts, they see gendered differences as representing men's inability to do what women do, reversing the outsider's presumption that privileges men's roles as aspirational. One woman describes the inequality by which men become priests and women become mothers as a repercussion of the fact that men cannot bear children, thus rebutting the presumption that becoming a priest is more aspirational than being a mother. Another describes the age differential of men and women's attendance at the missions (19 for men and 21 for women) as relating to the fact that adolescent males are less mature and need the missions to help them become men (Mihelich and Storrs, 2003, pp. 412–13). Again the outsider's presumption that going to mission is a sign of maturity is denied. The women themselves do not, either, recognize their actions in attending university as agentic (or at least they do not admit to it). They frame their decision to prioritize education over marriage within the discourse of womanhood, claiming it will strengthen their position within marriage. They managed to exercise freedom in the context of their basic duty of putting motherhood first, embedding their agency in the patriarchal ideological structure of the church as part of a dialectical process of negotiating hegemony.

Although it is the actions of the women inside the church taking advantage of opportunities for higher education that affect internal dynamics, these decisions by the women to prioritize education are related to pressures from outside the church for women's equality in the public sphere (Mihelich and Storrs, 2003, p. 419). The women, without articulating their actions as resistance, manage to change practices within the church, adapting them to pressures relating to education that come from outside the church. They affect the elements in circulation, how practices relate to each other. It is the wider context that facilitates change, although individuals who push the boundaries within redefine what these mean to fit their own circumstances.

Conclusion

I have suggested in this chapter that power practices affect how an individual responds to inequalities. Primarily, where the power relation either conceals the inequality through relations of nature or the individual accepts it due to their dependency on the relationship, relations of dependence, the individual is most likely to seek redress from within the relationship or the socio-legal order in which it is situated. Only if the subordinated individual rejects the consequences of inequality, which he or she experiences as maintained through force, is the individual likely to take recourse to a socio-legal order outside the relationship. Policy that aims to affect social reforms within cultural minorities tends to do so by offering solutions through state law apparatus that depend on the disadvantaged individual within that minority calling on state law for assistance. In other words it depends on the individual looking outside the power relation and its socio-legal order to find a redress. This is only likely in the exceptional circumstances of a power relation maintained through force. In most circumstances the high value put on the relationship itself, and the risk of excommunication for the individual if they take recourse to the state, makes this unlikely.

Though I use renegotiation as a diagnostic of power here, I have not found, as feminist studies of resistance tend to suggest, that its association with power acts as an obstacle, that it is subsumed within and subordinate to power. Rather I show that different forms of power practice lend themselves to different trajectories of renegotiation. The interplay between dominator and subjugator is part of the wider dynamic process of social change. Despite being internal to the power relation, non-compliance and counter-power affect processes within the relations of dependence and nature on which those social relationships are based. I explore in the next chapter how this is played out in the context of the arranged marriage process amongst a diaspora, British South Asians in England.

8
Forced Marriage: Engaging with Renegotiations Within

Forced marriage, defined as marriage without valid consent where duress[1] is a factor, often involving transcontinental movement of persons, provides a complex and interesting case study on which to test out my findings. As with the Santal, power practices characterize relationships within the family, South-Asian community and within the state. Different practices have emerged to counter domination and inequality within those relationships. This chapter examines how these play out in the context of the arranged marriage process within British South-Asian families. In arranged marriages parental and community interests are important factors in choice of spouse and timing of marriage. The prioritizing of parental and extended family wishes over individual choice, to a greater or lesser extent, means that pressure and coercion are pervasive and persistent characteristics of the marriage process. While some women's groups insist that this power dynamic makes negotiations futile, we will see that for the women and men who experience this pressure, negotiating with family and community is of paramount importance. Even those who look to outside agencies or the state for assistance tend to do so as part of a negotiating process, and maintaining links with family members is often a foremost concern. Investing in family bonds is a central part of socialization.

Although geographically and topically distant from my discussion on the Santal, the challenges of negotiating and modifying practices of arranged marriage amongst the South-Asian diaspora raises questions that are related to those I posed in my research on the Santal. Broadly, what are the dynamics, constraints, that affect the position of men and women and

---

1 Valid consent is often understood in the negative as the absence of duress and duress is defined in the Forced Marriage Act as 'to coerce by threats or other psychological means' and includes physical, psychological, financial, sexual and emotional pressure (see, for a detailed discussion, Anitha and Gill, 2009).

how they negotiate that position within relationships? The latter part of this question is particularly important because of the increased interest in state intervention against forced marriages globally and the recognition of the complexity of such intervention.

The UK provides a critical context for this discussion because the British state was the first to establish a dedicated Unit to develop policies and practices to help those facing forced marriages. The Unit has made remarkable progress in offering assistance, but the influence of a feminist agenda set by women's right groups has led to a move away from supporting renegotiations within to providing exit (Shariff, 2012). The Unit's focus on 'rescuing' women and men from their families and using statutory agencies to monitor and regulate them has raised concerns (Phillips and Dustin, 2004; Razak, 2004). This approach, modelled on the worst cases of abduction and force that characterized the Unit's early international work, has cut state policy off from a deeper examination of the causes of forced marriage and a wider engagement with less visible forms of coercion through the arranged marriage process (Shariff, 2012).

Current state interventions rely on the assumption that all those involved in marriages where parental pressure is present experience parental and community domination over their marriage choice as unacceptable and forced – relations of force. As an extension of this, it is assumed that the young person will accept 'exit' and terminate relations with their family and community, and even be prepared to sponsor the state in punishing them. In applying my three types of power practice and the forms of resistance and renegotiation that I identified in Chapters 5 and 6, I hope to demonstrate a more complex range of experiences of power within South-Asian families. In doing so, I highlight the fact that subordination of choice to parental wishes is an integral part of South-Asian culture and experienced by many as relations of nature and dependence and not as force. State strategies that rely on aggressive regulation and exit alone leave these other power practices untouched, and have little impact on the wider practice. On the other hand, internal renegotiation does exist in the context of these power practices and can offer an insight into how pressure within the marriage is being challenged. These challenges allow for small but significant changes in the meaning of practices.

Dilemmas of state intervention in forced marriage cases

The year before I set out to do the fieldwork on the Santal on which this book is based I was working at the British Foreign Office. I was seconded from an international human rights organization to assist with setting up a dedicated Forced Marriage Unit to offer support to women and men facing forced marriages abroad. The Foreign Office had been chosen as the seat for the new unit because staff in its consular division were receiving direct calls for assistance from British citizens taken abroad for a forced marriage. I remember the first case we received. A schoolteacher had received a battered hand-written letter sent from a village in Pakistan from one of her pupils. It was short and in the handwriting of a child. It said simply 'HELP ME' written in large letters across the page with scant details of an impending marriage that the girl had not agreed to. It was common to receive vague requests for assistance with little information about where exactly the person was being kept or under what conditions (whether they were locked in a room, and whether violence was being used). The challenges of locating individuals without raising suspicion in the villages where they were staying (news of a police visit could send the family into hiding) were complex. We also needed trustworthy staff and police on the ground able to travel to remote areas and speak to the person, away from their families, and ascertain if they were in danger. If the young man or woman was located and wanted assistance, he or she then needed to be escorted back to the main city and found somewhere safe to stay where the family could not find them until a replacement passport and tickets for a flight home could be arranged.

In the first year, we had pioneered procedures and agreements needed to locate and rescue those who requested assistance in Pakistan, India and Bangladesh – the three countries from which we had most requests. A Memorandum of Understanding with the Pakistani government allowed the British government to assist dual nationals facing forced marriage on Pakistani soil, who would otherwise have been beyond reach. Dedicated workers in the consular divisions of the Indian subcontinent gave us clear lines of cooperation on individual cases. Links between police forces in the Midlands and south-east England and forces in target regions in the subcontinent were established and a programme of information-sharing allowed for communication between forces across the continents. Funding was organized to work with safe-houses and NGOs in the subcontinent and key regions in Britain.

But these rescue missions posed significant challenges for the men and women concerned. Some, faced with the option of leaving their family under these dramatic circumstances, declined the offer to be taken to safety when a member of consular staff visited them. Some of those who did leave with the consular staff did so only to contact their parents when they found themselves alone in a safe-house with the realization of what had happened. Some reconnected with their family after they returned to the UK due to the total absence of any alternative support network. Those who chose not to make contact with their families were not able to return to their home town or contact friends, colleagues or extended family for fear they would be found by their families and punished. Many of the women we helped had no independent financial means either because they were still studying or because, if they did work, their salaries were paid into their parents' bank accounts. Women's shelters in the UK could provide them with temporary accommodation but were very alien experiences, and the feelings of guilt for having left their parents, confusion about unreciprocated filial love in light of the unwanted marriage and loneliness were common experiences.

After I left the Unit in 2002 the focus moved away from the international work to prevention and assistance by statutory agencies within the UK, but the aim of helping young men and women to exit from the family and community continued. The government passed civil, and later criminal, legislation to regulate acts associated with forced marriages (Forced Marriage (Civil Protection) Act 2007, Anti-social Behaviour, Crime and Policing Act 2014). The 2007 Act provided civil remedies in forced marriage cases and its principal provision, the forced marriage protection order, was designed to be used by public bodies to apply for prohibitions, restrictions and requirements against family members seeking to force a relative into a marriage. The broadening of government interventions was accompanied by a shift in language. In government papers on forced marriage, those seeking assistance from the state were referred to as 'abused children' and 'vulnerable adults'. Statutory guidance was drawn up to create a duty for statutory agencies, such as schools, local authorities, police and NHS trusts, to protect children, young people and adults facing forced marriage (HM Government, 2008). This signalled a turn to state regulation that was paternalistic in character.

But the challenge of what would happen to the individuals who sought assistance after the immediate threat of the forced marriage had passed posed persistent problems. Amongst the initiatives taken by the Unit was the production of a *Survivor's Handbook*, which prepares its reader for life without their family. The first edition of the booklet read as a practical guide to living in the UK, giving information on how to look after your finances, going back to education and finding a job, as well as more technical information about how to get a divorce, or, in the worst cases, get police protection or a new identity. Occasional pages left blank for the reader to enter their own notes and thoughts contain reassuring aphorisms that prepare the reader for the new life which they must make for themselves: 'You must be the change you wish to see.'; 'Instead of giving myself reasons why I can't, I give myself reasons why I can.'; and 'It's never too late to be what you might have been.' The subtext of such aphorisms was that the 'survivor' was responsible for finding ways to live a new life away from family and that to do so was a sign of wisdom and courage. The handbook spoke to a familiar type of aspirational personhood, independent from the binds of familial relationships, duty and culture. In a more recent version of the booklet, incorporating the new legislation, the aphorisms have been removed. Nevertheless, the strategy that underlies the state's approach – offering protection against the family and encouraging the individual to live independently – requires the individual in forced marriage to be emotionally and socially detachable from his or her family.

Admittedly, those who take recourse to the state for assistance have gone some way to rethinking their relations with their families. Their determination to avoid the marriage leads them to reject the process through which pressure is applied in the family and they experience their subordination in this process through relations of force. Relations of force describe moments in power relations where the individual feels they are being forced or compelled to accept the dominant party's will. While there is little or no room for negotiation within the relationship itself, the individual may take recourse to an external normative order or may remove themselves from the family temporarily. However, they often do so in anticipation that this will improve their negotiating power and many expect to resume contact with their parents.

In my research on the Santal I found that, where relations of force were present, engagement with the state process was part of a 'bargaining endowment' facilitating negotiations within the family or community. Recourse to the state did not demonstrate a commitment to the state process. Literature and testimonials on state intervention in forced marriage cases reveal this is also happening in that context. In Unni Wikan's (2000) account of the story of Nadia it is clear that, although the woman engages the state, she is deeply conflicted. At the time of her abduction Nadia is an 18-year-old Norwegian of Moroccan decent who has been in contact with the child welfare agency because her father beat her for being too Norwegian. Nadia has a job at a café, of which he disapproves, and wears Western clothing, and admits to having sexual relations with her boyfriend, all of which are unacceptable to her Moroccan parents. She voluntarily moves back into her parents' house after her 18th birthday, having spent three months under child welfare custody. Her family then takes her to Morocco to visit a sick grandmother. Nadia is told one evening that a friend has space in his van and they are leaving for Morocco the next morning. She is not able to inform her work of her departure but, while in Morocco, Nadia calls a work friend to say that she has been kidnapped and is to be forced into a marriage. The Ministry of Foreign Affairs liaises with the Norwegian ambassador in Morocco, where, given that Nadia is still considered a child, the ambassador negotiates with the parents to send Nadia back to Norway. The family rejects the invitation and the Norwegian government stops their welfare benefits. Nadia then appears back in Norway on her own. The family follow soon after and Nadia lives with them.

Up to this point the case appears to be a straightforward success story, but once back in Norway Nadia says she had invented the forced marriage claim because she wanted to leave Morocco. She is criticized by young Norwegian Moroccans for changing her story and later admits to doing so to protect her parents and younger siblings. The parents bring legal actions against the media and Ministry of Foreign Affairs for the bad reputation that they have suffered, but the state pursues a criminal case against the parents for kidnap. As time passes, fearful that her parents will try to arrange another marriage, Nadia again admits to her original account of the kidnapping and eventually supports a criminal prosecution. We assume that Nadia's decision to initially change her story when she arrived back in Norway is founded on an expectation that she will be able to resume relations with her family. It is only when she sees that her parents still intend to marry her, and because she fears that the state will not believe her in future, that she decides to support the case against her parents. Doing so comes at great personal cost and her father, who accuses her in court of lying and bringing shame on the whole family, dies shortly after the trial. During the trial Nadia lives in hiding and receives death threats on her life. Her Norwegian-Moroccan peers, who had supported her on her return from Morocco, criticize her for participating in the trial of her parents.

Nadia's story is complex, but demonstrates the enormous personal conflict involved in taking recourse to the state in these cases. The nature of family bonds within South-Asian families can lead to extraordinary displays of commitment by young people to their parents even in the face of cruelty and abuse. In *Shame*, the autobiography of Jasvinder Sanghera (2007), who set up an NGO to assist victims of forced marriage (Karma Nirvana) after escaping a forced marriage herself, the emotional conflict of leaving is well illustrated. Her parents arrange marriages for her sisters and insist they remain in the marriages even after it becomes apparent that their daughters are being physically abused – one of the daughters later commits suicide. When she turns 14, Sanghera is herself presented with a prospective husband from Germany. When she refuses the marriage her family prevent her from going out and she is locked in the house or in her room and closely monitored. One day she is left alone in the house and one of her sisters forgets to lock the front door and Sanghera has a chance to escape. Before she leaves, however, she takes time to write a note to her parents to explain why she is leaving, making three or four drafts to get the wording right. The letter ends 'hope I will see you again soon' (Sanghera, 2007, p. 70). At the time, she says that by running away she hopes to prompt her mother to take more notice of her wishes. Afterwards she tries desperately to get back in touch with her mother. Although it is months before her mother, or any of her sisters, will talk to her, she persists in trying to re-establish contact, calling her mother weekly despite silence on the other end.

In addition to the emotional strain of separating from their parents in this context is the difficulty of living without family support. Many of the young people involved in forced marriages are children or young adults who have little exposure to life outside the family. Sanghera was 15 when she fled her parents' house and Nadia was 18. They had nowhere to go, given that extended family supported their parents. Friends and acquaintances were unable to help because the family could easily identify and locate them. After she escaped from her home, Sanghera ran away with a friend's brother, Jassey, and she describes sleeping in his car for the first few nights and only being able to afford one meal a day. They eventually rent an unheated room, where they live with no money for food and vulnerable to petty crime. She describes comparisons she makes with her family life: a warm home, good food and a neighbourhood where she felt safe. She says 'images of home teased me'. She notes that as time passed she saw herself as at fault, having done wrong against her family (Sanghera, 2007, pp. 74–9).

The complexity of relying on state intervention to assist young men and women in these cases has led to a degree of cautiousness in some, though not all, international law provisions on forced marriage. The United Nations,[2] recognizing the complexity of the challenge, prioritizes information-gathering on best practice and encourages dialogue between stakeholders in the government and the communities affected. However, this cautious approach has not been followed elsewhere. The Council of Europe provides a single solution to the challenges of forced marriage. Its Convention on Preventing and Combatting Violence against Women and Domestic Violence, opened for signature in May 2011, requires signatories to criminalize the act of intentionally forcing someone to marry or luring someone into another state to force them to marry (Article 37). This situates the state in a position of exteriority and superiority to the communities concerned, regulating a deviant cultural minority through command and sanction. It treats the individual subjected to coercion as an independent entity requiring extraction.

---

2 At its 24th session in September 2013, the UN's Human Rights Council adopted a resolution on strengthening efforts to prevent and eliminate child, early and forced marriage (A/HRC/24/L35). See also General Assembly Resolution 'Recommendation on Consent to Marriage, Minimum Age for Marriage and Registration of Marriages' 2018 (XX) of 1 November 1965.

Following the Council of Europe's resolution, mentioned above, the British government passed a law in March 2014 (the Anti-social Behaviour, Crime and Policing Act) to criminalize forced marriage itself and to criminalize the breach of forced marriage protection orders. This move had historically been resisted and national consultations on the merits of criminalization had consistently warned government against this. The majority of respondents (including civil society, key public agencies and women and men who had had experience of a forced marriage) who responded to the government's 2006 consultation stated that criminalization would push the practice underground, that the young people affected would be isolated and that specific legislation on forced marriage would create racial segregation (HM Government, 2006, p. 11). Quotes reproduced in the government's report on the consultation highlight key objections: 'No child would want to prosecute his or her parents.'; 'Making forced marriage a criminal offence would make victims more reluctant to come forward in the first place.' (HM Government, 2006, p. 21) There were also concerns that creating a criminal offence would prevent young people moving on with their lives, some respondents noting that prosecuting family members would make it harder for a young person to later be reconciled with their families (HM Government, 2006, p. 22). Most favoured non-legislative routes, including better support for victims and survivors.

Despite this advice, the wording in the Act is broad: a criminal offence is committed by a person causing another to marry through violence, threats or 'any other form of coercion', as long as they 'ought reasonably to believe' that the person does not freely and fully consent (s. 1 21(1)). The inclusion of 'any other form of coercion' and the wording 'ought reasonably to believe' that they have not consented demonstrates an intention that the legislation should leave a surprisingly wide discretion to prosecute parents. It is hard to imagine the distinction between forced marriages and arranged marriage, which was critical to the state's early interventions in forced marriages being maintained (HM Government, 2000, p. 10). Because of this, the new legislation is likely to exacerbate the challenges for young people making the difficult decision of whether to seek state assistance and expose their family members to possible prosecution.

By the government's own admission, forced marriage is still underreported. While the Forced Marriage Unit gave advice or support to 1500 individuals in 2011, the Department for Children, Schools and Families estimates there may be 5000 to 8000 cases a year reported and many unreported (HM Government, 2012). In a report by Nazia Khanum (2008, p. 42) commissioned by the Home Office, few of those interviewed who experienced a forced marriage said they would approach a government agency. Lack of trust and familiarity was an important factor in this.

Khanum notes that these agencies are seen as unable to relate to South-Asian cultural norms and there was a fear that their intervention could lead to matters being taken out of their hands and parents being punished by the state. What young people approaching such agencies are likely to experience is very uncertain. While the government has issued statutory guidance for agencies on forced marriage (HM Government, 2008), there has been much concern over the reluctance on the part of some statutory agencies to commit to tackling the issue. A review of the success of the guidance in 2010 showed few agencies had integrated forced marriage into strategies and procedures (see discussion of the Bill, HM Government, 2013, para. 394). Schools in particular were reluctant even to put up posters or distribute leaflets for fear that these would stigmatize particular ethnic groups or provoke criticism from parents and governors (HM Government, 2013, para. 395). The complexity of using statutory bodies to regulate arranged marriages, and reluctance on the part of British South Asians to resort to them, means that states will have to think more broadly about this issue.

Power practices and the South-Asian marriage process

People designated South Asian represent a wide range of classes, religions and ethnicities, though they have some cultural practices in common and a sense of shared history. The term South Asian is used for people not only from Pakistan, India and Bangladesh but also those who relocated to Uganda, Kenya and Tanzania (East-African Asians). While I focus on the South-Asian diaspora, forced marriage is not exclusive to people from South-Asian backgrounds, or a feature of those communities, and other communities are affected including Irish travellers, Armenians, mainland Chinese, Eastern Europeans and people from Africa, the Middle East and the Caribbean (HM Government, 2006; Hester et al., 2008). Nevertheless, the majority of cases of forced marriage that are reported in the UK involve families who originate in Pakistan, Bangladesh and India (Strickland, 2013, p. 5).

Like the Santal, the South-Asian British diaspora have also migrated to alterity. Coming largely from poor rural villages in the subcontinent with high levels of illiteracy, they established themselves in Britain with few educational and social assets and were largely dependent on kin networks originating in the subcontinent for psychological and economic support. Their skills as agriculturalists, engineroom workers in British ships and sailors (*lascars*) did not prepare them well for finding employment in Britain. This trend continued into the second generation of settlers. In the early 1990s, Pakistani men were three times more likely to be unemployed than their white counterparts (Samad and Eade, 2001, p. 18). The areas where the majority of Pakistanis have settled in Britain, particularly in the Midlands, historically fell into the category of most deprived and were failing to meet national standards in education with the result that second-generation children, particularly male Pakistanis, have consistently underperformed at all early key stages of education.

When Pakistanis and Bangladeshis first migrated to Britain in the 1950s and 1960s, they intended to work for a period before returning to their homeland where most maintained family links and property interests. However, changes in immigration and nationality rules, which made it more difficult to move between Britain and the subcontinent, contributed to longer-term settlement. As the early male migrants were joined by wives and children, migrants' strategies changed and clusters began to take the form of family units. Roger Ballard's (1994) much-referenced edited volume *Desh Pardesh* illustrates that maintaining values of personal and family honour was important for first-generation migrants to establish familiar cultural practices within a very alien British culture. Power relations structured their lives and family and community disputes were first and foremost resolved there. Endogamous (marriage within one's caste and class) and intra-family marriage practices were central to this and the arranged marriage process was a convenient vehicle for implementing first-generation priorities, including maintaining links to brothers back home and keeping property within the family.

Within South-Asian families, roles and responsibilities, hierarchies, duties and benefits that are passed on to children provide a framework for familial and individual identity. Alison Shaw's (2000) study of Pakistanis in Oxford found that, despite being educated in Britain, traditional ideas from the subcontinent about gendered roles, sexuality and marriage were prevalent. Power relations within the family and community facilitate the maintenance of unequal distribution of status and with it the ability to control family assets and make decisions about key life-cycle events. It is possible to identify within the experiences of these power relations the three power practices I found in my research amongst the Santal: relations of nature, dependence and force. I examine these in the context of the arranged marriage process where parental input into choice of spouse and timing of marriage is the norm.

Khanum (2008, pp. 8–9) notes that, while parents and children rarely recognize pressure to marry, they believe that the parents' age and experience makes them well placed to find an appropriate spouse. According to a survey by Tariq Modood et al. (1997), 57 per cent of Pakistanis and 45 per cent of Bangladeshis aged 16–34 expected parents to have the final decision over choice of marriage partner. Empirical studies show passive agreement to arranged marriage by young South Asians who demonstrate a casual acceptance that marriage is inevitable and primarily a decision for their parents. Their subordinate position in the process is internalized through what I have called *relations of nature*:

> [Marriage] was something which, I suppose being brought up ... the only thing you are working towards is that one day you will get married and that's it. I suppose I wasn't forced into a marriage but having that drummed into you, well not drummed into you but having that, that's what happens in life, you get married. (Saira)[3] (Gangoli et al., 2006)

Saira situates her explanation of her own marriage in a process of socialization and, while her initial description frames this process as restrictive and coercive, she corrects herself and reconciles herself with the fact of her arranged marriage without questioning it. A middle-aged British Pakistani man, whom I will call Sadeq, interviewed by Yumas Samad and John Eade (2001, p. 68) also reconciled his arranged marriage as being 'how it happens in our community'. Despite the fact that he begins by saying he was upset when his marriage was arranged, he eventually accepts it, saying it is 'part of my life to go through'. One woman interviewed by Geetanjali Gangoli et al. (2006), Aisha, said it 'never occurred' to her that she should have an opinion in the matter. Other testimonials demonstrate a deep trust in parental guidance, and filial love between children and their parents features heavily. Some describe the process as exciting and 'the right thing to do'. Trust in parents is not only emotional but also pragmatic. The arranged marriage process is believed to provide an element of security because the parents, uncles and aunties consult through the grapevine to find a suitor of good character, financial means and family background. A marriage which has been supported by parents and extended family is also seen to have a better chance of success because of the benefits of support from extended family during times of difficulty.

While many arranged marriages are successful, and many British Asians acquiesce to them, either at the time of the arrangement or by reconciling themselves to it after the event, this is not always the case. Those who wish to delay marriage or disagree with parents about the choice of spouse, or find themselves in an unhappy marriage, may find a range of ideas and interests influence the willingness of parents to prioritize their preferences. Headline stories in the news tell of brutal parents using physical force and violence against their own children in the name of 'honour'. But honour is a complex concept and parental attitudes to these customary ideals vary

---

3 I attribute names to respondents from this and other studies for ease of reference.

enormously within the British-Asian community, which represents a wide variety of classes, castes, religions and ethnicities. The relationship between family members, the personality of parents and their attitude towards parenting and perceptions of what is acceptable to the community all have a bearing on how they are likely to respond to a son or daughter's decision to choose a partner against the parent's wishes. Samad and Eade captured two opposing views:

> When boys and girls choose their own partner for marriage you've got to accept ... It's better to them married ... What can you do? ... Parents might as well allow the marriage to take place. This is better than running away ... than doing something bad. (Parveen) [sic] (Samad and Eade, 2001, pp. 70–1)

Parveen, who is an older working-class Bangladeshi woman, exemplifies a pragmatic parent weighing up the alternatives: the consequences of a love marriage more easily adjusted to than the possibility of the daughter leaving home. Parents can make allowances for children's own choices, disguising love marriages as arranged. Despite challenging the basis of the arranged marriage process, love marriages do not necessarily lead to exclusion from the community, although their incorporation is not guaranteed. Many love-marriage couples do manage to renegotiate community reciprocities back into place. Ballard (2006, p. 6) notes that, even where couples have independently chosen to marry, this fact will often not be mentioned in order to maintain an appearance of cultural conformity. But not all parents are flexible. For Jamal, a Pakistani middle-aged working-class man, the possibility of a daughter marrying outside his religion is unthinkable.

> You know Islamically speaking, if my daughter went out of Islam, you know to get married, you know, I don't know, non-Islamic or in any other way, I would most ... definitely use force ... Q: To what extent, would you lock her up? A: ... well no, no ... Q: Drug her? A: ... I mean ... Q: What do you call force? A: ... Mainly it would be hard counselling you know, really to change her ways ... Q: Emotional blackmail [?] A: ... well, yeah, if you want to call it ... If you wanna call, to brainwash her mind ... (Samad and Eade, 2001, p. 71)

His approach – inflexible, defending his position by any means – is typical of a forced-marriage situation and references to emotional blackmail are common in the testimonials of those who acknowledge being forced to marry. They experience their subordinate position in the marriage process in terms of *relations of force*. Several men interviewed by Gangoli et al. (2006, p. 17) married after emotional pleas by a sick or dying parent and threats that they would be made to leave the family home. One man, Nazim, who acknowledged being forced into a marriage, explains that his father asked him to agree to the marriage for his sake and to prevent criticism from the community. He describes his father being 'the lowest I've seen my dad', crying and begging him to marry. Nazim agreed to the marriage because of this but refused to commit to the relationship. Nazim had an ongoing relationship with a woman from outside the South-Asian community and ultimately divorced his South-Asian wife despite strong disapproval from the family. That relationship had begun before the marriage was arranged and it had prompted the family to put pressure on Nazim to marry someone of their choice. Nazim's acceptance of the marriage process was a compromise to allow the family to restore its reputation in the short-term and demonstrated a sense of his commitment to them, but the marriage itself was not his choice and he never committed to it.

Gangoli et al. (2006) note that expectations of marriage differ between men and women. Men experience a higher status within the family and are more likely to be able to maintain some personal freedom, even to continue extra-marital relations, after an arranged marriage (see also Shaw, 2000, p. 190). Women have fewer options. Although there is little mention in the empirical literature about what happens to women after a forced marriage, in the early years of the Foreign Office's work on forced marriage, one in three of the women who contacted us had already gone through with a forced marriage abroad. Because they had been married to a foreign national, their spouses had had to go through a lengthy process to join them in the UK. Their parents were in the process of completing the forms needed to sponsor the new spouses' visas to enter the UK. The women who called the Unit continued to feign compliance to their parents and signed the forms, but requested to us directly that we refuse the visa so that the husband could not come to the UK. These cases posed considerable challenges for the state because reasons for refusing a visa had to be made public and this would have meant disclosing our communications with the British spouse to the family (see further Shariff, 2012). Nevertheless, in some cases the overseas spouse already had restrictions on his entry into the UK and the visa was refused on this basis.

The women presumed that if the husband's visa was refused then marital relations were impossible (relocating to the subcontinent was not contemplated) and the parents would have no choice but to arrange a divorce. Even if the refused visa was appealed in the courts, they considered that the long process of immigration appeals would buy them some time to find a way out of the marriage. These reluctant sponsors had recognized that the marriage was not their choice and sought a way to avoid the marriage without breaking ties with their parents. Like Nazim, they had no intention of accepting the marriage. They experienced the marriage through relations of force and, finding no opportunity to negotiate out of the marriage, they sought to use the immigration process as a way to prevent the marriage from being a de facto reality.

But not all of those who acknowledge pressure experience the power relations with their parents over marriage choice as relations of force. Some, who acknowledge that their own preferences are subordinated, nevertheless regard themselves as having had a choice. Modood et al. (1997) carried out a national survey on ethnic minorities in 1994 in which they recorded high levels of expectations of parental input into the marriage process. In this context the authors commented that some respondents overemphasized their sense of their own input, comparing it with other families. Ethnographic studies demonstrate that some young people turn the pressure inwards on themselves, marrying against their own preference, believing that this is necessary to protect their parents from extended family or community disapproval. Some respondents express deep feelings for their parents whom they understand to be under pressure from overseas relatives with an interest in the arrangement. This pressure to agree is experienced in the context of what I call *relations of dependence*.

> I was given a choice [about my marriage], my father did sit down with me and discuss it but I could see the pressure that he was under and I agreed. So is this a forced marriage then? (Ferhana) (Gangoli et al., 2006, p. 10)

While Ferhana, like Nazim, agreed to marry out of a sense of commitment to her father, she described herself as having an arranged rather than a forced marriage and described the process as one in which she was given a choice. The pressure need not only be from parents directly but may originate in a sense of wider responsibility to the family. In Sanghera's (2007, p. 140) autobiography she describes how she watches her older sisters get married to men whom their parents have chosen for them and struggle with abusive relationships. When she tries to reason with one of her sisters to leave her second marriage her sister tells her:

> [t]hat's easy for you to say. You don't have to think of the other. When you ran away with Jassey, you didn't think about us ... you didn't care about your duty, or your family. I'm not the same as you, I still have to put the family first.

Her retort reveals a strong sense that marriage symbolizes a commitment to the family, parents and other siblings. A woman, Fahmida, interviewed by Philip Lewis (2007, p. 162) explains how her older sister married their cousin out of commitment not just to her parents but also to her siblings and extended family. She describes her sister, then 19, feeling that she had a responsibility as the oldest sibling in the family to do what was expected. Her younger siblings would have been disadvantaged if she had not complied.

The ethnographic material discussed above demonstrates that marriage is not always experienced as an external force against individual choice. Power relations within the family, extended family and community shape expectations and perceptions producing a variety of responses. Those, like Saira and Sadeq, who anticipate their parents making a choice for them, accept their subordinate position in the way that I have described elsewhere as relations of nature. Others, like Ferhana, who come to a decision about their marriage while turning parental pressures in on themselves experience their family relationships through relations of dependence. They recognize the inequality of the relationship but accept it in the context of their dependence or interdependence with family members. Those, like Nazim and the reluctant sponsors who approached the Foreign Office in those early years, who went through with a marriage hoping for a divorce or maintained pre-marital relations with others, ultimately rejecting the marriage, were experiencing relations of force. They were looking outside of the relationship for a solution, despite the risks of rupturing familial relations. Identifying these different forms of power practice is instructive if we see that these influence the kinds of responses that people are likely to make to their situation.

Renegotiating relations of dependence and nature

Just as the testimonials seemed to suggest the prevalence of the three types of power practice I identified amongst the Santal, so too was there evidence of the three forms of response connected with these. Within the forced marriage and arranged marriage literature we see individuals taking recourse to alternative legal orders (usually the state, but also sometimes a community legal order), resorting to non-compliance and using counter-power. Those whom we assisted at the Foreign Office's Forced Marriage Unit were turning to an alternative legal order in the state to intervene in a matter arising from within the social and normative fields of the community and family. They had reached a point where they experienced their subordination in the marriage process as forced – relations of force – and were reverting to an alternative legal order for assistance. Others, who experienced their subordination in the family in the context of marriage arrangements as natural – relations of nature – or who turned the pressure to marry in on themselves – relations of dependence – were less likely to conceive of taking recourse to someone outside of the normative order of the relationship for help. In these cases, renegotiation was more likely to take place through the relationship.

While forced marriage policy focuses on the use of alternative legal orders, presuming relations of force, relations of nature and dependence are prevalent and, thus, closer investigation of the responses that correlate with these power practices is important. In the context of multicultural discourse, some authors refer to there being a 'third space' between the state and the community in which young women negotiate (Bhabha, 1990; An-Na'Im, 2000). Non-compliance and counter-power, both internal to the relationship, may not result in an immediate and irreversible change in the relationship, but may create a ripple that exposes practices to new meanings and contributes to a subtle reordering of relations over time. This has significant implications for the direction of policy on forced marriage, as I will suggest. As I discussed in Chapter 7, cultural practices are subject to a process of constant reiteration in which social norms are challenged and reinvented. Individuals within cultural minorities shape the evolution of practices through constant manipulations, creating new meanings. Being within the culture does not preclude dissent to some of its norms (Philips, 2007, p. 177). Shaw (2000) found that second and third-generation migrants within the British Pakistani community do challenge some cultural patterns and gender relations are always subject to renegotiation within families. Women debate over whether they should have more say in how *purdah* is interpreted and justified (Philips, 2007, p. 166). As second and third-generation South Asians have often had better opportunities for education than their parents, many use their access to information and their education to persuade parents of the need for change. In the interviews carried out by Samad and Eade (2001, p. 88), young men and women said they informed parents about the disadvantages of consanguineous marriage and the risk that children born from such marriages may be born with disabilities. Bredale (cited in Razack, 2004, p. 163) suggests young people spread stories of unhappy marriages, divorce and desperation to warn parents against undue pressure.

The resurgence of Islam as a cultural and spiritual identity, as well as a political identity, for second- and third-generation South Asians in Britain has also provided a new narrative with which to challenge South-Asian cultural practices. Islamic texts and teachings on equality and consent are used to present an alternative view of the ability of young people to refuse a partner chosen by their parents. One Pakistani man, Hasan, in Oxford, interviewed by Shaw (2000, pp. 189–90), critically contrasted community practices of arranged marriage with the treatment of marriage in Islam as a contract.

> In our religion it is wrong to force someone to marry. Both the girl and the boy should be asked if they consent. But very often our people don't even ask, they just go ahead because the marriage is in their interests, expecting everybody to agree so that no one loses face ... Our Muslim *nikahh* is a contract between a man and a woman who have to consent to the marriage in front of witnesses, that's all. You don't have to marry your cousin, that's just tradition.

He uses Islam to defend his own decision to break off a consanguineous marriage planned by his family. Hasan left home to marry a woman of his choice, a 'love' marriage. In a discussion recorded by Shaw in which several of his friends debate whether to attend his wedding, some criticize Hasan for failing his parents, while others defend the marriage as a legitimate Muslim marriage. They see Hasan's parents as wrong for expecting him to marry a woman from Pakistan, who would not be able to speak English or know anything of life in the UK. Their own logical arguments about what is 'reasonable' are contrasted with the parents' 'outdated tradition' and 'pride' and the parents are accused of failing to honour the 'genuine' spirit of Islamic marriage (Shaw, 2000, p. 190). This reference to Islam combines a Westernized reading of Islamic duties with a reflection on its authenticity, and therefore carries greater weight in comparison to the cultural traditions of his parents. Hasan and his supporters re-imagine the practice of marriage through a discourse of religion that fits with their assessment of what is logical, and this leads to a subtle but important change in the meaning given to his parents' dissent.

In Anshuman Mondal's (2008, pp. 165–88) interviews a young woman, Razia recounts her own arguments with her mother over the lack of equal treatment between her brothers and sisters. Razia is a British Bangladeshi student who considers herself a practising Muslim and began to wear a headscarf without consulting her parents as part of her own self-expression of her faith. She explains to the interviewer that the Qur'an states that sons and daughters should be treated equally and failure to do so will result in punishment. Her brother had a love marriage to a non-Muslim woman, a match that her parents initially resisted but eventually agreed to. Her sister had an arranged marriage and, although Razia expressed her own wish to choose her partner herself, her mother refused her request. She describes a conversation with her mother in which she asks: 'Am I not allowed a love marriage?'; 'What if he's Muslim?'; 'If he's a Muslim therefore it's not actually a sin'; 'What if you met him quite a few times and decided you really liked him?' Each time the mother replies 'no', but Razia's arguments seek to introduce doubt into the defensibility of her mother's stance through logical reasoning. She does this as much to convince herself as her mother and, in recounting it to the interviewer, to demonstrate the reasonableness of her own argument. She is testing out this new meaning to see if it holds any weight.

Unlike Hasan, however, Razia is ultimately submissive to her mother's preferences. Razia concludes '[s]o basically I have to have an arranged marriage with some Bengali guy'. She then adds:

> I think it would be best for everybody if I did have an arranged marriage. Because if I do have a love marriage chances are ... I would not feel right marrying someone, even if I did love them, hurting my parents like that.

Whereas Hasan, like Nazim above, experiences his parents pressure as relations of force and moves outside his family, breaking off his relationship with his parents to enter into a love marriage, Razia's experience, like that of Ferhana above, reflects her ultimate dependence on her parents – relations of dependence. She recognizes, and to some degree accepts, her subordination, turning the pressure in on herself. Although she tests out the argument of equal treatment, this is less important to her than maintaining relations with her mother.

She is described by Mondal as a 'spirited' woman who played football, had wanted to be a car mechanic and enjoyed the thrill of an argument. In her interview she oscillates between submitting to her mother and defying her. She recounts many conversations with her mother in which she reasons against her mother's determination to exert parental control, demonstrating through argument the folly of her mother's refusal to compromise. She says her parents restrict her too much and she does occasionally go out in secret without them knowing. Despite this, she is committed to maintaining her relationship with them. As such, whereas Hasan experiences his relations with his parents over marriage choice as a relation of force and leaves the family home, Razia ultimately gives more value to maintaining relations within the family.

The narratives of Hasan and Razia, which I correlate with relations of force and dependence, suggest a high level of personal conflict in their negotiations with parents over marriage choice. But conflict is not always this visible. Even those who ultimately accept their subordinate position in the marriage process and experience it through relations of nature regularly negotiate their position through non-compliance. In the marriage process, while many accept the inevitability of an arranged marriage as natural, ethnographic material shows young people regularly negotiate timing of marriage and choice of partner. The value put on a woman's education in the marriage process provides opportunities for young women to put off an early marriage in some situations. Nadia, discussed in Shaw (2000, p. 179), uses negotiations over her education and her career prospects to delay the marriage, showing that these will improve her marriage prospects (see also Abu-Lughod, 1990; Mihelich and Storrs, 2003).

Attitudes of parents may also change over time from one sibling to the next, suggesting that renegotiations by one sibling may impact on the flexibility applied to younger siblings. Shaw found in her study of Pakistanis in Oxford that parents were more flexible with younger children. Shaw notes that within one family there may be differences applied to siblings – the parents becoming less involved with younger siblings. Autobiographical accounts of forced marriage, such as Sanghera's autobiography *Shame* (2007), confirm this: after Jasvinder runs away to avoid an arranged marriage, her parents give more freedom to her younger sister to 'date' prospective husbands before marriage and accept her older sister's divorce and remarriage (a 'love' marriage, albeit one involving a man of the same caste).

Research has shown subtle changes in attitudes to dating and who is considered suitable over time. Muhammad Anwar's (1998, p. 108) research, comparing attitudes towards marriage amongst British Asians between 1975 and 1983, suggests that the custom of arranged marriage has become more flexible both in Britain and in the countries of origin over this period. Elsewhere there is evidence that the arranged marriage process is changing, with prospective spouses able to meet up together and spend time together, albeit with a chaperone, before marriage. Mondal's (2008) interviews amongst Muslims of South-Asian and North-African origin in London and Lancaster provide many examples of families where pre-marital relations are tolerated and marriage arrangements are less strictly controlled by parents. Use of marriage agencies, including online services, is now becoming more popular (Anwar, 1998; Ahmad, 2006). Online sites, such as Shaadi, have enjoyed surprising popularity. Reading the advertisements on these sites, there is a wide mix of perceptions about what is essential information about the person seeking a spouse: some prioritizing the person's height, educational achievements and salary, without mention of ethnic background, or sometimes religion; others clearly stating religion, sect and region of origin in South Asia as primary identifiers (Anwar, 1998, p. 111).

Conclusion

The cultural practice of arranged marriage within South-Asian families forefronts parental input into the choice of partner and timing of marriage and the dominant position of parents in the process is considered warranted by many. Many experience their inability to make a choice independently as an accepted practice and this explains why so many young people faced with parental pressure in marriage choice will never contemplate recourse to state law. Even when they take recourse outside the legal order of the family and community, the aim is often still primarily one of negotiating a change within the family and community. Life outside the family and community are often not contemplated.

Yet state policy has moved increasingly towards regulation of communities and offering exit as a prerequisite to assistance. State policy is more likely to be effective if it is premised on the understanding that recourse to the state happens in the context of internal negotiations and that those who do not engage the state may benefit from other types of state intervention as they are negotiating within families and communities under very difficult circumstances. Assistance that focuses on providing a way out of the family and community and a punishment to deter parents fails to engage with a complex of negotiations taking place in these families.

While there are no guarantees about what type of policies are likely to have a positive impact, a more productive way forward might be to engage communities in reflecting on the arranged-marriage process (see further Shariff, 2012). The aim of this would be not only be to improve awareness of the impact of pressure on young people but to alter the dynamic of the power relations: in Pierre Bourdieu's (1977) terms, to shift the practice from the doxa (that which is not discussed) to orthodoxy (open to challenge). Transforming marriage practices necessitates internal changes and negotiations. If state law focuses on exit, it misses a critical opportunity to engage with this. However, to do this the state is likely to have to undergo a cultural change within itself, a change captured in Abdullahi An-Na'Im's (2010) lecture on the 'Compatibility Dialectic'. This is not an easy task for the state and is likely to come up against the limitations of its own identity postulate. Engaging with communities that have a significantly different identity postulate will itself be transformative on the state and facilitating this process is only likely to happen at a time when other factors exist to affect the state's willingness to allow its own practices to be challenged and changed.

In short, my critique here is not suggesting that the state should do less to intervene, or should not assume it can help. The state will inevitably seek to intervene and the direct intervention of offering a way out may suit an individual experiencing relations of force. Beyond this, it is not the fact of intervention that is problematic but the match between this intervention and the dynamics of existing negotiations, particularly when power is experienced through relations of dependence and nature.

Whatever the state does it will create ripples that will disturb the existing patterns of practices within the community. What is important is that these ripples flow into and work with the direction and intention of the internal dynamics of change.

9
Conclusion

While policies relating to inequalities within minorities rely on actor-led change, there seems to be very little attempt to examine the heterogeneity of power practices within communities. Existing critiques of actor-led change highlight the shortcomings of using internal actors to implement external policies and treat the reliance on the disadvantaged to help themselves as misguided (Shachar, 2008) and as failing to account for power relations (Madhok and Rai, 2012). But these critiques are based on particular interventions where the agent/actor is tasked to transplant externally inspired notions of self within their communities. Ayelet Shachar's (2008) study of how the state should support minority ethnic women subordinated through customs and practices within their communities in multicultural societies finds fault with policies that rely on vulnerable women to make claims for gender equality. She advocates greater regulation of minority communities by the state to change practices. Sumi Madhok and Shirin Rai's study of illiterate women volunteers trained to introduce gender equality policies into rural India warns that agency puts women at risk of retaliation. These studies provide important caveats to the practice of state-sponsored change through internal actors but takes for granted that the solution must come from outside the communities and actors themselves.

Perhaps one reason why studies of agency tend to focus on externally inspired change is the presumption that internal renegotiations cannot be a catalyst for change, that they are circular, confined to function within the limits of the dominant ideology they seek to challenge. In many societies inequalities are deeply rooted and woven into the fabric of social relations and this poses significant challenges for those seeking to direct their own lives in a way not supported within existing practices. The complex and embedded nature of this inequality makes social change slow. Responses recorded by ethnographers within these communities are often not aimed at overturning the inequality itself or ending the relationship but in giving the subordinated individual the best possible outcome through the relationship. However, new forms of knowledge and practice do emerge within communities.

Using Foucault's theory of power and the free subject within power relations as a springboard, I have explored empirical evidence of individual external resistance practices and internal renegotiations amongst a minority people in South Asia and third-generation South Asians in Britain and used these to examine the qualities of power relations there. While micro-power within the social field of the family and minority community and within the state provides a context in which socialization and interdependencies differentiate and organize individuals, individual efforts to alter practices to meet that individual's needs in the moment are ubiquitous in both communities. Internal renegotiations were prevalent within the family and the village where disputes and tensions arose, and within the state in disputes between Santal and non-Santal citizens. In all these spaces, inequalities were accepted to a large degree, either through relations of nature or dependence, but individuals sought to modify their effect.

While it is difficult to prove that non-compliance and counter-power have the ability to change practices, the potential impact they have on the evolution of practices is relevant to our discussion. Society is organic and its process of change responds constantly to internal and external pressures. We know from historical studies that it is at the level of social relations that most fundamental transformations in culture take place (Moore, 1973). Renegotiations within relationships are countered by those who stand to lose, but the tensions that arise from this interplay transform practices of the relationship and their meanings (Stoler, 1986). As we saw in Chapter 5, older women seemed to have achieved a different consciousness about domestic violence that transcended Santali customary practices. Through the passage of time and experience they had come to a new expectation of marital relations. The proposal by one woman that men should discuss problems with their wives rather than using violence was founded on logic gained through her experience of life. Voicing these views to me in front of other women may have interrupted old patterns of expectation for those who were listening or seeking an answer to their own questions about men's responsibilities to women.

External pressures for change can be important in this context. The porous boundaries of each normative social field (family, village and state) means that each exists and reiterates its existence in the context of others. The fact that all normative social fields are only ever semi-autonomous (Moore, 1973) and exist in constant interaction with their others provides a critical factor in assessing the potential of internal renegotiations to facilitate real change. There is a subtle distinction between this kind of process of influence and the insertion of new practices from external bodies that I mentioned at the start of this chapter. The state, as an alternative legal order, inevitably influences internal pressures for change, but it does so by altering the ways in which social practices relate to each other and their trajectories (Shove et al., 2012, p. 146). These influences do not simply transfer, but undergo transformation as they are subsumed within existing practices. Experiences from outside the social field are let in but get reinvented within the imaginary of the culture (Mihelich and Storrs, 2003).

It is common to see references to the importance of dialogue in literature relating to the juxtaposing of different legal orders in the modern nation state. The American-Sudanese jurist, Abdullahi An-Na-Im (2010), writing in the context of multiculturalism and legal accommodation, argues for an inclusive dialogue that seeks to find compatibilities between the two conflicting legal orders. This ideal of mutually respectful dialogue, I believe, is critical. Admittedly, in most cases it is unlikely that either legal order will willingly, or with ease, concede to find compatibilities. But the process of dialogue itself introduces ideas from the other that take on an organic life of their own. Respect for the other's position and understanding can smooth this process. This needs very good dialogue of the sort that listens at least as much as it speaks.

Rather than seeking to regulate communities and provide exit for individuals within minority communities then, the state needs to invest in sharing ideas within communities, as part of a dialogue that allows practices within the state and the communities to change. We see the beginnings of this in the field of development studies. Studies of actor-led development (Burns et al., 2013) forefronting the experiences of the poor in the development process and anthropological and sociological analysis of development projects highlight the importance of engaging with local participants and the impact this can have on the success of the project (Cernea, 1991). Development agencies such as CARITAS, which worked in some of the villages where I stayed, have taken a first step in this direction by initiating programmes in the villages whereby women's committees meet weekly to hear from NGO workers about voting, hygiene, health and maternity practices advocated by the state. This gentle instruction makes no particular demands of the women and allows space for the women themselves to offer their own opinions and debate the merits and demerits of these practices.

In the 1970s, Sally Falk Moore suggested that, if state law was going to create social change, this had to happen through a reconfiguration of social relations within complex social and normative fields within society, existing semi-autonomously of the state. While anthropologists continue to investigate these places and legal anthropologists have made efforts to comprehend them, little progress has been made in understanding the latent potential for social reform from within. I want to invert the question of how policy creates change to say that change is a constant, policy can only hope to influence its direction. To do so it must engage with the existing forces endemic in power relations that agitate and provoke renegotiations in relationships. This engagement cannot rely on the individuals within these communities to seek assistance from the state as an alternative legal order. The presumption that all individuals will avail themselves of state assistance assumes that inequality is experienced as relations of force, and that those reaching out to the state will willingly disengage from the social relations in which their subordination arises.

The state must engage with the reality of relations of nature and dependence that represent the experiences of many individuals within minority communities. These power practices make recourse to the state to challenge practices within those communities less likely, but also provide a basis for a rich body of evidence that individuals are, from one moment to the next, seeking ways to adapt practices to best suit their needs within those relationships.

Glossary of Terms and Key Authors

adivasi means original inhabitant and is commonly used to refer to tribal people in South Asia (Hawkins, 1984). The term has taken on political meaning in the Indian subcontinent where its use to refer to chthonic people creates a platform to assert rights in international law associated with indigeneity.

Archer, William G, a British officer posted in rural areas of Bihar between 1931 and 1946. As Deputy Commissioner of the Santal Parganas he decided many cases involving Santals. While conducting his work, he came to the conclusion that, in any decision of the district court regarding civil suits where at least one of the parties was a Santal, Santal law should be applied. His book *Tribal Law and Justice: A Report on the Santal* (1984) was produced after official recommendation by the Santal Parganas Inquiry Committee and is the most comprehensive and most cited book on Santal law.

bhapla the Santal word meaning marriage, literally, the mutual strengthening of two families.

bhut the Santal word meaning ghost, referring to the interim status of the soul before it reaches spirit status.

biga a measurement of land – 1 biga in Bangladesh is equivalent to approximately one-third of an acre.

bitlaha a Santal ritual for excommunicating a Santal who has broken the rules of tribal endogamy or clan exogamy.

Bodding, Paul O, a missionary who spent 30 years in Mohulpahari in the Santal Parganas where he continued Reverend Skrefsrud's work and published more than 25 works on the Santal (Troisi, 1976, p. 4). Amongst these was a collection of Santal folktales in three volumes (Bodding, 1997). His final work before he died in 1938 was the translation of Skrefsrud's *Horkoren Mare Hapramko reak Katha* (*Traditions and Institutions of the Santals*) (Bodding, 1942). This book is a recounting of

Santal traditions and customs as told by an elderly man, referred to as a guru, named Kolean.

bongas spirits of the ancestors who are treated with respect in Santal traditions. The term is also used to refer to some spirits treated as deities, such as Marang Buru, the spirit of the great mountain remembered in their origin myth, which showed the Santal a path through as they sojourned across an impenetrable landscape where many had lost their lives.

bos a Santal word defined by Bodding as: 1. authority of, for example, the Manjhi or a parent; 2. the relationship of descendants, family lineage (generally agnate); 3. bos buda meaning one's race/genealogy or sept, such as *'Murmu bos budha kanae'* – 'I am of the Murmu clan/lineage' (Bodding, 2002, p. 345). See Somers' (1977, p. 79) description.

chaukidar a village police official.

clan a unilineal descent group with links to a common but uncertain ancestry.

diku the term used by adivasis to refer to non-adivasis.

FIR First Information Report, the police report that initiates a criminal case.

ghar jawae a son-in-law who lives with his wife's family and is entitled to inherit his father-in-law's property.

ghardi jawae a son-in-law who lives with and works for his in-laws without pay for a certain period after which he may receive an income or leave and set up home with his wife elsewhere.

gharonj the Santal word for a family or household.

gutias religious rites carried out once a year and usually dedicated to a single spirit ancestor.

hul an insurrection, a reference to the Santal insurrection against the British in 1855.

khas land government owned land, which is leased to people to cultivate annually.

Kolean a Santal elder interviewed by a missionary, Reverend Skrefsrud, in 1871. Kolean was from Pabea in Manbhum district of Santal Parganas. His words were taken down verbatim by Skrefsrud and later translated by Bodding. Skrefsrud told Bodding that he had hunted widely among the Santals for a man who knew his people and their customs and Kolean was without comparison the best authority he had come across (Bodding, 1942, p. 1). Bodding admits that having been passed down orally over several generations there may not be complete conformity between this text and others. He also admits that some of Kolean's statements differ from what was known about the custom in the Santal Parganas at the time it was written because Kolean had emigrated there from the west. Nevertheless, this text is the fullest indigenous account of information on the traditions and customs of the tribe, and one of the few records of the narrative of a Santal elder on the subject. It is frequently referred to by judges where Santal customs are in dispute (Troisi, 1976, p. 3).

oaris describes Santal family-related ties of a financial nature which provide a shared interest in goods and bind family members together, such as the bride-price. Bodding (2002, vol. IV, p. 447) defines the oaris as a 'claimant'.

paris refers to clan-related ties.

raiyat a person who has gained a right to hold land for the purpose of cultivation (by themselves, a relative or paid worker). A successor may inherit this right.

raiyati land describes land that belongs or belonged in the past to a landowner who permits or permitted people to reside and work on it as tenant farmers. Some tenant farmers farmed the land for a short time and gave part of their incomes to the landowner as payment. Others farmed land for longer periods and gained title rights to the land under legislation during British rule and after independence. However, this was not common in adivasi areas and living on raiyati land has left some tenant farmers vulnerable to land-grabbing.

sept *see* clan

sindur vermillion or 'red lead' used during marriage ceremonies.

Skrefsrud, Reverend Lars Olsen, a Norwegian missionary of the Lutheran Church who lived in the Santal Parganas from 1867 until his death in 1907 (Troisi, 1976, p. 3). Skrefsrud was keen to take down a record of customs that had been passed down orally from teacher (guru) to disciple over generations, which he claimed was a practice that had fallen into disuse.

zamindars landowners responsible for collecting land revenues on behalf of the ruling elite. They would keep a percentage of the revenue for themselves in payment for their services. The position was abolished in India in 1950 but the term is still used to refer to landowners.

Bibliography

Abrahams, R (1996) 'Vigilantism: Order and Disorder on the Frontiers of the State' in O Harris (ed.), *Inside and Outside the Law: Anthropological Studies of Authority and Ambiguity* (London: Routledge)

Abu-Lughod, L (1990) 'The Romance of Resistance: Tracing Transformations of Power through Bedouin Women' 17 *American Ethnologist* 41–55

Adas, M (1986) 'From Footdragging to Flight: The Evasive History of Peasant Avoidance Protest in South and South-East Asia' 13(2) *Journal of Peasant Studies* 64–86

Agarwal, B (1997) '"Bargaining" and Gender Relations: Within and Beyond the Household' 3 *Feminist Economics* 1–51

Ahmad, F (2006) 'The Scandal of "arranged marriages" and the pathologisation of BrAsian families' in N Ali, V S Kalra and S Sayyid (eds), *A Postcolonial People: South Asians in Britain* (London: Hurst)

Ain O Salish Kendra, Bangladesh Legal Aid and Services Trust and ODHIKAR (1997) *Human Rights in Bangladesh 1996* (Dhaka: University Press Ltd)

Ali, A (1998) *Santals of Bangladesh* (Midnapur: Institute of Social Research and Applied Anthropology)

Allen, A (2000) 'The Anti-subjective Hypothesis: Michel Foucault and the Death of the Subject' 31 *The Philosophical Forum* 113–30

Anderson, M (2003) *Access to Justice and Legal Process: Making Legal Institutions Responsive to Poor People in LDCs* IDS Working Paper 178 (Sussex: Institute of Development Studies)

Anitha, S and A Gill (2009) 'Coercion, Consent and the Forced Marriage Debate in the UK' 17 *Feminist Legal Studies* 165–84

An-Na'Im, A (2000) *Forced Marriage* (unpublished report) (London: Centre of Islamic and Middle Eastern Law, SOAS) www.soas.ac.uk/honourcrimes/resources/file55689.pdf

An-Na'Im, A (2010) 'The Compatibility Dialectic: Mediating the Legitimate Coexistence of Islamic Law and State Law' 73(1) *Modern Law Review* 1–29

Anwar, A (1984) 'The Question of Tribal Identity and Integration in Bangladesh' in M S Qureshi (ed.), *Tribal Cultures in Bangladesh* (Rajshahi: Institute of Bangladesh Studies)

Anwar, M (1998) *Between Cultures: Continuity and Change in the Lives of Young Asians* (New York: Routledge)
Ara, S, N Sandoval, M M Amin and A Clemett (2007) 'Institutional Analysis for Wastewater Agriculture and Sanitation in Rajshahi, Bangladesh' WASPA ASIA (Wastewater, Agriculture and Sanitation for Poverty Alleviation in Asia) citing compliance with the government of Bangladesh's (1976) 'The Rajshahi Town Development Authority Ordinance' www.ngof.org/nrc/reports/Asia%20Report-5.pdf
Archer, W G (1974) *The Hill of Flutes: Life, Love and Poetry in Tribal India – A Portrait of the Santals* (London: George Allen & Unwin Ltd)
Archer, W G (1984) *Tribal Law and Justice: A Report on the Santal* (New Delhi: Concept Publishing Company) (published under the authority of the Bihar Government)
Ashley, C and Sustainable Livelihood in Southern Africa Team (2003) 'Right Talk and Rights Practice: Challenges for Southern Africa' 34(3) *IDS Bulletin* 97–111
Austin-Broos, D J (1996) '"Two Laws", Ontologies, Histories: Ways of Being Aranda Today' 7(3) *Australian Journal of Anthropology* 1–20
Awasthi, S K (2002) *The Prevention of Witch (Daain) Practices Act, 1999* (Allahabad: Rajpal & Co.)
Bailey, F G (1971) 'Gifts and Poison' in F G Bailey (ed.), *Gifts and Poison: The Politics of Reputation* (Oxford: Basil Blackwell)
Ballard, R (1994) 'Introduction: The Emergence of Desh Pardesh' in R Ballard (ed.), *Desh Pardesh: The South Asian Presence in Britain* (London: Hurst)
Ballard, R (2006) 'Forced Marriage: Just Who is Conspiring against Whom?' conference paper, University of Roehampton, 12 January 2006 www.casas.org.uk/papers/networks.html
Bandyopadhyay, P K (1999) *Tribal Situation in Eastern India: Customary Laws Among Border Bengal Tribes* (Calcutta: Subarnarekha)
Banerjee, S (1981) *Impact of Industrialisation on the Tribal Population of Jharia-Ranigung Coal Field Areas* (Calcutta: Anthropological Survey of India)
Barkat, A, S U Zaman, A Rahman and A Poddar (1997) *Political Economy of the Vested Property Act in Rural Bangladesh* (Dhaka: Association for Land Reform and Development)
Barman, D C and M S Neo (2012) 'Human Rights Report 2011 on Indigenous Peoples in Bangladesh' (Dhaka: Kapaeeng Foundation) http://kapaeeng.org/wp-content/uploads/2012/06/Human-rights-report-2011.pdf
Baskey, B N (2002) *The Tribes of West Bengal* (Kolkata: Subarnarekha)
Batra, S L (1999) *Study of Land Alienation of Tribals In Dumka and Ranchi Districts of Bihar* (New Delhi: Council for Social Development)
Baxi, U (1986) 'Discipline, Repression and Legal Pluralism' in P Sack and E Minchin (eds), *Legal Pluralism: Proceedings of the Canberra Law Workshop VII* (Canberra: Australian National University)
Becker, G (1981) *A Treatise on the Family* (Cambridge MA: Harvard University Press)
Benda-Beckmann, F Von (1981) 'Forum Shopping and Shopping Forums: Dispute Processing in a Minangkabau Village in West Sumatra' 19 *Journal of Legal Pluralism* 117–59
Besra, B D (1995) *Problems and Precedents in Santal Female Succession in Santal Parganas* (Dumka: Santal Social Institute)

Besra, B D (2002) *Santal Laws: Marriage, Succession, Adoption, Guardianship*, draft circulated for discussion (Jamtara: Santal Education Institute) (copy with author)

Bhabha, H (1990) 'The Third Space: Interivew with Homi Bhaba' in J Rutherford (ed.), *Identity: Community, Culture, Difference* (London: Lawrence & Wishart)

Bhattacharya, P K (c. 1991) *Witchcraft Among the Santals: A Study of Fifty Cases in Three Districts of West Bengal* (Kolkata: LAMP)

Biswas, P C (1956) *Santals of the Santal Parganas* (Delhi: Bharatiy & Adimjati Sevak Sangh)

Bodding, P O (c. 1920) 'Some Remarks on the Position of Women Among the Santals' 2(III) *Journal of the Bihar and Orissa Research Society* 239–49

Bodding, P O (1942) *Traditions and Institutions of the Santals*, translated from the Santal, L O Skrefsrud (1887) *Horkoren Mare Hapramko Reak Katha* (New Delhi: Bahumkhi Prakashan)

Bodding, P O (1997) *Santal Folk Tales* vols I, II and III (New Delhi: Gyan Publishing House) (originally published 1925)

Bodding, P O (2002) *A Santal Dictionary* vols I–V (New Delhi: Gyan Publishing House) (originally published in Oslo 1932–1936)

Bouez, S (1985) *Reciprocite et Hierarchie: L'Alliance chez les Ho et les Santal de l'Inde* (Paris: Societe D'Ethnographie)

Bourdieu, P (1977) *Outline of a Theory of Practice* (Cambridge: Cambridge University Press) (reprinted 2008)

Bourdieu, P (1984) *Distinction: A Social Critique of the Judgement of Taste* (London: Routledge)

Bourdieu, P (1992) *The Logic of Practice* (Cambridge: Polity Press)

Bouysse-Cassagne, T (1996) 'In Praise of Bastards: The Uncertainties of Mestizo Identity in Sixteenth- and Seventeenth-Century Andes' in O Harris (ed.), *Inside and Outside the Law: Anthropological Studies of Authority and Ambiguity* (London: Routledge)

Burns, D, E Lopez-Franco, T Shahrokh and J Wheeler (2013) *Work with Us: How People and Organisations Can Catalyse Sustainable Change* IDS report www.ids.ac.uk/files/dmfile/Workwithus_Howpeopleandorganisationscancatalysesustainablechange FINAL.pdf

Butler, J (1993) *Bodies that Matter* 2011 edn (Oxford and New York: Routledge)

Butler, J (2010) 'Performative Agency' 3(2) *Journal of Cultural Economy* 147–61

Caldwell, R (2007) 'Agency and Change: Re-evaluating Foucault's Legacy' 14(6) *Organization* 769–91

Castelfranchi, C (2003) 'The Micro-Macro Constituition of Power' 18–19 *ProtoSociology: An International Journal of Interdisciplinary Research* 208–65

Cernea, M (1991) *Putting People First: Sociological Variables in Rural Development* (Oxford: Oxford University Press)

Chattopadhyay, K P (1979) 'Santal Sibs: Their Transitional History and Observed Inter-Marriage Frequencies' in J Troisi (ed.), *The Santal: Readings in Tribal Life* (Delhi: Indian Social Institute)

Chaudhuri, A B (1987) *The Santals: Religion and Rituals* (New Delhi: Ashish Publishing House)

Chaudhury, R P C (1961) 'Bitlaha, a Santhal Ritual' LII *Quarterly Journal of the Mythic Society* 1

Chiba, M (1998) 'Other Phases of Legal Pluralism in the Contemporary World' 11(3) *Ratio Juris* 228–45
Claessen, H J M and P Skalnik (1978) 'The Early State: Theories and Hypotheses' in H Claessen and P Skalnik (eds), *The Early State* (The Hague: Mouton Publishers)
Cohen, P N and D MacCartney (2004) 'Inequality and the Family' in J Scott, J Treas and M Richards (eds), *The Blackwell Companion to the Sociology of Families* (Oxford: Blackwell Publishing)
Comaroff, J (1985) *Body of Power, Spirit of Resistance: The Culture and History of a South African People* (Chicago: University of Chicago Press)
Culshaw, W J (1942) 'The "Folk Consciousness" of the Santals' in J P Mills, B S Buha, K P Chattopadhayay, D N Majumbar and A Aiyappan (eds), *Essays in Anthropology* (Lucknow: Maxwell Co.)
Curtis, R (1986) 'Household and Family in Theory on Inequality' 51 *American Sociological Review* 2
Das, A K (1967) 'Scientific Analysis of "Santal" Social System' 6(1–2) *Bulletin of the Cultural Research Institute* (West Bengal) 5–8
Das, U K (1996) 'Ethnic Communities of North Bengal Face Uncertain Future' 2 *Earth Touch* 37–40
Day, S (1996) 'The Law and the Market: Rhetorics of Exclusion and Inclusion among London Prostitutes' in O Harris (ed.), *Inside and Outside the Law: Anthropological Studies of Authority and Ambiguity* (London: Routledge)
Delsing, R (1991) 'Sovereign and Disciplinary Power: A Foucaultian Analysis of the Chilean Women's Movement' in K Davis, M Leijenaar and J Oldersma (eds), *The Gender of Power* (London: Sage Publications)
Ekka, A (2000) 'Jharkhand Tribals: Are They Really a Minority?' *Economic and Political Weekly*, 30 December, 4610
Fiske, J and P J Ginn (2000) 'Discourse and Defiance: Law, Healing, and Implications of Communities in Resistance' 45 *Journal of Legal Pluralism* 115–35
Fitzpatrick, P (1988) 'The Rise and Rise of Informalism' in R Matthews (ed.), *Informal Justice?* (Middlesex: Sage Contemporary Criminology)
Foucault, M (1977) *Discipline and Punish* (London: Penguin Books)
Foucault, M (1980) 'Lecture Two: 14 January 1976' in C Gordon (ed.), *Power/Knowledge: Selected Interviews and Other Writings 1972–1977* (Harlow: Longman)
Foucault, M (1981) *The History of Sexuality vol. 1: The Will to Knowledge* (London: Pelican Books)
Foucault, M (1988) 'The Ethic of Care for the Self as a Practice of Freedom' in J Bernauer and D Rasmussen (eds), *The Final Foucault* (Cambridge MA: MIT Press)
Foucault, M (1994a) 'Truth and Power', interview of June 1976, in J D Faubion (ed.), *Power: Essential Works of Foucault 1954–1984* vol. 3 (London: Penguin Books)
Foucault, M (1994b) 'The Subject and Power' English translation from 1982, in J D Faubion (ed.), *Power: Essential Works of Foucault 1954–1984* vol. 3 (London: Penguin Books)
Fraser, N (2000) 'Rethinking Recognition' 3 (May/June) *New Left Review* 107–20
Fraser, N and A Honneth (2003) *Redistribution or Recognition: A Political–Philosophical Exchange* (London: Verso)

Furer-Haimendorf, C (1985) *Tribal Populations and Cultures of the India Sub-Continent* (Leiden Koln: EJ Brill)

Galanter, M (1981) 'Justice in Many Rooms' 19 *Journal of Legal Pluralism* 1

Galanter, M (1984) 'Worlds of Deals: Using Negotiation to Teach about Legal Process' 34 *Journal of Legal Education* 268

Gangoli, G, A Razak and M McCarry (2006) *Forced Marriage and Domestic Violence among South Asian Communities in North East England* (Bristol: University of Bristol, School for Policy Studies)

Gausdal, J (1960) *The Santal Khuts, Contribution to Animistic Research* (Oslo: Aschehoug & Co.)

Gautam, M K (1977) *In Search of an Identity: A Case of the Santal of Northern India* (Leiden: Rijksmuseum voor Volkenkunde)

Genovese, E (1976) *Roll, Jordan, Roll: The World the Slaves Made* (New York: Vintage Books)

Ghosh, G K and S Ghosh (2000) *Legends of Origin of the Castes and Tribes of Eastern India* (Calcutta: Firma KLM Private Ltd)

Gluckman, M (1955) *The Judicial Process among the Barotse of Northern Rhodesia* (Manchester: Manchester University Press)

Government of Jharkhand (Official Website) 'About the State: Jharkhand at a Glance' www.jharkhand.gov.in/AboutState_fr.html

Gramsci, A (1971) *Selections from Prison Notebooks of Antonio Gramsci*, Q Hoare and G Nowell Smith (eds) (London: Lawrence & Wishart)

Griffiths, A (1990) 'The Woman Question in Kwena Family Disputes' 30–31 *Journal of Legal Pluralism* 223–54

Griffiths, J (1985) 'Introduction' in A Allott and G Woodman (eds), *People's Law and State Law: The Bellagio Papers* (Dordrecht: Foris Publications)

Griffiths, J (1986) 'What is Legal Pluralism?' 24 *Journal of Legal Pluralism and Unofficial Law* 1–56

Griffiths, J (2006) 'The Idea of Sociology of Law and its Relation to Law and to Sociology' in M Freeman (ed.), *Law and Sociology* (Oxford: University Press)

Guha, R (1983) *Elementary Aspects of Peasant Insurgency in Colonial India* (Delhi: Oxford University Press)

Guha, R (1997) *Dominance without Hegemony: History and Power in Colonial India* (Cambridge MA: Harvard University Press)

Harris, O (1996) *Inside and Outside the Law: Anthropological Studies of Authority and Ambiguity* (London: Routledge)

Hawkins, R E (1984) *Common Indian Words in English* (New Delhi: Oxford University Press)

Haynes, D and G Prakash (1991) 'Introduction: The Entanglement of Power and Resistance' in D Haynes and G Prakash (eds), *Contesting Power: Resistance and Everyday Social Relations in South Asia* (Delhi: Oxford University Press)

Hellum, A (1995) 'Actor Perspective on Gender and Legal Pluralism in Africa' in H Petersen and H Zahle (eds), *Legal Polycentricity: Consequences of Pluralism in Law* (Aldershot: Dartmouth)

Hembrom, T (1996) *The Santals: Anthropological–Theological Reflections on Santali and Biblical Creation Traditions* (Calcutta: Puthi Pustak)

Herring, R (1981) 'Embedded Production Relations and the Rationality of Tenant Quiescence in Tenure Reform' 8(2) *Journal of Peasant Studies* 131–72

Hester, M, K Chantler, G Gangoli, J Davgon, S Sharma and A Singleton (2008) 'Forced Marriage: The Risk Factors and the Effect of Raising the Minimum Age for a Sponsor, and of Leave to Enter the UK as a Spouse or Fiance(é)' Home Office www.endviolenceagainstwomen.org.uk

HM Government (no date) *A Survivor's Handbook* www.mensadviceline. org.uk/data/files/forced_marriage__survivors_handbook.pdf (original edn); www.gov.uk/government/publications/survivors-handbook (updated edn)

HM Government (2000) *A Choice by Right: The Report of the Working Group on Forced Marriage* (London: HMSO)

HM Government (2006) *Forced Marriage: A Wrong Not a Right* (London: HMSO)

HM Government (2008) *The Right to Choose: Multi-Agency Statutory Guidance for Dealing with Forced Marriage* (London: HMSO) (revised 2010)

HM Government (2012) *Forced Marriage – Consultation: A Summary of Responses* (London: HMSO)

HM Government (2013) *Anti-Social Behaviour, Crime and Policing Bill*, Public Bill Committee, Hansard, 9 July 2013 (morning) www.publications.parliament. uk/pa/cm201314/cmpublic/antisocialbehaviour/130709/am/130709s01.htm

Hoare, Q and G Smith (1971) *Selections from Prison Notebooks of Antonio Gramsci* (London: Lawrence & Wishart)

Horowitz, D L (2001) *The Deadly Ethnic Riot* (California: University of California Press)

Hossain, K T K and S Z Sadequ (1984) 'The Santals of Rajshahi: A Study in Social and Cultural Change' in M S Qureshi (ed.), *Tribal Cultures in Bangladesh* (Rajshahi: Institute of Bangladesh Studies)

Hunter, W W (1868) *The Annals of Rural Bengal* West Bengal District Gazetteers, Government of West Bengal (Calcutta: K R Biswas) (reprinted 1996)

Jenkins, R (1996) *Social Identity* (London: Routledge)

Kabeer, N (2002) *Citizenship and the Boundaries of the Acknowledged Community: Identity, Affiliation and Exclusion* IDS Working Paper 171 (Sussex: Institute of Development Studies)

Katz, E (2010) 'The Intra-Household Economics of Voice and Exit' 3(3) *Feminist Economics* 25–46

Khan, B U and M M Rahman (2011) 'Human and Minority Rights in Bangladesh' in R Hofmann and U Caruso (eds), *Minority Rights in South Asia* (Frankfurt: Peter Lang GmbH)

Khanum, N (2008) *Forced Marriage, Family Cohesion and Community Engagement: National Learning through a Case Study of Luton* (Watford: Equality in Diversity/Bartham Press) www.reducingtherisk.org.uk/cms/sites/reducingtherisk/ files/folders/resources/hbv_forced_marriage/FM_family_cohesion_community_ engagement.pdf

Kochar, V K (1963) 'Kinship Terms and Usages among the Santals of Bolpur Area, Birbhum' 12(1–2) *Bulletin of the Anthropological Survey of India* 47–58

Kochar, V K (1964) 'Attributes of Societal Status among the Santals' 3(3–4) *Bulletin of the Cultural Research Institute* 20–9

Kochar, V K (1966) 'Village Organization among the Santals' 5(1–2) *Bulletin of the Cultural Research Institute* 11–19

Kochuchira, J (2000) *Political History of Santal Parganas from 1765 to 1872* (New Delhi: Inter-India Publications)

Kumar, S (1997) 'In Bihar Witch Hunting is Not Just a Metaphor' 18 *Exchanges: A Quarterly Publication of ActionAid India* (no page nos)

Kymlicka, W and W Norman (2000) 'Introduction' in W Kymlicka and W Norman (eds), *Citizenship in Diverse Societies* (Oxford: Oxford University Press)

Layton, R (1997) *An Introduction to Theory in Anthropology* (Cambridge: Cambridge University Press)

Levi-Strauss, C (1969) *The Elementary Structures of Kinship* revised edition, J H Bell (trans.), J R Sturmer and R Needham (eds) (Boston: Beacon Press)

Lewis, P (2007) *Young, British and Muslim* (London: Continuum International Publishing Group)

Liddle, J and S Rai (1998) 'Feminism, Imperialism and Orientalism: The Challenge of the "Indian Woman"' 7(4) *Women's History Review* 495–520

Madan, T N (1998) 'Coping with Ethnicity in South Asia: Bangladesh, Punjab and Kashmir Compared' 21(5) *Ethnic and Racial Studies* 970–89

Madhok, S and S M Rai (2012) 'Agency, Injury, and Transgressive Politics in Neoliberal Times' 37(3) *Signs* 645–69

Mahapatra, S (1976) 'The Insider Diku: Boundary Rules and Marginal Man in Santal Society' 56 *Man in India* 1

Mahapatra, S (1986) *Modernization and Ritual: Identity and Change in Santal Society* (Calcutta: Oxford University Press)

Malinowski, B (1939) 'The Group and the Individual in Functional Analysis' 44(6) *American Journal of Sociology* 938–64

Maloney, C (1984) 'Tribes of Bangladesh and Synthesis of Bengali Culture' in M S Qureshi (ed.), *Tribal Cultures in Bangladesh* (Rajshahi: Institute of Bangladesh Studies)

Manning, C (1999) *God Gave us the Right: Conservative Catholic, Evangelical Protestant, and Othodox Jewish Women Grapple with Feminism* (New Brunswick: Rutgers University Press)

Mardi, S (1997) 'The Santal Law' XIX(4) *Bulletin of the Cultural Research Institute*

McCue, M L (2008) *Domestic Violence: A Reference Handbook* (California: ABC-CLIO Inc.)

McNay, L (1991) *Foucault and Feminism: Power, Gender and the Self* (Cambridge: Polity Press)

McNay, L (2000) *Gender and Agency: Reconfiguring the Subject in Feminist and Social Theory* (Cambridge: Polity Press)

Medeirost, C L (1984) 'Kwandu Law: The Evolution of a Juridical System among an Herero People of South-West Angola' 28(1–2) *Journal of African Law* 80–9

Melissaris, E (2004) 'The More the Merrier? A New Take on Legal Pluralism' 13(1) *Social and Legal Studies* 57–79

Melissaris, E (2009) *Ubiquitous Law: Legal Theory and the Space for Legal Pluralism* (London: Ashgate)

Merry, S E (1988) 'Legal Pluralism' 22(5) *Law and Society Review* 869–96

Merry, S E (2009) 'Relating to the Subjects of Human Rights: The Culture of Agency in Human Rights Discourse' in M Freeman and D Napier (eds), *Law and Anthropology* Current Legal Issues Series (Oxford: Oxford University Press)

Mihelich, J and D Storrs (2003) 'Higher Education and the Negotiated Process of Hegemony: Embedded Resistance among Mormon Women' 17 *Gender and Society* 404–22

Mitchell, T (1990) 'Everyday Metaphors of Power' 19 *Theory and Society* 545–77

Modood, T, R Berthoug, J Lakey, J Nazroo, P Smith, S Virdee and S Beishon (eds) (1997) *Ethnic Minorities in Britain: Diversity and Disadvantage* (London: Policy Studies Institute)

Mohsin, A (2000) 'State Hegemony' in R D Roy, A Mohsin, M Guhathakurta, P Tripura and P Gain (eds), *The Chittagong Hill Tracts: Life and Nature at Risk* (Dhaka: Society for Environment and Human Development)

Mohsin, A (2003) *The Chittagong Hill Tracts, Bangladesh: On the Difficult Road to Peace* (London: Lynne Rienner Publishers Inc.)

Mondal, A (2008) *Young British Muslim Voices* (Oxford: Greenwood World Publishing)

Moore, D (1998) 'Subaltern Struggles and the Politics of Place: Remapping Resistance in Zimbabwe's Eastern Highlands' 13(3) *Cultural Anthropology* 344–81

Moore, S F (1973) 'Law and Social Change: The Semi-Autonomous Social Field as an Appropriate Subject of Study' 7 *Law and Society Review* 719

Moore, S F (1978) *Law as Process: An Anthropological Approach* (London: LIT James Currey with the International African Institute)

Moore, S F (2001) 'Certainties Undone: Fifty Turbulent Years of Legal Anthropology, 1949–1999' 7 *Journal of the Royal Anthropological Institute* 95–116

Nader, L (1990) *Harmony Ideology: Justice and Control in a Zapotec Mountain Village* (Stanford CA: Stanford University Press)

Naqavi, S M (1979) 'Santal Murders' 23 *Man in India* 3, reproduced in J Troisi (ed.), *The Santal: Readings in Tribal Life* (Delhi: Indian Social Institute)

Newman, P (2010) 'Glimpses of Exploited Jharkhand' posted 17 June 2010 on South Asia Speaks http://southasiaspeaks.wordpress.com/2010/06/17/glimpses-of-exploited-jharkhand

Okin, S (1998) 'Feminism and Multiculturalism: Some Tensions' 108(4) *Ethics* 661–84

O'Malley, L S S (1910) *Bengal District Gazetteers: Santal Parganas* (Calcutta: Bengal Secretariat Book Depot)

O'Malley, L S S (1916) *Bengal District Gazetteers: Rajshahi* (Calcutta: Bengal Secretariat Book Depot)

Ong, A (1988) 'Colonialism and Modernity: Feminist Re-presentations of Women in Non-Western Societies' 3(4) *Inscriptions* 79–93

Ortner, S (1995) 'Resistance and the Problem of Ethonogrphic Refusal' 37 *Comparative Studies in Society and History* 173–93

Philips, A (2007) *Multiculturalism without Culture* (Oxford: Princeton University Press)

Phillips, A and M Dustin (2004) 'UK Initiative on Forced Marriage: Regulation, Dialogue and Exit' 52 *Political Studies* 531–51

Prakash, A (2001) *Jharkhand: Politics of Development and Identity* (Hyderabad: Orient Longman Ltd)

Putnam, R D (1993) *Making Democracy Work: Civic Traditions in Modern Italy* (New Jersey: Princeton University Press)

Rao, N (2005a) 'Questioning Women's Solidarity: The Case of Land Rights, Santal Parganas, Jharkhand, India' 41(3) *Journal of Development Studies* 353–75

Rao, N (2005b) 'Displacement from Land: Case of Santhal Parganas' 40(41) *Economic and Political Weekly* 4439–42

Rao, N (2008) *'Good Women Do Not Inherit Land': Politics of Land and Gender in India* (New Delhi: Social Science Press and Orient Blackswan)

Ray, P C (1975) *Socio-Cultural Process and Psychological Adaptation of the Santal* (Calcutta: Anthropological Survey of India, Government of India)

Razak, S (2004) 'Imperiled Muslim Women, Dangerous Muslim Men and Civilised Europeans: Legal and Social Responses to Forced Marriages' 12 *Feminist Legal Studies* 129–74

Reckwitz, A (2002) 'Toward a Theory of Social Practices: A Development in Culturalist Theorising' 5(2) *European Journal of Social Theory* 243–63

Risley, H H (1891) *The Tribes and Castes of Bengal* vol. II (Calcutta: P Mukherjee) (reprinted 1998)

Risseeuw, C (1988) *The Fish Don't Talk about the Water: Gender Transformation, Power and Resistance among Women in Sri Lanka* (Leiden: EJ Brill)

Roberts, S (2005) 'After Government? On Representing Law without the State' 68 *Modern Law Review* 1–24

Roy, P N (1997) 'The Problem of Female Inheritance in Santhal Tribal Society' 18 *Exchanges* (no page numbers)

Roy, R D, A Mohsin, M Guhathakurta, P Tripura and P Gain (2000) *The Chittagong Hill Tracts: Life and Nature at Risk* (Dhaka: Society for Environment and Human Development)

Sachchidananda (1955) 'Bitlaha' 9(1) *Eastern Anthropologist* 42–7

Sachchidananda (1969) 'Bitlaha: Analysis of a Santal Institutions' 49(3) *Man In India* 281–88

Saha, N K (1969) 'Husband, Wife and Children in a Santal Village: A Study on Role Analysis' 8(3–4) *Bulletin of the Cultural Research Institute (West Bengal)* 97–102

Samad, Y and J Eade (2001) *Community Perceptions of Forced Marriage* (unpublished) www.portmir.org.uk/assets/pdfs/community-perceptions-of-forced-marriage.pdf

Sanghera, J (2007) *Shame* (London: Hodder & Stoughton)

Santos, B de Sousa (1977) 'The Law of the Oppressed: The Construction and Reproduction of Legality in Pasargada' 12(1) *Law and Society Review* 5–126

Santos, B de Sousa (1995) *Toward a New Common Sense: Law, Science and Politics in the Paradigmatic Transition* (New York: Routledge)

Santos, B de Sousa (2002) *Toward a New Legal Common Sense: Law, Globalisation, and Emancipation* 2nd edn (London: Butterworths)

Sattar, A (1983) *In the Sylvan Shadows* (Dhaka: Bangla Academy)

Scott, J (1985) *Weapons of the Weak: Everyday Forms of Peasant Resistance* (New Haven and London: Yale University Press)

Scott, J (1986) 'Everyday Forms of Peasant Resistance' 13(2) *Journal of Peasant Studies* 5–35

Sen, A (1990) 'Gender and Cooperative Conflicts' in Irene Tinker (ed.), *Persistent Inequalities: Women and World Development* (Oxford: Oxford University Press)

Sen, N (c. 2002) *Citizenship as Practice: Meanings and Identities of Citizenship amongst Santals in Jharkhand* conference paper, 14 March (Dumka: PRIA/Agrarian Assistance Association)

Sen, J, S C Sinha and S Panchbhai (1969) 'The Concept of Diku among the Tribes of Chotanagpur' 49(2) *Man in India* 121–38

Shachar, A (2001) *Multicultural Jurisdictions: Cultural Differences and Women's Rights* (Cambridge: Cambridge University Press)

Shachar, A (2008) 'Privatising Diversity' 9 *Theoretical Inquiries in Law* 573

Shah, A (2010) *In the Shadows of the State: Indigenous Politics, Environmentalism, and Insurgency in Jharkhand, India* (Durham and London: Duke University Press)

Shakil, M and R Hasnat (2013) 'Systematic Persecution of Religious Minorities: Bangladesh Perspective' 7(3) *IOSR Journal of Humanities and Social Science* 9–17

Shariff, F (2007) 'Micro Level Factors in the Pursuit of Social Justice: A Study of Power Relations in the Santal Village' 2007(1) *Law, Social Justice and Global Development Journal* (LGD) 1–23

Shariff, F (2008) 'Power Relations and Legal Pluralism: An Examination of "strategies of struggles" amongst the Santal Adivasi of India and Bangladesh' 57 *Journal of Legal Pluralism* 1–43

Shariff, F (2012) 'Towards a Transformative Paradigm in the UK Response to Forced Marriage: Excavating Community Engagement and Subjectivising Agency' 21(4) *Social and Legal Studies* 549–65

Shariff, F (2013) 'Harmony Ideology Revisited: Spatial Geographies of Hegemony and Disputing Strategies amongst the Santal' 45(1) *Journal of Legal Pluralism* 124–43

Shariff, F (2014) 'Establishing Field Relations through Shared Ideology: Insider Self-positioning as a Precarious/Productive Foundation in Multisited Studies' 26(1) *Field Methods* 3–20

Shaw, A (2000) *Kinship and Continuity: Pakistani Families in Britain* (London and New York: Routledge)

Shove, E, M Pantzar and M Watson (2012) *The Dynamics of Social Practice: Everyday Life and How It Changes* (London: Sage)

Siddiqui, A (1972) *Bangladesh District Gazetteers: Dinajpur* (Dacca: Bangladesh Government Press)

Silvester, T (2003) *Wordweaving: The Science of Suggestion* (Cambridge: Quest Institute)

Singh, H and P Singh (2011) *Indian Administration* (Delhi: Pearson Education India)

Singh, K M, S S Meena, R K P Singh, A Kumar and A Kumar (2012) *Rural Poverty in Jharkhand, India: An Empirical Study Based on Panel Data* (New Delhi: ECARRCER: Patna and NCAP) Munich Personal RePEc Archive http://mpra.ub.uni-muenchen.de/45258/1/MPRA_paper_45258.pdf

Singh, S K (2000) 'Panchayats in Scheduled Areas' in *Status of Panchayati Raj in the States and Union Territories of India 2000* (New Delhi: Concept Publishing Co.)

Sinha, A C (1967) 'Leadership in a Tribal Society' 47(3) *Man in India* 222–7

Sinha, K K (2000) 'Bihar' in *Status of Panchayati Raj in the States and Union Territories of India 2000* (New Delhi: Concept Publishing Co.)

Sinha, S P (1990) *Santal Hul (Insurrection of Santal) 1855–56* (Ranchi: Bihar Tribal Welfare Research Institute for the Government of Bihar Welfare Department)

Snyder, F (1981) 'Colonialism and Legal Form: The Creation of Customary Law in Senegal' 49 *Journal of Legal Pluralism* 81

Somers, G (1977) *The Dynamics of Santal Traditions in a Peasant Society* (New Delhi: Abhinav Pulbications)

Stoler, A L (1986) 'Plantation Politics and Protest on Sumatra's East Coast' 13(2) *Journal of Peasant Studies* 124–43

Stone, J (1966) *Social Dimensions of Law and Justice* (London: Stevens & Sons Ltd)

Strathern, M (1985) 'Knowing Power and Being Equivocal: Three Melanesian Contexts' in R Fardon (ed.), *Power and Knowledge: Anthropological and Sociological Approaches* (Edinburgh: Scottish Academic Press)

Strauss, C and N Quinn (1997) *A Cognitive Theory of Cultural Meaning* (Cambridge: Cambridge University Press)

Strickland, P (2013) 'Forced Marriage' Standard Note to House of Commons, Home Affairs Section, SN/HA/1033 16 September

Tamanaha, B (1993) 'The Folly of the "Social Scinetific" Concept of Legal Pluralism' 20 *Journal of Law and Society* 192–217

Tamanaha, B (2000) 'A Non-Essentialist Version of Legal Pluralism' 27 *Journal of Law and Society* 296–32

Tamanaha, B (2001) *A General Jurisprudence of Law and Society* (Oxford: Oxford University Press)

Taylor, C, A Appiah, J Habermas, S Rockefeller, M Walzer, S Wolf and A Gutmann (eds) (1994) *Multiculturalism: Examining the Politics of Recognition* (Princeton NJ: Princeton University Press)

Teubner, G (1992) 'The Two Faces of Legal Pluralism' 13(5) *Cardozo Law Review* 1443–62

Thompson, E P (1963) *The Making of the English Working Class* (London: Gollancz)

Timm, Father R W (1991) *The Adivasis of Bangladesh* (London: Minority Rights Group International) 92/1

Troisi, J (1976) *The Santals: A Classified and Annotated Bibliography* (New Delhi: Manohar)

Troisi, J (1979) 'Social Organisation of a Santal Village: Expanding Socio-Economic Frontiers' 24 *Social Action* 4, reproduced in J Troisi (ed.), *The Santal: Readings in Tribal Life* (Delhi: Indian Social Institute)

Tuck, D R (1976) 'Santal Religion: Self-Identification and Socialization in the Sohrae-Harvest Festival' 56(3) *Man in India* 215–36

Vanderlinden, J (1989) 'Return to Legal Pluralism: Twenty Years Later' 28 *Journal of Legal Pluralism* 149–57

Wagner, R (1981) *The Invention of Culture* (Chicago and London: University of Chicago Press)

Wanitzek, U (1990) 'Legally Unrepresented Women Petitioners in the Lower Courts of Tanzania: A Case of Justice Denied?' 30–1 *Journal of Legal Pluralism* 255–71

Weber, M (1978) *Economy and Society* vol. 1, G Roth and C Wittich (eds) (Berkeley CA: University of California Press)
Westergaard, K (1986) *State and Rural Society in Bangladesh: A Study in Relationship* (New Delhi: Select Book Service Syndicate)
Whitaker, B (1982) *The Biharis in Bangladesh* 4th edn (London: Minority Rights Group)
Wikan, U (2000) 'Citizenship on Trial: Nadia's Case' 129(4) *Daedalus* 55–76
Wills, C (2001) 'Women, Domesticity and the Family: Recent Feminist Work in Irish Cultural Studies' 15(1) *Cultural Studies* 33–57
Wolf, E R (1990) 'Distinguished Lecture: Facing Power – Old Insights, New Questions' NS 92(3) *American Anthropologist* 586–96
Wolf, E R (1999) *Envisioning Power: Ideologies of Dominance and Crisis* (Berkeley and Los Angeles CA: University of California Press)
Wood, G (1994) *Bangladesh: Whose Ideas, Whose Interests?* (London: Intermediate Technology Publications)
Woodman, G (1998) 'Ideological Combat and Social Observation: Recent Debate about Legal Pluralism' 42 *Journal of Legal Pluralism* 21–59
Young, K, C Wolkowitz and R McCullagh (eds) (1981) *Of Marriage and the Market: Women's Subordination in International Perspective* (London: CSE)

Index

Abu-Lughod, Leila 5, 9, 115, 164
abuse
　domestic *see* domestic violence
　of power 37, 41, 86, 119, 123
actor-led change 8, 15, 128, 167, 169
Adithio 119–21, 134
adivasis 34n, 40, 43–5, 48, 49, 106
　Bangladesh 50n, 109, 124
　women 49, 87, 14
　see also land and rights
agency 4, 9, 12, 117, 123, 128, 142–4, 167
Anti-social Behaviour, Crime and Policing Act 149, 153

Bangladesh, war of independence 35, 39, 40–1, 43, 47, 109
bargaining power 52, 64, 91, 141, 150
beliefs, of Santal
　ancestors 6, 7, 36, 59, 68
　origin myth 3, 35–6, 53, 172
　see also bongas; division of labour; witchcraft
benefits 13, 14, 18, 20, 32, 42, 48, 51–2, 55, 64, 65, 73, 78, 83, 85, 101–8, 113–14, 121–2, 126, 133–4, 135, 151, 155, 156
bitlaha 118, 171
Bodding, Paul Olson 8, 171
bongas 64, 67, 70, 93–5, 172
Bourdieu, Pierre 103
　discourse 28, 138
　habitus 20, 136
　practice 8, 21, 130
British Asians 2, 154, 156, 164 *see also* diaspora
British rule 7, 13, 36–8, 39, 49, 88, 103, 109
Butler, Judith 21, 130–1, 133, 143

case studies
　diku thief 53–4, 111
　stolen ducks 76–8, 97–8, 140, 142
Christianity 11, 40, 43, 91, 109, 133, 134, 139
clan 35, 61–2, 64, 70, 72–6, 118, 172, 173
coercion 18, 19, 27, 146, 147, 152, 153
commitment 99, 111, 114, 135, 150, 151, 158–9
compromise 158, 163
Constitution of Bangladesh 43n, 44, 124
Constitution of India 41–2, 47, 48, 65
counter-power 14, 102–4, 106, 109, 121–2, 125, 128, 131, 133–6, 142, 143, 145, 161, 168
courts
　recourse to state
　　in forced marriage cases 158
　　by Santal 36, 65, 79–81, 84–5, 87–92, 103, 108–9, 125
　Santal system 49, 59, 61, 76–7, 81, 83–6, 98, 100–2, 131–3, 140, 142
criminality 32–3, 53
　forced marriage 149, 151–3
　in India and Bangladesh 37, 50, 54–5, 92, 124
　in Santal law 62, 67
　see also witchcraft; witch-hunting
culture 7–9, 17, 25, 43, 53, 97, 122–3, 130, 137–44, 168–9
　of Santal 118 *see also* Santal culture
　of South-Asian diaspora 148, 150, 155, 161

Dharma, Raja 103
diaspora, British-Asian 145, 146, 154
　see also settlement

187

Index

disadvantage 3, 9, 10, 14, 24, 34–5, 42, 45, 47, 65, 76, 79, 90, 99, 122, 133, 142, 160, 161
discourse *see* Bourdieu, Pierre
division of labour 13, 59, 62–3, 65–6, 78
domestic violence 54n, 80, 81–5, 91, 111, 113, 116, 132, 134, 136, 152
and forced marriage 151

East Pakistan 39–41, 55
education 42, 48, 50, 66, 70, 99, 140, 143–4, 155, 161, 164
embedded agency 143 *see also* agency
empowerment 141
enlightenment 122
ethnicity 25, 50
everyday resistance 115, 128, 134
exploitation 28, 37, 42, 128, 138

family inequalities
  gender inequality 63, 161
  generational inequality 155, 161
  see also division of labour
fear 45, 53, 123–5, 154
feminism 1, 9, 14, 115, 122, 125, 133, 142–3, 147
filial love 2, 149, 156
folk tales 53, 63, 81, 82, 115–16
Forced Marriage (Civil Protection) Act 149
Forced Marriage Unit 147, 153, 160
Foreign and Commonwealth Office (UK) 2, 3, 15, 147–8, 158, 160
Foucault, Michel
  agency 122, 125, 136, 168
  disciplinary power 19–20
  History of Sexuality, The 22
  panopticon 19
  power relations 22, 102
  self, the 122
  visibility 20

Gantzer Report 88

gender inequality *see* division of labour; family inequalities; witchcraft
Genovese, Eugene D 103
Gram Sabha 48
Gramsci, Antonio 18–19, 24–6, 47
  consciousness, theory of 23
  Prison Notebooks 18

Hara 120–1
harmony ideology 14, 97, 99
headman *see* manjhis
Hinduism 35, 43, 65, 88–9, 110, 139
honour 54n, 155, 156
housework *see* division of labour
Hul, Santal 38, 106, 172
human rights 2, 4, 6, 7, 9, 44, 89, 105, 122–3, 142

immigration 155, 158, 159
indigenous peoples *see* adivasis
Indo-Pakistan war 40
inheritance 85–90, 99
  Indian Supreme Court ruling 65, 87, 88
insurrection *see* Hul, Santal; Nachol insurrection
interlegality 31
Islam
  Bengal and 39, 43
  forced marriage and 157, 161–2

Jharkhand, Indian state of 42–3, 47, 48, 139
Jharkhand Mukti Morcha (JMM) 42

kinship 13, 46, 71–4, 139 *see also* Santal culture
Kolean 8, 60, 80, 94, 112–14, 172

land
  land-loss 38, 45, 105, 107, 109
  ownership of 36–41
  rights/disputes 54, 108–9
  see also inheritance

legal anthropology 3, 29, 92
legal orders 30–2, 80–1, 100, 133, 160, 165, 169
legal pluralism 3, 29–33, 131, 137
liberalism 46, 123, 142
life-cycle events 35, 59–62, 67, 155
literacy 42, 50
litigotiation 14, 91

Magli 87, 117, 141
manjhis 13, 49, 67–8, 80, 84, 132
 relations with state 49, 99
 voting 51–2
 wife of 69
 see also domestic violence; witchcraft
Mary 58, 83–5, 90–1, 111, 112, 116–18, 132, 140–1
micro-power 4, 12, 19, 101
migration 3, 35–41, 55, 139
minority rights 6–7, 41–5, 52
Mitchell, Timothy 19, 27–8, 115, 122, 143
Mitra, Ila 40n

Nachol insurrection 40
negotiation 5–6, 14–15, 24–6, 65–6, 91, 101, 115–16, 123, 127–32, 136–7, 142–3, 147, 150, 160–5, 168
Nepal 35
non-compliance 14, 102, 115–22, 128, 131, 133–7, 143, 161, 163

origin myth see beliefs, of Santal

Panchayat Raj 42, 47–9
paradigm shift 24
paris see clan
Partition (India–Pakistan) 39–40
patron–client relations 142
power
 practices 4, 6, 8–9, 129–42, 154–60
 product 20, 27, 103–15
 relations 4–5, 8–9, 22–6, 30, 101–3, 118, 123, 128–30, 155, 165

 see also Foucault, Michel; Gramsci, Antonio; micro-power; Santos, Boaventura de Sousa; Wolf, Eric R
 practices see power
pradhans 12, 49

rational subject 121–5
Rao, Nitya 63, 65, 86–90, 92, 99, 106–8, 117, 126, 132–3, 137
reciprocity 20
relations of dependence 14, 131, 133–6, 138, 144, 159, 160, 163, 165
relations of force 5, 14, 15, 129, 131, 132, 134, 142, 147, 150, 157, 159, 160, 161, 163, 165
relations of nature 14, 65, 128, 131, 136–7, 138, 142–3, 144, 147, 155, 156, 160–1, 163, 168
religion see Christianity; Hinduism; Islam
remuneration see salary
renegotiation see negotiation
resistance 4–6, 12–15, 22–9, 32, 33, 92, 101, 103, 115, 122, 127–31, 168
 see also everyday resistance
responsibilities, familial 66, 78, 90, 99, 118, 132, 155, 168
rights see Constitution of Bangladesh; Constitution of India; human rights; minority rights
 Santal customary see benefits
Risseeuw, Carla 28, 115, 138

salaries 119, 135, 142, 143, 164
Sama 117, 141
Santal culture
 clan structure see clan
 hierarchy 66–78
 kinship 73
 village officers 67–9
Santal customary rights see benefits
Santal insurrection 1855 see Hul, Santal
Santal Parganas 11, 12, 36–8, 48–51, 52, 55, 88, 99, 106–7

Santos, Boaventura de Sousa   30–1, 92, 130–1
Sapha   39, 40, 49, 91–2
Sathins   123, 141
Scheduled Tribes   41–2
Scott, James   27, 115, 128, 131, 135
semi-autonomous social field   31
sept   *see* clan
settlement
  of Santal   125
    in Bangladesh   138–41
    in India   136–8
  South Asians in Britain   155
sharecropping   11, 40n, 70, 107, 142
Skrefsrud, Reverend Lars Olsen   8, 60, 112, 171, 172, 173
slaves   103
social change   3, 4, 5, 14, 15, 128, 137, 143, 145, 167

spirits   *see* bongas
Suphol   53, 54
Supreme Court, Indian, ruling of   *see* inheritance law
symbolic violence   20, 103

village officers   3, 67–70, 87   *see also* Santal culture
violence   *see* domestic violence; symbolic violence

wages   *see* salary
wars   40 *see also* Hul, Santal
witchcraft   69, 76, 80, 85, 92–7, 100   *see also* witch-hunting
witch-hunting   93, 95–6, 118
Wolf, Eric R   21, 129, 131

zamindars   37, 38, 173